S.W.B.

in memory of

H.A.H.

Dec. 1975.

(June Bayliss)

Sport in Britain

by the same author

Greek Athletes and Athletics
Sport in Greece and Rome

Dedication

This book is dedicated to all those who have ever enjoyed playing games, not very well, but as well as they could.

Sport in Britain

Its Origins and Development

H A Harris

Stanley Paul, London

Stanley Paul & Co Ltd
3 Fitzroy Square, London W1

An imprint of the Hutchinson Publishing Group

London Melbourne Sydney Auckland
Wellington Johannesburg and agencies
throughout the world

First published 1975

Set in Monotype Baskerville
Printed in Great Britain by The Anchor Press Ltd
and bound by Wm Brendon & Son Ltd
both of Tiptree, Essex

ISBN 0 09 124960 0

Contents

Preface 6

1 The Problem 9
2 The First Stage: Roman Britain 15
3 The Beginning of Modern Sport: Royal Tennis 20
4 The Beginning of Organized Team Games: Cricket 35
5 Cricket: The Later Stages 51
6 Rowing and other Aquatic Sports 79
7 Football 102
8 Athletics 135
9 Other Ball Games 154
10 Combat Sports 170
11 Winter Sports 177
12 The Olympic Games 180
13 Sport and Broadcasting 191
14 Sport and Literature 198
15 The Future 210

Index 221

Preface

When I was invited to write on sport in Britain, my first impulse was to decline with the historian's usual excuse, 'Outside my period'. Yet the prospect was attractive, and I began to deceive myself into believing that I might have some qualifications for the task.

I have always been glad that I started life in the same way as Jack Hobbs. We were both sons of college servants, he at Cambridge, I at Oxford. (We also both loved cricket, but where cricket is concerned, resemblance between us ended at that point.) The great university cities before the First World War were wonderful places for a small boy destined to have any interest in games. Amateur sport at its best was going on all round him. One of my earliest memories is of seeing A. N. S. Jackson, gold medallist at 1500m in the Stockholm Olympics of 1912, winning a race on the Iffley Road track, and I often used to watch R. C. Bourne, the only man ever to stroke four winning crews in the Boat Race, rowing in his college eight. The enthusiasm thus aroused led to an enjoyment of sport over a wide field at the modest level of school, college and club. I have played and umpired cricket, played and refereed soccer and rugby, run on the track and across country, rowed in a college eight and dabbled in other games as opportunity offered. Most writers on sport have achieved eminence in one or two fields, and their outlook, though profoundly informed, is necessarily narrow. This I have escaped. Nor have I ever been closely concerned with the administration of any one sport. For years I was treasurer of the central sports fund of a college, and in that capacity I had to maintain at least the appearance of impartiality among the claims of many games.

Such long and wide experience, even at a humble level, is useful equipment for writing on sport; there are many thousands who possess it. In one respect only can I claim a special qualification. I have long devoted myself to the study of sport in the ancient civilization of Greece and Rome, and this has given me standards of comparison not available to all. In some respects that sporting world was startlingly like ours, in others it was very different; a knowledge of it reveals that much that we take for granted as essential in our sport is in fact accidental. Acquaintance with this vanished world makes possible a detached outlook on the modern scene which is particularly valuable in a field where tradition is as powerful as it is in sport.

In two respects my experience of sport differs from the average. It is normal for a young boy to acquire a devotion to a county in cricket, and a famous league club in soccer. My formative years coincided with the First World War, when there was no league football and no county cricket. School games were well organized throughout the war, but spectator sport ceased, and I had no opportunity to form such ties.

Sixty years ago the path from elementary school to university, though open, was not the broad and easy highway it has since become. As a carrot to inspire effort I could dangle before my eyes the prospect of the opportunities for games enjoyed by undergraduates, but sport could never be the first aim in life. From an early age I was well aware that a single break in the line of scholarships would mean the end of the road. Work had to come first. There was never a chance of my becoming an example of that absurd contradiction in terms, a dedicated sportsman. Here too I differ from most enthusiasts.

Such then is the background from which this book has emerged. A work on a theme so comprehensive as sport in Britain inevitably has its limitations. The sporting scene is made up of a large number of games and pursuits, and a mosaic treatment is unavoidable. Before we can usefully consider the scene as a whole, we must attempt to establish the facts of the diverse elements. I have tried to be accurate about facts, but anyone interested only in the history of a particular game will not turn to a book like this. A satisfactory account of sport during the last four centuries must be more than a collection of separate descriptions of these various activities. The games have been influenced by one another, and all of them have been affected by the social and economic changes of the period. To examine these aspects of sport is the main purpose of this book. It has also a secondary intention. I differ from many historians – especially from the scientific school – in believing that the sole purpose of studying the past is to improve the present and future. I have therefore not hesitated to suggest ways in which a knowledge of sport in the past can help us to do just that.

Everyone who has played games will have his favourites among them. I have tried not to allow my preferences to sway my judgement, but I have not made any conscious effort to conceal my prejudices. A subject so close to men's hearts does not call for a clinical impersonality.

It is not possible for me to thank individually everyone with whom I have played, watched and discussed games. They have all contributed something to this book, and I am deeply grateful to them all. I must thank the staff of Bury Knowle Branch Library at Headington, who have been tireless in obtaining books for me to read in the only place where books on sport should be read – in my own armchair.

H. A. Harris
Oxford

Professor Harris died on 29 August 1974, a few days after sending the typescript of this book to the publishers. It has therefore not been possible to incorporate any references to subsequent events, and the text represents the author's final views. As an old friend and colleague, I have done my best to see that the work appears in the form he would have wished.

Ian M. Barton

I
The Problem

Almost everyone interested in the world of sport agrees that all is not well with it. The reasons for dissatisfaction are varied. Many of the old are sure that the level of skill and performance has fallen since their youth. Still more are convinced – and with far greater justification – that standards of conduct and sportsmanship on the field have declined, and that this decline has been accompanied by an increase of hooliganism on the terraces. Organizers and administrators are dismayed by the drop in the numbers of spectators.

Some critics attribute every defect in sport to lack of money, and call for the injection into it of ever greater sums. Others regret that sport has come to depend so much on money, and particularly lament the ever-growing connection between sport and gambling; the clearer-sighted realize that as more and more money comes into sport, the menace of corruption increases proportionately. Many regret bitterly the lack of success of their own country in winning Olympic medals and international cups and championships, while some of the older generation, who remember the great hope that international sport would promote friendship among peoples, see with dismay that the increase of chauvinism in the realm of games and the intrusion of international politics into sport is leading to nothing but bitter hatred. Serious-minded young reformers of left-wing tendencies suspect that enthusiasm for league football has replaced religion as the opiate of the masses, and are compelled to admit the truth of Chesterton's dictum that the British working man cannot be persuaded to dedicate himself to the cause of the equality of man because he is much more interested in the inequality of horses.

All this amounts to a formidable indictment. Yet an ordinary man in late middle age, looking back on his own experience of sport and what it has meant to him in his lifetime, sees a rather different picture. He can recall a time when his highest ambition in life was to secure a place in a school team and to perform with some distinction on his school's Sports Day. Many of his happiest memories are of games played for his school, club or college, and of the friends he made in these encounters. He may have met his wife at a tennis club. He may still play golf or bowls. If he has children and grandchildren, he watches them passing through the same stages and deriving the same enjoyment from them. Perhaps he is one of those who think it right after their active days to give back something to the games to which they owe so much, and who undertake the thankless post of secretary or treasurer of their old club, or turn out to umpire or referee the countless matches which take place every week in public parks and playing fields. Here too he sees a new generation with far more opportunities for enjoying games than ever he experienced in his youth. He is probably aware of periods of anxiety in his private life when he was infinitely grateful for a game which compelled him for an hour or two to withdraw his mind from everything else in order to concentrate on winning; he will remember too times of national crisis during war when sport afforded a similar distraction. In fact he will realize that sport has contributed not only to his physical well-being but also to his mental health, and that it has done much to ensure that balance which is an indispensable part of the good life to which we all aspire.

At this level of sport, then, though there may be room for improvement, there is little cause for gloom. This is the level at which games are played for the enjoyment of the players; it covers at least nine-tenths of the total sporting activity of the country. The sector of sport about which so much anxiety is felt is that small area in the top reaches which engages almost all the sports pages of the press and the time devoted to sport on television and radio. In this area there are three primary considerations: the entertainment of huge numbers of spectators, with all the financial problems which this entails; the maintenance of an essential part of a vast gambling industry; and the supposed advancement of national prestige by success in international encounters. Superficially, of course, this section of the sporting scene is identical with the other. The FA Cup Final is played under the same rules as a friendly match between two boys' clubs, and except for the skill of the players, the games are recognizably the same. Yet there is a fundamental difference between them. It is a sound moral and legal principle that the validity of an action depends on the motive behind it. To play a game for enjoyment is completely different from performing the same actions in order to earn money by entertaining spectators. Almost all the problems of modern sport are the result of attempts to carry over the ethical assumptions of the first department into the second.

There is no realm of human activity about which it is more difficult to think clearly than sport. This is because it is completely paradoxical. From one point of view it is utterly useless and aimless. It is the antithesis to a man's work in life by which he serves the community and earns his living, and it is precisely because it is the opposite of that purposeful business that it affords an incomparable medium of refreshment and recreation in leisure hours. Yet at the same time, if sport is to be enjoyable, it is essential that during the short time which a game or contest requires to complete, every player should behave as if nothing in the world mattered except winning by fair means; there is nothing more intolerably boring than games played half-heartedly. The operative phrase is 'by fair means'. We all recognize that when sport is at its best, a player would rather lose than win by unfair tactics. Human nature being what it is, this ideal is not easily achieved in any circumstances; it is impossible unless the rest of the paradox is maintained – that while winning is supremely important during the game, as soon as the game is finished, nothing is so unimportant as who did win. At the top level of sport, organized as it is today, this is unattainable. The result of a game matters a great deal; the very existence of a club may depend on it; the standard of living of the players for years ahead may be determined by it. In these circumstances it is absurd to expect an altruistic attitude towards fair play and keeping the rules.

The confusion in the outside world of sport is matched by a similar uncertainty in the minds of sports lovers. It is natural for those who practise any activity and realize its difficulties to admire those who reach the highest levels of skill in it. Our middle-aged enthusiast will have memories not only of his own modest achievements but of a time in his boyhood when he was a fanatical admirer and supporter of a first-class football team in the winter and of a county cricket team in the summer. Often this enthusiasm was bound up with natural local loyalties. He would have to be a very old man indeed to remember the days when members of a football club had to qualify for FA competitions by birth or residence within six miles of the club's headquarters; but until very recent years first-class cricket teams were genuinely representative of the counties whose names they bore. Our elderly sports lover may cynically reflect that nowadays a first-class cricket or football team represents nothing except the ability of the club management to buy its raw material in a vastly inflated market. Yet he still finds himself turning every morning to the sports pages in the papers to learn how Everton or Sussex have fared, and he feels vaguely that there is something wrong with a world in which Blackburn Rovers or Preston North End are in the Third Division. He may know perfectly well that international sport fosters far more hatred than friendship between nations. He may be convinced intellectually that the Olympic Games would be better abandoned and that the World Cup is more likely to provoke a war than to conduce to international peace. But he is also well aware that if Britain is engaged in the World Cup or the Olympic Games, he desperately wants Britain to win.

Another reason for the confusion in the world of sport and in the minds of those who try to think about it lies in the fact that our games are not rational and logical products of human intellect. All our important sports have been shaped by centuries of traditional practice. Their origin lies in games like those still played by children in their playgrounds. The rules for these games are not written, but they are none the less mandatory for that. Each child as he is taken into the group picks them up the hard way; woe betide him if he violates one of them, even in ignorance; in a few years he will be handing them on to newcomers. The national – and often international – codes of laws which now exist for adult games were not invented out of the blue by the first organizers of the modern versions; they were simply clear statements of the best practice which the legislators could find – the embodiment, in fact, of tradition. And wherever tradition is concerned, our emotions are far more powerful than our intellect. This is one of the reasons why obviously necessary improvements in rules have often been so slow to be adopted.

The conservative force of tradition is not the only obstacle confronting those who would like to bring about some improvement in the world of sport. That world is made up of innumerable games and pastimes, each of them by now furnished with a governing body, all of them fiercely independent and only too often bitterly jealous of one another. Naturally enough, the governing body of each sport is composed of those who have achieved eminence in the game, and in these days of increasing specialization in every field, such eminence can be attained only at the expense of ignorance of most other games. So the history of sport during the last century shows all too many instances of ruling bodies not only failing to profit from the experience and mistakes of other games, but sometimes flatly rejecting obvious improvements simply because they had been adopted by 'the other Code'. In every game the authorities are increasingly obsessed by financial problems; generally they are convinced that the solution to these depends on their tempting spectators away from other games. To do this, they modify the rules of their game in the hope of making it, not more enjoyable for the players, but more exciting for the onlookers. These efforts rarely achieve their aim, and they merely spoil the game for everyone by the changes involved.

Another problem arises from the importance of sport in our daily press and radio. The first duty of those responsible for these media is to secure good and lively reporting of current events. For many years now this has been very well done; Britain may well be proud of her best sports journalists, who are probably unequalled anywhere in the world. (Today we are able to see this world of sports journalism from the inside, thanks to four delightful books, *Autobiography* and *Full Score* by Sir Neville Cardus, Henry Longhurst's *My Life and Soft Times*, and E. W. Swanton's *Sort of a Cricket Person.*) But the high standard demands that each writer must be a specialist in his own game, and as every sport tends more and more to become an all-the-year-round occupation, he tends to be tied more and more to a single track. The requirements of day-to-day reporting prevent him from taking a long look into the history and development even of his own sport, much less of any other. Often the leading players about whom he is writing are his personal friends, and this also prevents him from taking a detached view. The best of these journalists are clearly disturbed by some recent developments in sport, and call attention to the dangers involved. But naturally they do not wish to decry the games which they love and to which they owe their daily bread. Inevitably they fall back on platitudinous expressions of hope that by some miracle all will be well, and they justify their hopes by pointing to problems in the past which have been successfully solved. In doing this they are using a legitimate historical method, but the validity of their optimistic conclusion depends on whether the problems of the past were in fact identical with ours, and whether our society is identical with the society of the past which solved them. To examine these two questions is the aim of this book.

Anyone with a lifetime's experience of the world of sport has seen many changes in it, and further changes are bound to come. Every lover of sport is concerned to see that these changes shall be improvements, and that the mistakes of the past shall not be repeated. Before we can hope to alter any part of the multifarious sporting scene for the better, we must understand how it has grown to be what it is now. Reform must not be long delayed. For the world of sport, like our churches and universities, is rotten at the top. In all these spheres, there is plenty that is healthy in the lower reaches. But rot spreads downwards all too quickly.

2
The First stage: Roman Britain

Human play and games are as old as humankind, but the history of a country's organized sport cannot begin until the country has achieved law and order, reasonable periods of freedom from war, good facilities for communication and some degree of civilization. Britain first enjoyed these advantages when the country became a Roman province in the first century A.D.

The Roman domain had been growing for centuries under a republican régime, but it had been given its final consolidation by the first Emperor, Augustus, less than a hundred years before Britain was added to it. It included all the lands with a Mediterranean seaboard, and some lying beyond these. The subjects of this Empire enjoyed many advantages. They were protected by the Roman armies on the frontiers. The provincial administration gave them the security of a system of law which, if sometimes cumbersome in its machinery, was firmly based on justice. Trade and commerce flourished, and movement within the Empire was made easy by an abundance of well-constructed roads and by ships which sailed across seas kept free from pirates. The central government was tolerant of local variations of culture and religion, and, provided that taxes were paid and law and order maintained, interfered little.

The heterogeneous provinces which made up this huge complex fell naturally into two groups. The Mediterranean countries east of Italy, long before Rome had entered their world, were heirs of great civilizations far older than Rome herself; as a result of the conquests of Alexander the Great, they already enjoyed a unified Greek culture when they became part of the Roman Empire. Greek was the common language of the East Mediterranean, and the Romans accepted this. In this part of the Empire, Greek was an official language, and Latin was little used outside the army and government circles. In the West, on the other hand, Rome for the most part brought a superior civilization to the provinces she annexed, and it was natural for Latin to become the lingua franca of these countries. The distinction between the Greek East and the Latin West persisted until the Empire collapsed, and it has left its mark even today in the existence of the Latin Roman Catholic Church of the West and the Greek Orthodox Church of the East Mediterranean.

One of the minor differences between the two halves of the Empire lay in the field of sport. By the first century A.D. spectator sport was as comprehensively organized throughout the whole Empire as it is in our world. In the Greek East the popular sport was athletics, on which by this time the Olympic Games had bestowed a tradition and prestige of more than eight centuries. Alexander the Great had carried the cult of athletics beyond its Greek homeland into Asia Minor, Syria, Mesopotamia, Palestine and Egypt; in all these countries every city had its stadium in which meetings were regularly held. Uniformity was ensured, because the programme, procedure and rules of the Olympic Games set a pattern for the whole of the Greek world. At the most important of these meetings valuable money prizes were given, and by the beginning of the Christian era Greek athletics were as fully professional at the highest level as soccer is in our world, and its highly paid leading figures were darlings of the people as our top stars are today.

From time to time attempts were made to popularize Greek athletics as spectator sport in the Latin West, just as today efforts are made to convert the United States to professional soccer, and the city of Rome had a permanent stadium for such meetings. But Greek athletics never caught on in the West, which had its own institutions for the entertainment of crowds. One of these consisted of the gladiatorial contests and fights between men and animals in the arena, and vast amphitheatres were built to accommodate the spectators at these exhibitions. The Colosseum in Rome is the best known of these; the wealthiest cities of the provinces had equally impressive structures, some of which still survive, at Arles and Nîmes in France, at El Djem in Tunisia and at Pula in Istria. More deserving of the name of sport was chariot racing, which was highly organized throughout the Roman world, with the statistics of performances of horses and drivers during their careers as carefully kept and recorded as those on the Turf today. For centuries the sport attracted enormous crowds; the Circus Maximus at Rome could accommodate a quarter of a million spectators. Every great city had its racecourse. In the Roman world, chariot racing occupied the place of football in the modern.

The most striking difference between the sporting scene in antiquity and our own is the lowly position of ball games in Greece and Rome. A ball is a natural object for games, and ball-play is shown in Egyptian paintings before 2000 B.C. Homer tells how Nausicaa and her attendants amused themselves by throwing a ball at one another while they were waiting for the palace washing to dry, and from that time on, both Greeks and Romans enjoyed a variety of ball games. Alexander the Great was a keen player; the earliest recorded courts constructed especially for ball-play date from his lifetime. Some of these courts were public, attached to the concourse of sports buildings – stadium, gymnasium and baths – which was a feature of every Greek city. Others were privately owned; the younger Pliny had one in each of his two country houses in Italy.

Of the many games played in these courts we know little. The most popular was one in which the players stood in a circle or in two rows and threw catches to one another, while a man in the middle tried to intercept or to avoid being hit by the ball. None of these games appears to have attracted more than a handful of spectators. The reason for this, no doubt, was the strange lack of competitive spirit in most of the games. In the whole of Greek and Latin literature, there is no mention before the first century of the Christian era, a thousand years after Nausicaa had played on the Phaeacian shore, of a ball game being lost or won. Both Greeks and Romans found their pleasure from ball games in the sheer manipulative skill of the players – the same satisfaction as we derive from a juggler. For contention they turned to athletics or chariot racing.

Such was the sporting scene when Britain, or that part of it which is now England and Wales, was annexed to the Empire. Britain was not a wealthy province, but it was thoroughly Romanized and civilized, and although direct evidence is lacking, there is no reason to suppose that the provincials in this country did not enjoy the same sports as their contemporaries in neighbouring provinces. It is unlikely that these sports ever included athletics meetings on the Greek pattern. The nearest point to Britain at which such meetings are known to have been held is Vienne, in the Rhône valley near Lyons. The athletics festivals in this city, established by a bequest in the will of a citizen, were abolished about A.D. 100 by a magistrate, and on appeal to the Emperor his decision was upheld. The reason for the abolition was that the meetings constituted a danger to the morals of the citizens; such was the reputation of Greek professional athletes in the Roman world at this time. If Greek sport was on the retreat in this way in a part of Gaul where, owing to the influence of the Greek cities of Marseilles, Nice and Antibes, it had earlier been strong, it is highly improbable that it would have crossed the Channel into Britain.

On the other hand, it is certain that the exhibitions of the arena were available in Britain. A dozen amphitheatres have been identified in the province. Two of them are well known, Maumbury Rings at Dorchester in Wessex and the arena of the legionary fortress at Caerleon. These do not compare in size with the vast structures on the Continent. The oval arena of each is roughly half the size of a soccer pitch; the amphitheatre of the small fort at Tômen-y-Mûr, beautifully situated among the hills of Merioneth, would hardly accommodate a tennis court. There is little direct evidence of the entertainment provided in these places, but there is no reason to suppose that in this respect Britain differed from other parts of the Empire. A vase in Colchester Museum depicts gladiators and bear-baiting; it was almost certainly made in East Anglia, and this suggests a familiarity with these subjects in the province. The smaller arenas may well have exhibited cock-fighting, a popular pursuit among the Romans.

The same degree of uncertainty hovers over the question whether the provincials of Roman Britain were able to enjoy chariot racing. A mosaic found in a Roman villa at Horkstow in Lincolnshire and now in the British Museum depicts a chariot race. This of course merely shows that the owner of the villa was interested in racing; it does not prove that the racing took place in Britain. But most racing mosaics found in the provinces of the Empire depict four-horse chariots among the splendours of the Circus Maximus in Rome. The Horkstow picture has two-horse chariots and the very simplest of equipment, merely the two turning-posts and the wall joining them – the kind of course we might expect in a remote and poor part of the Empire. There would have been less difficulty in providing such a track than there is today in laying out the course for the point-to-point races of a local hunt. So, although no circus has yet been identified in Britain, there is every likelihood that chariot racing did in fact take place here.

The same is true of ball games. Historians of football sometimes state that the game was introduced into Britain by the Romans. There is no ground whatever for this assertion. Nor indeed is there the slightest evidence that either Greeks or Romans ever played any game which we should recognize as football. Equally there is no reason to suppose that the provincials of Britain did not enjoy the same simple ball games as the inhabitants of other parts of the Western Roman Empire.

3
The Beginning of Modern Sport: Royal Tennis

During the time when Britain was part of the Roman Empire, a development took place which was to change the whole history of the world – the spread of the Christian religion. When Britain was first annexed by Rome, the Church was still in those early stages of its struggle for existence which are described in the New Testament in *Acts*. When the Empire of the West collapsed some four centuries later, Christianity was its official religion and the majority of its subjects were Christian. Inevitably every aspect of life was affected by this revolution, even such minor activites as games and entertainments, and from this time on, the historian has constantly to take into account the impact of the Church on sport.

The earliest Christians, convinced that the Second Coming of Christ would occur in their lifetime, naturally believed that this world should be sacrificed to secure happiness in eternity. But as this hope evaporated, it became obvious that Christians must make some compromise with existing society. The Church has never been able to reach a common mind about the proper degree of this compromise. From the beginning there have been some who believe that concessions to the outside world must be kept to the minimum, that the Church should form a closed community with as little contact as possible with those outside. Others have taken the more humane view that if Christians are to act as the leaven of society they must mingle freely with society, and that a Christian is not called upon to eschew anything unless it is positively and demonstrably sinful. For them the Christian life is identical with the good life, and the secret of the good life is a proper balance of all its constituent elements.

This controversy in the Church is closely connected with a curious trait in human nature which is far older than Christianity and which emerges from time to time in history to affect the conduct and development of individuals and societies – a deep distrust of pleasure and a suspicion that unmixed pleasure is somehow morally wrong. It may be that the basis of morality is felt to be self-mastery, and there is nothing more destructive of self-mastery than the pursuit of pleasure. There is a widespread feeling that:

Man was made for Joy and Woe;
And when this we rightly know
Thro' the World we safely go.

Undue prosperity or happiness has to be paid for somehow. In some Christians the distrust of pleasure has led to a complete rejection of it and to a renunciation of this world to achieve everlasting life; this is the basis of monasticism. Others have tried to counteract the supposed evils of pure pleasure by balancing it with some degree of self-imposed asceticism such as formal fasts.

One of the considerations which justify us in regarding sport as a microcosm of life is that this avoidance of pure pleasure has always been fundamental to sport itself. The Greeks, who are responsible for the beginning of our thinking about sport as about many other subjects, regarded a certain degree of suffering as a necessary element in their athletics – the exhaustion of the runner, and the blows and throws of boxer or wrestler. Today we still recognize that hard knocks and endurance are an inseparable part of any sport of real importance, and that self-control in face of these is the mark of the true sportsman. A corollary of this is that anyone who knows sport only as a spectator simply does not know what sport is.

The attitude of the early Church towards sport was probably influenced by the fact that St Paul was an enthusiast for athletics. In his writings he constantly uses imagery drawn from sport. In particular he depicts the Christian life in terms of the athlete's, the painful struggle rewarded in the end by the victor's palm and crown. This was taken up by the Early Fathers and has been part of Christian imagery ever since; the word 'ascetic', for instance, is the Greek technical term for an athlete in hard training. The most important influence of the Church on public entertainment in the Roman Empire resulted in the abandonment of the brutal gladiatorial fights of the arena. Chariot racing and athletics were occasionally deprecated by Christian writers because of the pagan associations of some of the festivals at which they were held, but Christian opposition to them went no further than this. And before the final dissolution of the Western Empire we have evidence of positive encouragement by authorities of the Church of healthy physical activities among the young. In the fifth century A.D., Sidonius Apollinaris was Bishop of Clermont in Gaul. He is the only writer in Greek or Latin who has left us a description of a contemporary chariot race; it is an account of an event for amateur drivers, won by a young friend of his. Even more important is what he tells us about his attitude towards ball games. In one of his letters he describes the scene outside a church in Lyons, where he and several others were waiting for Mass. Some of the congregation went off to gamble at dice, but not the Bishop.

> I was the first to call for a ball game, which, as you know, is as true a friend to me as are my books. . . . I played for some time with a group of students, until I had thrown off that sluggishness which inevitably results from my sedentary occupation. Among those present was an elderly man, Philomatius, who had been a first-class player in his young days; now he joined the spectators round the game. While he stood looking on, the 'middle runner' several times bumped into him, and this made him join in the game. But he found that he could no longer intercept the ball as it flew past him, nor dodge it; often he almost went flat on his face as he ducked, and only just saved himself from a nasty tumble. So he was the first to drop out of the game, puffing hard and sweating all over.

Whatever the game may have been, the Bishop was obviously a keen lover of it, and that 'muscular Christianity' which we regard as belonging particularly to the nineteenth century was flourishing fourteen hundred years earlier.

As a result of the collapse of the Empire of the West, nothing in the nature of nationally organized games was possible for several centuries after the time of Bishop Apollinaris. This does not, of course, mean that there was no sport. From time to time during the Middle Ages we hear of running, jumping, weight-throwing, wrestling, single-stick and quarter-staff, football and golf; the evidence mostly comes from attempts by legal authority to suppress these pastimes in order to encourage archery, which was useful in war. The essence of modern sport is the existence of widely accepted codes of rules for various games. This first happened with the game of Royal, Real or Court Tennis. Significantly, the game seems to have originated in the Church.

Most people in Britain today probably owe such knowledge of Royal Tennis as they possess to a visit to Hampton Court. There they will have walked through the Tennis Court and seen its curious construction, with penthouse, gallery, grille and dedans. If they have been fortunate, they may have watched a game in progress, noted the oddly shaped rackets and heard the esoteric language of the sport, the 'boasted force into the dedans' or 'laying down chase better than 2'. But they will have felt more at home with other aspects of the game, as they see the ball being hit backwards and forwards over a net, and hear the score being called in the familiar but mysterious terms, 15–love, 40–30, deuce, and so on.

There are many ways in which a ball can be treated in play. It can be thrown to be caught; it can be bounced against the ground or a wall and kept bouncing; it can be aimed at a target, a goal, another ball, a hole in the ground or a space marked out in the playing area; it can be dispatched to a distance to afford time for a manoeuvre such as the scoring of runs. These activities can be made more difficult by interposing some obstacle such as a net, a bunker or a line on a wall; most of them can be performed either with the hand or with some kind of club. Royal Tennis exploits all these possibilities except the first and the last.

The strange features of the court are almost certainly derived from monastic buildings, the penthouse representing the cloisters, and the grille and dedans being stylized versions of the buttery hatch and the opening for the bell rope. It would seem that the monks of one such community developed their own game in their cloisters, incorporating into it these features of the buildings in which they lived their daily lives, and that early in the Middle Ages the game was seen by some French king who was so attracted by it that he had a court constructed for his own use embodying these peculiarities. From this source the game was carried to Italy and Britain. Because of the strange features of the court and the consequent complexity of the rules, the spread of the game necessarily carried the rules with it. There is an obvious parallel in the game of Eton Fives. This game originated in an identifiable place in Eton College grounds where there is a step near the back wall, and where a buttress of the Chapel protrudes into the playing area; these features were duly incorporated into the game, and have been reproduced in stylized form all over the world wherever the game has been taken. With Eton Fives we know the place of origin of the peculiarities. What particular monastery was the source of the tennis court has long been lost in the mists of time, and probably the secret will never be recovered.

It is good to know that the Church's encouragement of ball games which we encountered in Sidonius Apollinaris had this result. Yet in the Middle Ages, as always, the mind of the Church was divided on this subject. In 1245 priests in France were forbidden to play the game, and the ban was repeated several times during the next three centuries. In Britain too, ecclesiastical authority did not view the game with unmixed approval, at any rate when it was played on Church property by the laity. In 1447 the Bishop, Dean and Chapter of Exeter Cathedral petitioned the Mayor about the conduct of some of the citizens, and their indictment included this article:

> Atte which tymes, and in especial in tyme of dyvyne service, ungoodly ruled peple, most custumably yong peple of the saide Comminalte, within the saide cloistre have exercised unlawfull games, as the toppe, penny prykke and *most atte tenys*, by the which the walles of the saide Cloistre have been defowled and the glas wyndowes all tobrost, as it openly sheweth, contrarie to all good and goostly godenesse.

The game is first heard of in France in the twelfth century; two hundred years later it was well established in Britain. Where evidence is slight and accidental, it is never easy to ascertain the degree of popularity of a game in a country, but if we find writers using allusions to the technical terms of a game and expecting them to be understood by their readers, we may deduce that the game is fairly widely known. Chaucer clearly expected this acquaintance with tennis in his readers. When Pandarus is urging Troilus to abandon Criseyde for another love, the hero objects,

> But canstow pleyen raket, to and fro,
> Netle in, dokke out, now this, now that, Pandare?

This was written about 1370. A few years later, Chaucer's younger contemporary John Gower has an even more explicit allusion to the game. In his poem *In Praise of Peace* he is driving home the truism that 'The fortune of the warre is ever unknowe' and writes:

> Of the Tenetz to winne or lese a chace
> May no lyf wite, or that the bal be ronne.

(In Tennis, no man knows whether he wins or loses a chase, until the ball has run its course.)

Clearly the members of the courtly circles for whom Chaucer and Gower wrote could be relied upon to grasp a reference to the technical terms of the game.

In the course of the next century the popularity of tennis spread far beyond this narrow circle. Public courts were built in London, Oxford and Cambridge which could be hired by players. Demand for the implements of the game became so great that in 1446 Edward IV was petitioned to prohibit the import of tennis balls, and in 1459 a monopoly of their manufacture was granted to – rather oddly – the Ironmongers' Company. The accounts of the Company reveal some interesting details. In 1459 the price was 20d. a gross, and most purchasers took forty or fifty gross at a time. By the beginning of Richard III's reign the price was down to 16d., and at the end of the reign to 1s. In 1529 comes the intriguing entry, 'Payd to parson for tyth of the balls, 2s.' Already there were strange vested interests in the manufacture and sale of sports equipment.

The public courts in London were licensed under Queen Elizabeth in order to regulate conduct in them. The caretakers who looked after them acted as markers and no doubt played against patrons when required. They are the first professionals in the history of modern sport. In France there were enough of them at the beginning of the seventeenth century to form a trade union (*Communauté des Maîtres Paumiers-Raquetiers*). Later in the same century, five professionals were granted the privilege of playing matches in Paris twice a week and advertising publicly 'like the Comedians'. Almost certainly to this professional class belonged the first modern sportswoman, one Margot, in the fifteenth century. She could beat most men, and she appears to have been the inventor of backhand strokes ('*Elle jouoit devant main derrière main*').

Elizabethan England may not have experienced quite the explosion of enthusiasm for the game which was felt in contemporary France. The Venetian ambassador to that country at the end of the sixteenth century reported, 'There were more than 1800 Tennis courts in various parts of Paris, and it was calculated that more than 1000 crowns was daily spent in the purchase of rackets.' But in 1558 a Frenchman, E. Perlin, wrote in his *Description of England and Scotland*:

> This country is very rich, and people in trade gain more in one week than those in Germany or Spain do in a month; for here you may commonly see artisans, such as hatters and joiners, playing at Tennis for a crown, which is not often seen elsewhere, particularly on a working day.

And ordinary Londoners in the audience at the Globe knew enough about the game to be able to follow the speech of Henry V in reply to the Dauphin's insulting gift of tennis balls:

> When we have matched our rackets to these balls,
> We will in France, by God's grace, play a set
> Shall strike his father's crown into the hazard.
> Tell him he hath made a match with such a wrangler
> That all the courts of France will be disturbed
> With chases.

One of the minor mysteries of tennis is the origin of its name. Although it has never been used in France, where the game has always been called *Jeu de Paume*, the word is almost certainly the French *Tenez*, used by a player to warn his opponent that he is about to serve, where a player today calls 'Service'. In the best early account of a match we have – it is in Latin – the server calls '*Excipe*', the exact Latin equivalent of *Tenez*.

The French name of the game is a reminder that in it the ball was originally struck with the palm of the hand. When tennis rackets were introduced is uncertain; Chaucer's use of the word suggests that they were well established by the fourteenth century. It is usually stated that the racket was developed from a glove with strings stretched across the palm, but the evidence for this is unsatisfactory. (It goes back no further than the eighteenth-century French historian, Saint Foix.) Improbable as it may appear, rackets were almost certainly borrowed from the game of polo. The earliest mention in literature of a racket occurs in the twelfth-century Byzantine historian Cinnamus. Having occasion to relate how the Emperor Manuel Comnenus fell when playing polo and was rolled on by his pony, he takes the opportunity to describe the game, and in the course of his account writes, 'Each player has in his right hand a club of a length to suit him. The club broadens out at the end into a flat curved head, fitted inside with a kind of net woven of dry gut.' But we can take the racket back further than this. A picture in marble inlay has survived from the secular basilica of Junius Bassus, built in Rome shortly before A.D. 350. This depicts four horsemen, each of them holding at the slope a racket exactly like that described eight hundred years later by Cinnamus. It is reasonable to deduce that polo and the racket go back as far as this; it is interesting too to notice that polo is still played with rackets in Russia.

Like most innovations in sport, the tennis racket was not immediately welcomed by everyone, as a passage in the *Colloquies* of Erasmus suggests. (In the Latin of this dialogue, rackets are called 'nets' (*reticula*). There is no ambiguity here, for what we call a tennis net had not yet been invented. The ball was hit over a cord stretched across the court; the only device to help the marker to decide whether the ball had passed over or under the cord was a row of tassels hung from it. The net for this purpose appears first in the eighteenth century.) One of Erasmus' young men proposes a game of tennis (*pila palmaria* – the Latin equivalent of *Jeu de Paume*); the other objects that it is too hot a game for summer, and suggests that they will sweat less if they use rackets. To this his companion rather snootily rejoins, 'Let us leave "nets" to fishermen; it is more elegant to use the hand' (*elegantius est palma uti*).

The best contemporary account of a game of Royal Tennis in its heyday is also in Latin. Even the requirements of the hexameters in which it is composed and the fact that it is an allegory of a war between France and Spain cannot altogether conceal the liveliness of the narration. It is the work of a Frenchman, R. Frissart, *Carmen de Ludo Pilae Reticulo Bello comparato* ('Poem on a game of Rackets compared to War'), dedicated to Cardinal Richelieu and published in 1641. There are three characters, the Kings of France and Spain and the marker:

F. Toss the racket for service . . . (He calls) Smooth. Smooth it is. I serve; you are striker . . . Here is a trial ball (*En praelusio*). Now for the real thing . . . Service! (*Excipe*). (He serves) Your shot was under the cord. 15 to me. . . . Look at that stroke of mine. It hit the foot of the wall and shot off.

S. Yes. A rotten fluke (*Hic etiam fortuna valet*).

F. Not at all. Sheer skill. A very pretty shot of mine. 30 to me. Service!

S. I took that on the first bounce. (To the marker) Your decision?

M. On the second.

F. 45 to me . . . Service!

S. There's a volley for you! . . . I can keep this up for ever.

F. But there's one straight into the grille. First game to me.

The curious method of scoring, by which each point won counts 15, has been taken over into Lawn Tennis. (The score at the third point was originally 45, now abbreviated for convenience to 40.) The clue to the origin of this is to be found in Perlin's statement that he had seen artisans in England playing *for a crown*, the total of the stakes put up by the players; these stakes were deposited during the game underneath the centre cord. A crown was 60d. Thus each of the four points which constituted a game counted 15d. towards winning the stakes. The use of 'love' for 'no score' in games, which is not found before the eighteenth century, is obviously derived from the very old antithesis 'for love or money'. The suggestion that it is *l'œuf* – the 'duck's egg' of cricket, now always abbreviated to 'duck' – is a guess without any foundation whatever.

The stake of a crown was not confined to tennis. It was customary also in bowls, and this explains a play on words in a sad little poem on Charles I, who towards the end of his life played a few games at Colins End in Oxfordshire:

> Stop, traveller, stop! In yonder peaceful glade
> His favourite game the Royal Martyr played;
> Here, stripped of honours, children, freedom, rank,
> Drank from the bowl, and bowled for what he drank;
> Sought in a cheerful glass his cares to drown,
> And changed his guinea ere he lost his crown.

In golf, the custom of a stake of half a crown by each player survived until decimalization.

The method of scoring 15–30–45 is found in the earliest printed set of rules, in Scaino's *Trattato della Palla*, published in

Italy in 1555, together with the provision that if the score reaches 45 all, *a due* or deuce, a two-point lead, is needed for game; the term *vantaggio* is also already established. A fuller set of rules, drawn up in Paris in 1592 and published in 1632, fixes the height of the cord, provides for the spinning of a racket to decide service and for the trial ball (*coup des dames*), and lays it down that the winner of the stakes shall pay for the court, the marker, firewood and drinks. Already the tradition existed that any possible asperities of a sporting contest should be forgotten in a social get-together after the match. Urquhart's translation of Rabelais gives us a brief but pleasant picture of the scene: 'After playing, when the game is done, they refresh themselves before a clear fire, and change their shirts; and very willingly they make all good cheer, but most merrily those that have gained; and so, farewel.' The custom of teams meeting their opponents after a match for drinks or a meal happily survives in some circles; elsewhere it has vanished, a sad symptom of the decline of the true spirit of sport in our world.

Tennis appears to have reached the height of its popularity about 1600 and thereafter to have declined slowly, in France as well as in England, but in England there was a brief revival of interest after the Restoration. Both Charles II and James II were keen players, and because of this royal patronage the game figures a good deal in Samuel Pepys, though the diarist was prevented by his poor eyesight from being a player himself. He records the building of a new court for Lord Sandwich, but he also mentions courts which had been converted to other purposes, notably one which had been turned into the best theatre in London. One anecdote told by Pepys about Charles reveals the intellectual curiosity of that many-sided king:

> [2 September 1667] I observed in the morning that the King, playing at tennis, had a steelyard carried to him, and I was told it was to weigh him after he had done playing; and at noon Mr Ashburnham told me that it is only the King's curiosity, which he usually hath of weighing himself before and after his play, to see how much he loses in weight by playing; and this day he lost $4\frac{1}{2}$ lbs.

Charles encountered the problem which always confronts the great when they take part in sport. On 4 January 1664, Pepys reports:

> To the Tennis Court, and there saw the King play at tennis and

> others; but to see how the King's play was extolled, without any cause at all, was a loathsome sight, though sometimes, indeed, he did play very well and deserved to be commended; but such open flattery is beastly.

Alexander the Great had to give up athletics, which he loved, because other runners always allowed him to win.

On another occasion, the King and his brother were discussing the reluctance of Quakers to take an oath. Pepys reports a pleasant contribution to the conversation:

> [4 April 1668] My Lord of Pembroke says he hath heard the Quaker at the tennis court swear to himself when he loses.

In the eighteenth century the game, deprived of royal support, lost further ground. It was kept alive in the courts of great houses, at Oxford and Cambridge, and at a few public courts in London. At the beginning of the next century there was a renewal of interest; Wellington and Napoleon were both players. The crowning achievement of this revival was the building of the court at Lord's cricket ground in 1839. Twenty years later the first Oxford and Cambridge match was held. The game had survived in France too; at the end of the century it was introduced into the USA and later into Australia. This prevents the championships, amateur and professional, from being parochial. Within the last few years an old court has been brought back into use at Canford School and another at Petworth, and recently two new courts have been opened in Melbourne, the first to be built since before the First World War. Building costs will inevitably prevent the game from achieving wide popularity, but anyone who values tradition in sport must hope that there will always be sufficient enthusiasts to prevent this ancient game from dying.

Not surprisingly, Royal Tennis gave rise to several other games embodying the same principle, the bouncing of a ball off walls, games which could be played in situations where a tennis court was not available. One of these is fives, developed especially in the public schools. Instead of the ball being hit over a net, it has to be hit above a line on the end wall of the court, from which it rebounds. Three schools have produced three different patterns of court, the Eton version with its step and buttress, the Rugby court with a back wall, while the Winchester court lacks this back wall. The game has generally, like Royal Tennis in its early days, been played with the hand, and the name 'fives' is almost certainly derived from a cant term for a hand. But *Tom Brown's Schooldays* reveals that in the 1840s fives bats were used at Rugby, where they survived until the twenties of this century.

The most important of the surrogate forms of Royal Tennis is rackets. The hazards of the tennis court – penthouse, grille and dedans – are omitted from the rackets court, and the net is replaced by a line on the end wall; this reduces the size of the court considerably, and enables it to be more cheaply built. The scoring is also simplified, points being scored one at a time.

The early history of rackets has been inadequately explored. Search into it will never be easy, if only because Royal Tennis was often called rackets. Moreover, such investigations as have been undertaken have been hindered by a curious accident. The earliest mention in literature of a rackets court is in *Pickwick Papers* (1837); the court is in the Fleet debtors' prison. Dickens describes it thus:

> The area formed by the wall in that part of the Fleet in which Mr Pickwick stood, was just wide enough to make a good racket court, one side being formed, of course, by the wall itself, and the other by that portion of the prison which looked (or rather would have looked, but for the wall) towards St Paul's Cathedral.

The results of this chance mention by Dickens afford an interesting example of the way in which sports history comes to be written. In the *Encyclopaedia of Sport* (1897), a work of very uneven merit, E. O. P. Bouverie in the article on rackets writes: 'The debtors' prisons and the public houses were the places in which it grew into vogue, and it is said that until the time of Mr (now Sir) William Hart-Dyke's championship, all those who successfully competed for the position of champion rackets player were born or brought up in one of the debtors' prisons.' 'It is said' is all too often the introduction to a statement for which there is no evidence whatever. Bouverie gives no authority for his dogmatic statement about debtors' prisons and public houses. Nor have subsequent writers filled the gap; they have been content to repeat and elaborate Bouverie's surmises.

Even R. J. McNeill, in his admirable article in the *Encyclo-*

paedia Britannica (1911), writes: 'The 19th century was far advanced before the racquet court was promoted from being an adjunct of the pot-house and the gaol . . . to a position scarcely less dignified than that of the tennis-court with its royal and historical associations.' Careful writer though he is, he gives no evidence for his statement about pot-houses. As recently as 24 March 1973, an article appeared in *The Times* under the heading, 'Rich man's sport that began in debtors' prison'. In it Bouverie's guesses are expanded. 'Racquet Court in Fleet Street is the site of the old Fleet Debtors' Prison, and it is thought that the game was developed there around 1800. It has been said that Mr W. H. Dyke (later Sir William Hart-Dyke), who won the title in 1862, was the first world champion to come from outside the walls of that prison.' 'It is thought that . . . ', 'It has been said that . . .': the least captious reader must surely ask at last, 'By whom?'

The impression produced by these writers that rackets originated in conditions of squalor is most improbable. There is a much more likely interpretation of such evidence as exists. There must always have been a tendency to simplify the highly complicated game of Royal Tennis. The earliest book on it, Scaino's of 1555, in its description of the court, does not mention the hazards, but it does speak of courts of different sizes for different forms of the game. The only fundamental difference between tennis and rackets is the replacement of the net by the line on the back wall, with the consequent reduction in the size of the court. When the first of these smaller courts was built is not known; it must have been before 1800. The earliest known date for the building of a rackets court is 1822, at Harrow School, but as one R. Mackay was claiming the title of champion in 1820, there were obviously courts in existence before that time. These smaller courts, no less than the larger tennis courts, needed money to build and caretakers to look after them, and these caretakers were the 'professionals' who provided the early champions. If there had been no wealthy patrons of the game, there would have been no one to pay for the building of the courts or to provide the stakes for the championship matches. By far the likeliest originators of the game were men of some means who did not have access to a tennis court.

The debtors' prisons which figure so conspicuously in the

'histories' of the game appear to have no other authority than *Pickwick*. Dickens' description makes it clear that the 'court' in the Fleet was not constructed for the purpose, like that at Harrow, but a part of the prison yard where the layout of the walls happened to make it possible to play a game of some kind. A debtors' prison housed many from the prosperous classes who had come down in the world, and others who were suffering temporary financial embarrassment. They were glad enough to fill their idle hours with the nearest approximation they could contrive to the rackets of their happier days, while their humbler fellow-prisoners, as Dickens tells us, played skittles at the other end of the same area. No doubt the extraordinary popularity of *Pickwick* led to some wag suggesting that skill at rackets must be the outcome of a sojourn in a debtors' prison, just as a similar wit originated the oft-repeated theory that success at billiards is a sign of a dissipated youth. But a writer in a standard encyclopaedia of sport should have demanded better authority than this.

We are so accustomed to a sporting world in which every game down to tiddly-winks has its national, if not international, association to lay down the rules and arrange the major competitions, that it is difficult for us to envisage a scene in which no such bodies existed and players made their own arrangements. In some games this was possible because all players accepted the rules observed by a prominent club, MCC in cricket, the Royal and Ancient in golf, the Portland Club in card games. Sometimes a leading club promoted a competition, the winner of which came to be regarded as the Amateur Champion in the game; Wimbledon in Lawn Tennis is a reminder of this. In Royal Tennis, the MCC's competition in its court at Lord's fulfilled this function. The first of these contests to be accepted as the Amateur Championship took place in 1889. In rackets, the Prince's Club provided the first Amateur Championship in 1862 and added a Public Schools' Championship in 1868. The Tennis, Racquets and Fives Association was not founded until 1908.

Rackets has the distinction of being one of the earliest sports to inspire a match between Oxford and Cambridge, in 1858. Only the Boat Race and the Cricket Match have a longer history; they started a quarter of a century before. Royal Tennis followed a year later.

Just as Royal Tennis gave birth to rackets, so rackets has produced its own progeny in squash. One of the chief nurseries of rackets players has always been Harrow. Towards the end of the nineteenth century it was found that the number of boys wishing to play was far greater than could be accommodated by the school court. Accordingly a variant of the game was devised to initiate younger boys and to prepare them for senior rackets. By the use of a larger and softer ball the game was slowed down, and, more important, a much smaller and therefore cheaper court was needed. Thus squash rackets was born, and it has become a game in its own right, a very valuable addition to the sports repertory. Even in large cities, where space is impossibly costly for most games, squash courts can be built in such places as the basements of office blocks. Sedentary workers can go straight from their desks at the end of a day's work, enjoy a game of squash and a shower, and so avoid the discomforts of rush-hour travel. It is not surprising that the game is growing in popularity more quickly than any other, but this sudden growth brings its dangers. Squash is a perfect game for playing by friends where the result does not matter in the least. Unfortunately there are ominous signs that it may be spoilt, as many other games have been ruined, by an over-elaborate organization of leagues, cups, championships and sponsorship. Squash is an ideal second sport, but a squash court is no place for a young man or woman on a fine afternoon.

Fives, rackets and squash all eliminate the net from Royal Tennis and utilize the bounce of the ball from wall and ground. From the eighteenth century onwards there have been attempts to take tennis out of the enclosed court into an open space; this meant abandoning the bounce off the walls and demanded the retention of the net. The first hint of such an attempt comes from the *Sporting Magazine* for 29 September 1793: 'Field Tennis threatens ere long to bowl out Cricket'. Cricket survived the threat, and no historian appears to have discovered anything further about this Field Tennis. Eighty years were to pass before Royal Tennis was successfully freed from its walls in the game which used to be called Lawn Tennis. The results of that success were so important that they will demand full treatment in the proper place.

4
The Beginning of Organized Team Games: Cricket

The reasons for the decline of Royal Tennis at the opening of the seventeenth century are not easy to find. In our own day, when a game loses popularity, it is because players or spectators find some other pursuit more attractive. But there is no evidence of an upsurge of activity in any other sport during Tudor times. The most likely explanation is to be found in the social and religious movements of the sixteenth century which we sum up under the title of the Reformation.

By pointing to obvious instances of licentious conduct in some clerics of the Roman Church, the reformers were able to appeal to that ascetic and puritan element which lurks in every society and most individuals. The extreme Protestant sects resembled the Marxists of today both in their fanaticism and in the methods which they used to secure power over their fellow-citizens. They aimed at achieving control over local authorities and trade guilds, institutions which affected everyday life far more than did the remote central government at Westminster. One of their chief weapons was the rigid enforcement of the Fourth Commandment, which could be embodied in stringent regulations against Sabbath-breaking. Thus puritanism impinged strongly on sport, since for the majority of people Sunday afforded the traditional and indeed the only leisure for recreation. The sectarians had other resources. Tennis courts were required to be licensed, and local authorities could refuse or cancel licences. Before the end of Elizabeth's reign the City Fathers of London, a stronghold of puritanism, succeeded from time to time in closing the theatres, using outbreaks of the plague as a pretext. As an actor, Shakespeare was inevitably affected by this, and puritanism was obviously much in his mind when he wrote *Twelfth Night*. In the character of Malvolio he brought to bear against it the most effective weapon, ridicule, but by this time ridicule was not enough.

The Crown made occasional attempts to protect its subjects from this oppression by a minority. A declaration of James I, dated 24 May 1618, reads thus:

Whereas we did justly, in our progresse through Lancashire, rebuke some puritans and precise people, in prohibiting and unlawfully punishing of our good people for using their lawfull recreations and honest exercises on Sundayes and other holy days, after the afternoone sermon or service; it is our will that, after the end of divine service, our good people be not disturbed, letted or discouraged from any lawful recreation, such as dauncing, either for men or women; archery for men, leaping, vaulting, or any other such harmless recreation. . . . But withall, we doe here account still as prohibited all unlawfull games to be used upon Sundayes onely, as bear and bull-baitings, interludes, and at all times in the meaner sort of people by law prohibitted, bowling.

This proclamation was renewed by Charles I early in his reign. But the Crown was unpopular for reasons quite unconnected with sport, and these well-meant efforts had less effect than they deserved. With the defeat of the royal cause and the establishment of the Commonwealth, the rigorists were left in full control. Probably at no time in human history has the effect of religion on sport been so decisive or so deadly.

The Restoration brought a revival in Royal Tennis, but the popularity of the game did not spread widely among the middle classes as it had done a century and a half earlier. The reaction against Commonwealth austerity, in this as in other spheres, was slow to extend beyond court circles. When at last the relaxation of puritan severity in behaviour allowed the mass of the people once again to indulge freely in sport, the game which began to appeal to them particularly was cricket.

The earliest reference to the name of cricket so far discovered is in the Borough Records of Guildford under the year 1598:

John Denwick of Guldeford . . . one of the Queenes Majesties Coroners of the County of Surrey, being of the age of fyfty and nyne yeares or there aboute . . . saith upon his oath that hee hath known the parcell of land . . . for the space of Fyfty years and more, and saith that hee being a schollar in the Free schoole of Guldeford, hee and several of his fellowes did runne and play there at Creckett and other plaies.

This makes it clear that the game was being played before the reign of Queen Elizabeth. Two other fragments of evidence from the next century reveal that the puritan prohibition of Sunday play did not always deter cricketers. In a biography published in 1672 we read: 'Maidstone was formerly a very prophane town, inasmuch that before 1640 I have seen morrice dancing, cudgel playing, stoolball, *crickets*, and many other sports openly and publickly on the Lord's Day.' And there is an entry in the Churchwardens' Overseer's Book of Eltham for the year 1654: 'An accompt of all such moneys as hath bene receved for misdemeners of whom and howe disposed of; – Cricket players on ye Lord's Day.' Seven names follow, and each culprit was fined two shillings.

The most romantic of these early references to the game comes later in the same century. In 1676 a British fleet operating off the Levantine coast sent a body of men ashore. The log-book of one of the ships, HMS *Assistance*, records that on 6 May some members of her crew played cricket at Antioch. Though cricket is very much a game of the sun, we tend to think of it against a background of English green fields. It is curious that this first game to which an exact date can be assigned should be set in the parched land of Syria.

There is no certainty that any of the cricket so far mentioned consisted of formal matches between teams. It may well have been no more than the kind of informal knockabout seen today when a group of small boys have a bat and ball. The first recorded match took place in 1700. In March of that year, a newspaper published an advertisement of a 'Cricket Match, the best of five games, to be played on Clapham Common on Easter Monday next for £10 a head a game and £20 the odd one'. Already cricket was following tennis and bowls in being played for stakes; the terms appear to mean that each player staked £10 on each game, while if the rubber went to the fifth game for decision, the stakes on this last game were doubled. Clearly if five games could be finished in a day – they would presumably be single-innings and almost certainly single-wicket – scoring cannot have been high. The fact that the match was advertised implies that the organizers hoped to attract spectators.

In the year in which this match was played, a young man named Goldwin went up from Eton to Cambridge. In 1706 he published a book of Latin poems, one of which, 'On a Ball-game' (*In Certamen Pilae*), clearly describes a cricket match. Nowadays this would be suspected of being a rather pretentious pastiche of phrases from ancient authors, valueless as evidence for details of a game. But in Goldwin's time, many cultured Englishmen still felt that they could convey their meaning and even their deep feelings more adequately in Latin than in their native language, as Milton had done not many years before. So Goldwin's poem may be regarded as perfectly trustworthy. The curious will find in it a dropped catch very prettily described in hexameters; for the historian the opening of the poem is more important. As soon as the teams meet, there is a heated discussion about the rules under which the game is to be played:

> Soon they were hurling insults at one another and almost coming to blows, because everyone wanted to have the game played according to his view of the laws.
>
> (*Mox iurgia miscent*
> *Civilesque iras, quod vult imponere ludo*
> *Quisque suas leges.*)

Happily among those present was an old player, a Nestor:

> Although he had long since laid aside bat and ball and was enjoying the privileges of a veteran, he remembered his former prowess and played the part of a just arbitrator. He laid down reasonable rules and put an end to the quarrel.
>
> (*Vice fungitur aequi*
> *Iudicis, et quanquam positis campestribus armis*
> *Iamdudum indulsit senio, non immemor artis*
> *Proponit iustas leges, et temperat iras.*)

Such waste of time before play could start must always have been likely until laws were printed. In important games it was guarded against by rules for each match being put in writing beforehand. A copy of such 'Articles of Agreement' has survived, dated 11 July 1727. It covers two matches between teams captained by the Duke of Richmond and Mr Broderick. Several of the conditions are interesting. The teams are twelve a side, the stakes twelve guineas a side, the wickets 23 yards apart. 'A ball caught, cloathed or not, the striker is out'; 'If any of the gamesters shall speak or give their opinion on any point of the game, they are to be turned out and voided in the Match; this not to extend to the Duke of Richmond and Mr Broderick'; 'The Batt Men for every One they count are to touch the Umpires Stick'.

From this it appears that the modern soccer rule which permits only a captain to ask the referee the reason for a decision has a respectable ancestry; but unhappily not every footballer who violates this regulation is 'turned out and voided in the Match'. Another interesting point is the reference to umpires' sticks. These are to be seen in several cricket pictures of the eighteenth century, but, except here, have never figured in the laws. In cricket, by some atavistic folk memory, prehistoric habits survive in a remarkable way. A few years ago, a preparatory school headmaster stated in a letter to *The Times* that when his boys were called upon to umpire, they felt it necessary to carry a bat as a symbol of office. I have myself heard the umpire of a village team, before calling 'Play', ask the opening batsman if he would like a trial ball. This has never appeared in the laws of cricket, though it was customary in Royal Tennis in the sixteenth century.

Goldwin's Latin poem and the Duke's Articles show how pressing was the need for a published set of laws. So far as our present knowledge goes, this was first met in 1752, when a code, 'Rules of the game of cricket as played on the Artillery Ground, London', was printed in *The New Universal Magazine*; with a statement that it had been drawn up eight years earlier. This is undoubtedly the most important document in the history of cricket, and it repays endless study. The code presumes in its users a general knowledge of the game; there is no attempt at a description. The rules simply deal with a number of points over which disputes might arise. Clearly whoever was responsible for compiling it was wise enough to secure the help of an old player – one just like Goldwin's Nestor – and to record his pronouncements with a minimum of editing. The direct language is in refreshing contrast to the gobbledegook of the committees who nowadays produce or revise the rules of games.

> If ye Wicket is Bowled down, its Out.
>
> If a Striker nips up a ball just before him, he may fall before his Wicket, or pop down his Batt before she comes to it, to save it.

Even when the complications of a rule involve the lawgiver in constructions at which a pedantic syntactician might frown, the meaning is perfectly clear.

> If he delivers ye ball with his hinder foot over ye bowling Crease, ye Umpire shall call No Ball, though she be struck, or ye Player is bowled out, which he shall do without being asked, and no Person shall have any right to ask him.

On the wickets of those days the behaviour of the ball was no doubt as unpredictable as a woman's, and fully justified the delightful use of the feminine pronoun.

Very occasionally the hand of the editor peeps through:

> Ye Umpires are sole judges of all Outs and Ins, of all fair and unfair play, of frivolous delays, of all hurts, whether real or pretended, and are discretionally to allow what time they think proper before ye Game goes on again.

'Frivolous' and 'discretionally' are hardly words which the veteran would have used. It is interesting that while the old man spoke of 'Notches', the editor seems to have preferred 'Runs'. If 1744 is the true date of the code, this is the earliest recorded use of the words. In the *Oxford Dictionary* the first quotation for 'run' in this sense is from 1746, the first for 'notch' is dated 1755.

The game mirrored in these laws is astonishingly like the cricket played today. The most important difference is that in 1744 a batsman was allowed to obstruct an opponent to prevent him from making a catch:

> When ye ball is hit up, either of ye Strikers may hinder ye catch in his running ground, or if she's hit directly across ye wickets, ye other Player may place his body anywhere within ye swing of his Batt, so as to hinder ye Bowler from catching her, but he must neither strike at her nor touch her with his hands.

(This law contains the only slip in the whole code; 'Strikers' in the first line should be 'Batsmen'. The end of the law shows that the rule for the striker is not the same as for the batsman at the bowler's end.) The other noteworthy difference, as Sir Neville Cardus has pointed out, is that there is no mention in the code of Leg Before Wicket. There were no pads in those days.

There are sad signs in the section on 'Laws for ye Umpires' that the heavy betting of the time had already caused corrupt practices which had to be guarded against. The ominous reference to 'hurts, whether real or pretended' appears more appropriate to professional soccer than to cricket; equally significant is the law that it is the duty of the umpires:

> To mark ye Ball that it may not be changed.

It is worth noting that the 1744 laws include the term 'popping crease'. The *Oxford Dictionary* derives this from a rare and obsolete use of 'pop' in the sense of 'strike'. John Nyren in his *Cricketers of My Time* (1833) has a more probable explanation:

> Between the stumps a hole was cut in the ground, large enough to contain the ball and the butt-end of the bat. In running a notch, the striker was required to put his bat into this hole, instead of the modern practice of touching over the popping crease, The wicket-keeper, in putting out the striker when running, was obliged, when the ball was thrown in, to place it in this hole before the adversary could reach it with his bat. Many severe injuries of the hands were the consequences of this regulation; the present mode of touching the popping crease was therefore substituted for it.

This is supported by the use of the phrase 'pop down his Batt' in the 1744 laws. The hole into which the batsman 'popped his bat' before the keeper could 'pop' the ball into it was pushed forward from the wicket to the 'popping crease'. No known version of the Laws mentions the hole, yet today there are still batsmen who are not content when taking guard until they have banged out a quite unnecessary hole in the crease, and others who at the end of a run feel an atavistic urge to ground the bat in this block-hole (a term still current). This habit is the cause of those frequent and disastrous collisions between running batsmen. For some reason, Australian cricketers are particularly prone to this failing.

Even before the appearance of the Laws of 1744, the game was already attracting the attention of the sociologists. In 1743 an author calling himself the 'British Champion' launched a furious attack on cricket. When he declares, 'It is a most notorious and shameless breach of the laws, as it gives the most open encouragement to gambling', the reader might allow that he had detected a real danger to the game; but when he goes on, 'It is highly unseemly that lords and gentlemen, clergymen and lawyers, should associate themselves with butchers and cobblers in such diversions', all sympathy with him evaporates. It is worth noting that he denounces the 'crowds of idle spectators' which cricket attracted, evidence of its place in the life of the country even at that early date.

The lucubrations of the 'British Champion' had little effect. On 18 June 1744, the first match was played of which a complete score has survived; it was between Kent and All England, and among the spectators was Frederick, Prince of Wales, himself a keen player, who seven years later was to die untimely as the result of a blow from a cricket ball. The game, which was won by Kent, was celebrated by James Love in poetic English far more flowery than Goldwin's Latin.

> A place there is, where City-warriors meet,
> Wisely determined not to fight, but eat.
> Where harmless Thunder rattles to the Skies,
> While the plump *Buff-coat* fires, and shuts his eyes.
> Here, in the Intervals of Bloodless War,
> The Swains with milder Pomp their Arms prepare.

Thus the poet describes the Artillery Fields, for many years used for cricket when not required by the owners, the Honourable Artillery Company. He tells us that while Kent included Lord John Sackville, one of the All England team was a bricklayer:

> Next Bryan came, whose cautious Hand could fix
> In neat disposed Array the well-pil'd Bricks.

So much for the 'British Champion'.

At the beginning of his poem Love reveals that already in 1743 rivalry among the counties dominated the game:

> And see where busy Counties strive for Fame,
> Each greatly potent at this *mighty* Game!
> Fierce *Kent*, ambitious of the first Applause,
> Against the World combin'd asserts her Cause;
> Gay *Sussex* sometimes triumphs o'er the Field,
> And fruitful *Surry* cannot brook to yield.

So it is not surprising that one of the earliest revisions of the Laws, published in 1774, was announced as the work of 'A committee of Noblemen and Gentlemen of Kent, Hampshire, Surrey, Sussex, Middlesex and London'. For the first time, rules covering betting on matches were included, destined to remain for half a century. Rather strangely these rules had already been dropped when in 1835 a law forbidding betting by umpires was introduced. This survived until after the Second World War, and then unobtrusively disappeared from the book; presumably it was thought to be obsolete, a sadly over-optimistic view, as developments of the last few years are showing.

In 1787 occurred an event crucial in the history of cricket. An enterprising enthusiast, Thomas Lord, became tenant of a field in London, and a club was formed to play on it, the Marylebone Club or MCC. Twice Lord was compelled to move to a new field, but each time he stripped the turf and took it with him. The second of these changes, in 1813–14, brought him to the present Lord's ground. One of the first actions of the newly formed MCC was to settle the code of laws under which they would play. This was not published until 1796, but its title page bore the imprint, 'Revised by the Cricket Club at St Mary-le-Bone, May 30th, 1788'. The prestige of the club grew steadily. Its rules were accepted as the standard for the game, and little by little, often unwillingly, it became the governing body of cricket.

This is an example of a curious phenomenon in the social life of Britain. The British are by nature democratically minded; certainly in their political life they have made a democratic constitution work better than any other nation in the history of mankind. But they are also intensely pragmatic; if a piece of social machinery works satisfactorily, they are content to let it go on working, whatever its ideological imperfections. This is particularly evident in the field of sport. The MCC is the very antithesis of democracy. Like the Jockey Club, founded a quarter of a century earlier, it is aristocratic in origin, and it still retains abundant traces of its origin; it is self-elected and self-perpetuating. So far from aiming at power, it has constantly tried to avoid responsibilities which the cricket world has wished to thrust on it. In fact a cynic might point out that it is only since the MCC attempted to democratize its functions by means of elected boards and committees that first-class cricket has fallen into the state of ruin in which it now lies.

One of the founders of the MCC was the fourth Duke of Richmond, grandson of the second Duke who drew up the Agreement for the match in 1727; the third Duke was also a keen cricketer. The teams which these noblemen organized included many of their employees from their considerable estates at Goodwood. These men were not expected to lose any wages by playing, but cricket was in no sense a career for them; the enthusiasm of their patrons made it possible for these humbler lovers of the game to take part in it. They were, in fact, the first 'broken-time' professionals – though the terms 'amateur' and 'professional' applied to cricketers still lay a hundred years in the future. In the eighteenth century the distinction was between those who were 'gentlemen' and those who were not.

Today it is conventional to regard any stratification of society into a class structure as an unmitigated evil. Certainly it is not easy to find any theoretical justification for such distinctions, and those whose political career depends on their ability to arouse envy and hatred in their supporters find 'class' a convenient target for their attacks. Yet there is another side to the question. Shakespeare and Dr Johnson were in many ways very different men, but they were both highly intelligent and enriched with a wide experience of life. Neither had been born in the purple or anywhere near it; they had known poverty in their youth. Both were convinced that a breakdown of 'degree' or 'subordination', as they called the class structure, was the greatest danger to which society was exposed. Until recent times, social class was regarded almost universally as one of the facts of life, to be accepted without bitterness. Today we are supposed to have achieved a classless society, yet there is more talk about class and class warfare than ever before; if the beneficiaries of this state of affairs have achieved by it any greater degree of happiness than their grandfathers enjoyed, they contrive to conceal it very successfully. The class-structured society of the eighteenth century had its unpleasant side, which appears for instance in the 'British Champion's' objections to lawyers and gentlemen associating with butchers and cobblers at cricket. But we must remember that few took any notice of him. From the time when the Dukes of Richmond played with the workers on their estates, it has always been one of the great glories of the game that men of all classes can meet on friendly terms on the field.

Sociologists sometimes speak of society as if it consisted of two classes, rich and poor, employers and employed, but, at any rate since the Middle Ages, society has always been far more diverse than that. At the top were the aristocracy and landed gentry, both 'gentlemen' beyond a doubt. Then there were the prosperous commercial class, at first looked down on as being 'in trade', but after a generation or two able to buy themselves into the rank of landed proprietors. There were also yeoman farmers and tenant farmers, skilled artisans and master craftsmen, men of substance well above the breadline of agricultural labourers and urban poor. We have seen that the town-dwelling section of this diversified middle class made a considerable contribution to the game of Royal Tennis in the time of Elizabeth I. In the eighteenth century the country dwellers were the backbone of the cricket of their day.

By good fortune we know a good deal about this aspect of cricket. In 1756 there was a match between Hambledon and Dartford; this is the first mention of one of the most remarkable clubs in the history of the game. Hambledon is a small village in Hampshire. It was the home of Richard Nyren, heir to a proud cricketing tradition. He was the nephew of Richard Newland, who had played for All England in the match against Kent in 1743, hymned by Love:

> On th'adverse Party, towering o'er the rest
> Left-handed Newland fires each arduous Breast.

Richard Nyren, a farmer and innkeeper, was the moving spirit in the Hambledon club, which in its heyday, the thirty years after its first recorded match, could hold its own against any opposition; when he left the club in 1791, it broke up. His son John, an enthusiast for the game from boyhood, wrote an account of the club in a book, *The Young Cricketer's Tutor and the Cricketers of My Time*, published in 1833, with which begins the vast literature of cricket, unmatched by any other sport.

Perhaps John Nyren's keenness and the charm of his short book have led us to overrate the abilities of the men of Hambledon when they are judged against absolute standards. We have to remember that when we read of Hambledon defeating 'Surrey' or 'All England', those terms do not mean what they would today. There were no county clubs or selection committees then. The titles of these teams were assigned to them by the aristocratic patrons who assembled them.

One of Nyren's anecdotes gives a lively picture of the mingling of different social classes at cricket. Among the Hambledon men was Lambert, the 'Little Farmer', who had discovered how to bowl off-breaks (the natural ball in right-handed underarm bowling was the leg-break), 'And egad! this new trick of his so bothered the Kent and Surrey men that they tumbled out one after another, as if they had been picked off by a rifle corps. For a long time they could not tell what to make of that cursed twist of his.' But Lambert was a man of very limited intelligence, and for a long time he persisted in bowling at the wicket with the result that he constantly missed the leg stump. At last Richard Nyren got him to pitch the ball a little to the off-side of the wicket.

> Before he had got into this knack, he was once bowling against the Duke of Dorset, and, delivering his ball straight to the wicket, it curled in and missed the Duke's leg-stump by a hair's breath. The plain-spoken little bumpkin, in his eagerness and delight, and forgetting the style in which we were always accustomed to impress our aristocratical playmates with our acknowledgment of their rank and station, bawled out, 'Ah! it was *tedious* near you, Sir!' The familiarity of his tone, and the genuine Hampshire dialect in which it was spoken, set the whole ground laughing.

The great growth in the popularity of cricket at the end of the eighteenth century produced some changes. More and more working-class men took to the game, to their great financial profit, for they could now command more than the 'broken-time' equivalent of their wages. The usual payment was five guineas for a win, three for a lost match; later the figures rose to six and four. The Reverend James Pycroft, who published a history of cricket in 1851, points out that money of this kind was a strong temptation when the wage of a farm labourer was 10s. a week. A natural result of this was that these professionals – or 'players' – soon far excelled the 'gentlemen' in skill. But there was another and less happy development, the intrusion of corruption into the game. From the beginning, matches had normally been played for stakes, as was the practice in every other sport. Nyren tells us that the 'great matches' of the Hambledon club were for £500 a side, their own stakes being put up by two local landowners. This in itself constituted a danger to the game; an even greater peril lay in the heavy side betting on matches. The 'legs', the unscrupulous bookmakers who frequented Lord's and other grounds, would stoop to any measures to 'fix' matches, and it was not only the 'players' who took their bribes. The Reverend Lord Frederick Beauclerk, the only 'gentleman' of his time who was said to be the equal in skill of the 'players', admitted to making £600 a year from the game – the equivalent of at least £10 000 today – and it was widely suspected that he owed a great deal of his financial success to backing his opponents in matches in which he was playing himself.

Pycroft's book has 'A Dark Chapter', which makes sad reading. He tells of games which were sold by both sides. A cricket match which both teams are trying to lose has comic or indeed farcical possibilities, but it does not betoken a healthy state of the game. Pycroft pictures the scene: 'Lord's was frequented by men with book and pencil, betting as openly and professionally as in the ring at Epsom, and ready to deal in the odds with any and every person of speculative propensities.' It is not surprising that early in the nineteenth century there was a decline in the popularity of cricket at the top level. In the previous century, aristocratic patrons in Surrey had raised many teams to which they gave the county name; between 1801 and 1844 hardly any such matches are recorded.

There is no doubt whatever about the cause of this corruption and decline. It was the intrusion of money – especially the hot money of gambling – into the game; for more than 2000 years this intrusion has been fatal to any form of sport at any level. Far more mysterious is the reason why cricket was able to emerge from this slough and to rise into the Golden Age at the end of the century. The subject is of great interest today, when the top stratum of the game is in the same parlous state as 150 years ago, and for the same reasons. Nowadays we have a succession of committees of inquiry into the state of the game, but the deterioration is so swift that the reports of the commissions are out of date by the time they are published. Cricket before 1850 was at least free of these nuisances.

Part of the reason for the improvement was no doubt simply a change of fashion. Some of the raffish aristocrats who had been responsible for the corruption of cricket grew old and dropped out of the game. Others transferred their patronage to horse racing or prize fighting; in these pursuits they could see the outcome of their bets more speedily than in cricket, where matches of two or three days were already common. A younger generation of amateurs, then as now, had no wish to support the first-class game which had fallen into such disrepute, but they still loved and played cricket, and there is plenty of evidence that at club level it flourished and expanded. The disappearance of the first-class matches reduced the demand for the services of the 'players'. Towards the middle of the century a man named Clarke of Nottinghamshire organized some of these professionals into what he called the All England XI; they toured the country playing against local clubs, which were allowed to field teams of sixteen to twenty-two to meet their powerful opponents. The fee charged was £70, and sometimes a share of the gate money. There were enough prosperous clubs to make the enterprise a success; it lasted for thirty years, and provoked several imitators. Such a project had become a possibility owing to the improvements in communications, first the turnpike roads with reliable services of stage coaches, and then the railways. Tom Brown travelled to Rugby by stage coach on the morning of the famous football match. Seven years later, when he was captain of cricket, the MCC came by train to play against the school. This match can be accurately dated to 1841, the year in which Hughes, who was obviously the Tom Brown of his book, was cricket captain at Rugby.

The clean-up of cricket did not come entirely or even mainly from within the game; it must be seen against an improvement in morality in the social scene generally. In the eighteenth century the distress caused by the influx of workers into the factories of the towns had been disregarded by a Church which was complacent and worldly. The universities of Oxford and Cambridge, still a preserve of the Church, followed the same line. Yet in both there were small bodies of serious-minded undergraduates who were keenly aware of what was going on, and formed groups for study and mutual support. These earnest young men were not well regarded either by their contemporaries or by the university authorities; they were assailed as 'Methodists' and 'Enthusiasts', terms of abuse at that time. Yet when they went out into the world, the influence on the working class of such men as John Wesley and George Whitefield was considerable.

In the universities the number of undergraduates who felt a personal commitment to Christianity slowly grew. Early in the nineteenth century some of them were elected to fellowships of their colleges, and this gave further impetus to the movement; the dominant element in the quality of any university, ancient or modern, has always been the character of the younger

(Above) An illustration found in a fourteenth-century manuscript, which suggests hockey, but could equally well show a pair of medieval gardeners. *(British Museum)*
Women playing bowls, *c.*1340, with an intensity and concentration that is familiar to modern players. *(Bodleian)*

(Above) The Countess of Derby playing cricket in 1779. *(MCC)*
A cricket match in Mary-Le-Bone Fields, 1748. *(A. Lockwood)*

dons. The reformation thus engendered spread much more widely through all classes of society than had the Methodism of the previous century. Many of the reformers belonged to the Oxford Movement, highly influential until it was shattered by the defection of Newman to Rome and driven to a concentration on ecclesiastical haberdashery and similar trivia. More significant if less spectacular were the Evangelicals, prime movers in the abolition of slavery and in much social legislation, but even more important for their insistence on high moral standards in the everyday life of the individual. Nor must we underrate the effects of the accession of Queen Victoria, whose unimpeachable private character, markedly different from that of some preceding monarchs, set new standards in court circles which spread downwards.

With the increasing seriousness among undergraduates came a change in the amusements of their leisure hours. It is impossible to say whether or not there was any connection between the two, and if there was a link, to decide which was cause and which was effect. In the eighteenth century when men came up to the university, they abandoned the games they had played at school and for recreation relied mainly on activities based on the horse: hunting, steeplechasing, and driving extravagant vehicles which were the counterpart of the modern sports car. Games were on the whole frowned on by the authorities, and they conferred no social prestige in undergraduate circles. With the turn of the century came a gradual change, signalized by the first Oxford and Cambridge Cricket Match at Lord's in 1827. This was arranged by Charles Wordsworth, a nephew of the poet. He was in residence at Christ Church, Oxford, and his father was Head of a Cambridge college, so he had a foot in both camps. To the modern generation of students it will seem incredible that the players had to resort to considerable subterfuges and deceptions in order to escape from their colleges for the game. Two years later, Wordsworth arranged the second match, played at Oxford. On the previous day he had rowed at Henley in the first University Boat Race, which he had also done much to promote; happy days of the all-rounder! The third Cricket Match was not played until 1836, the fourth in 1838. Since then, thanks to improved communications, it has been played annually, except during two World Wars.

It is said that all the members of the Oxford crew in that first Boat Race took Holy Orders; Charles Wordsworth became a Bishop. At last the tension between Christianity and sport, which had existed for 1500 years and had been particularly marked in Britain since the puritans of Elizabeth's reign, was coming to an end. John Wesley, who had played and enjoyed Royal Tennis at Oxford, came in his later years to regard this as part of his unregenerate youth. Now the attitude had changed. Our sniggering satirists find something funny in the idea of 'muscular Christianity'. People of greater intelligence and a more adult sense of humour know that there is nothing incompatible between physical excellence and the deepest spiritual sensitiveness.

The part played by Oxford and Cambridge in the history of cricket is not nearly so important as in football, rowing and athletics. Indeed it might easily be argued that the game would not be significantly different had these universities never existed. It is true that until 1939 a stream of first-class amateurs came from them into county cricket, and even since the Second World War there has been a trickle. But perhaps their greatest contribution to the development of cricket was indirect, in that their influence on the general moral standards of society during the first half of the nineteenth century had much to do with rescuing the game from its earlier corruption.

5
Cricket: The Later Stages

As cricket emerged from its period of corruption, the landed gentry and professional classes renewed their enthusiasm for the game at its highest level and took the step which was responsible for the development of the first-class game as we know it – the foundation of the county clubs. The dates of the founding meetings of these clubs extend from Sussex (1839) and Surrey (1844) to Somerset (1875), Essex (1876) and Leicestershire (1878). The clubs have an unbroken history to the present day, but they are very far now from their founders' intentions.

Today the member of a county cricket club is little more than a glorified season-ticket holder. The committee of the club is indistinguishable from the board of directors of a professional soccer club. It runs a heterogeneous team of players, most of whom have little connection with the county and all of whom are under contract, and runs it as a commercial enterprise. When the clubs were founded, the members were men who wanted to play the game themselves at the highest level, and the committee was appointed to run the club with that end in view. In order that there might always be someone to bowl to members and their sons when they wanted to practise, the clubs employed professionals, who could also be called upon to play in matches, but in many counties a member with any pretensions to ability expected to play a few games in the county XI, even if this meant dropping a professional of superior skill. The committees also made arrangements for members and their families to watch matches in comfort and to enjoy other amenities of a social club.

Whether or not the founders of these clubs realized it, they were in fact performing a completely revolutionary act. The history of sport was already 3000 years old in their day, but now for the first time a game was being organized at top level purely for the enjoyment of the participants, without any consideration for the supposed interests of gamblers, advertisers, crowds of spectators or anyone else. The other games and sports, which were then beginning to achieve organization for the first time, tried to follow the example of cricket, and for this reason the Victorian age is rightly regarded as having exhibited first-class sport at its peak. Little by little, almost inevitably, the outside considerations crept in, always with plenty of interested parties to justify the intrusion and always with disastrous long-term results, as we can see only too well; for it is a curious paradox, proved true time and time again in this century, that whenever a game is modified to make it more attractive to spectators, the spectators themselves are less and less attracted to it. Today, happily, there are hundreds of thousands of moderate performers playing games for pure enjoyment, but it has become increasingly difficult and now almost impossible for a player of first-class ability to do so with his equals.

The distinction between the members of the county cricket clubs and the professionals employed by them now became the dividing line between 'gentlemen' and 'players'. These terms remained in use, especially for the matches between them which sadly came to an end in 1962, but were gradually superseded by 'amateur' and 'professional', which came into vogue at about this time. (The earliest date recorded by the *Oxford Dictionary* for 'professional' in a sporting context is 1850, for 'amateur', 1885.) There were some anomalies in the distinction between employer and employed. The secretary of a club was no less an employee than the playing professionals, but he was regarded as an amateur. Within living memory, V. W. C. Jupp, who had played as a professional for Sussex, became Secretary of Northants CCC, and captained the county team; until well after the Second World War it was thought essential that no matter how many professionals played in a county XI, the captain should be an amateur. But the Victorian attitude towards professionals in cricket was very different from that in rugby football. In that game, to have been a professional conferred – and still confers – a lifelong stigma, and the amateur is still not allowed to play in company with anyone who has incurred that disgrace. Cricketers never took this attitude. Amateur and professional had been playing together happily for a hundred years and continued to do so. A professional could at any time become an amateur simply by ceasing to take money for playing. The most famous of those who took this step was W. R. Hammond, who suffered so little from having been a professional that he captained England.

Young and ignorant journalists sometimes give the impression that in the days before the distinction was abolished in 1963, cricket professionals were a depressed, servile and miserable class of men. It is true that none of them acquired great wealth. Many of them had abilities which would have brought them success in other walks of life, but they preferred cricket. In those leisurely days a man could stay in the profession well into his forties. When Jack Hobbs and Frank Woolley opened the England innings in the Lords Test in 1930, their combined ages numbered ninety, and the elder George Cox took all ten Yorkshire wickets in an innings in his fiftieth year. The season being short, any cricket professional had to be able to keep himself by some other occupation during the remainder of the year, so when their playing days were over, they had resources to fall back upon, or if they preferred, they could remain in the game for many more years. Some became umpires, others took a post as coach at a public school, which offered them the pleasures of a schoolmaster's life without its most trying burdens, as they grew old in the company of eternal youth in its happiest hours on the playing fields. Anyone who has played cricket over a number of years will have met some of these old-timers and will remember them with infinite delight; others can enjoy them in the pages of Sir Neville Cardus. In conferring honours on the worlds of sport and entertainment, the Crown has often been badly served by its advisers, but no one has ever cavilled at the distinction bestowed on Sir John Berry Hobbs.

There was, of course, another side to the picture. Any man in the sporting limelight is exposed to temptation. There are always far too many people anxious to stand him a drink, hoping to share his glory by being seen in his company; and there are other social pressures. It is not surprising that a few succumb. Everyone acquainted with the world of sport knows of some such tragedies, not all in the game of cricket, and by no means all among professionals. In this as in many other aspects, sport is only a microcosm of life.

There is one general consideration which does much to account for the happiness of the county cricket scene before 1914 – the absence from it of people lusting to organize it. This is hardly credible today, when every game teems with hangers-on who yearn to sit on committees to run it or boards to reform it, and who even long for that ultimate degradation of sport, a government enquiry to investigate it. The lack of organization explains the vague way in which the county championship came into existence. Cricket was the first team game in which the idea of a championship arose, though the institution had existed for many years in sports for individuals, boxing, sculling, tennis and rackets. In these a man claimed the title of champion and arranged contests with challengers until one of them beat him. Sometimes he would resign the title while still undefeated, and then matches were arranged between likely candidates to find a successor.

For obvious reasons most of the cricket matches played by the counties were from the beginning against other counties; there were few other clubs strong enough to give them a good game. It was no doubt the rivalry thus engendered that led to the MCC in 1862 laying down a rule of qualification to play for a county – birth or two years' bona fide residence. This was eminently reasonable and proved satisfactory for a century. Today, with cricketers moving from county to county as freely as soccer players jump from club to club, we can see that the abandonment of the rule was one of the chief causes of the decline of the first-class game. With the honourable exception of Yorkshire, still faithful to birth, any of our county teams might more aptly be entitled 'the Rest of the World'. One of the most valuable elements in a man's character is his proper loyalty, to school, club, university, regiment, city, county or country. The old loyalty to a sports team genuinely representing one of these was innocent enough, but now this has been replaced by a spurious loyalty to a cricket or football team which may bear the name of Surrey or Leeds, but which in truth represents nothing whatever. To replace the genuine by the spurious is always dangerous, and it may well be that the hooliganism among spectators which disfigures modern sport is to some extent due to this.

Modern lists of the champion counties start at 1864, but it is not easy to discover how the early holders were decided. The counties did not all play against all the others, and they did not all play the same number of matches. In many years, then as now, the best team was obvious; otherwise the matter seems to have been decided at the end of the season by a general consensus of opinion at the MCC, a method far superior to any that has been devised since. But it was theoretically indefensible, and in 1872 the MCC tried to regularize the position by offering a challenge cup to be competed for at Lord's by six leading counties, to be selected by the MCC. Oddly enough, the counties showed no enthusiasm for the scheme, and the offer was withdrawn. The reason which Lancashire gave for refusing showed knowledge of past history and prescience of future dangers: 'It was unnecessary and might encourage gambling.' In 1887 the MCC, anxious as always to avoid responsibility where possible, persuaded the counties to set up a County Cricket Council to administer their activities.

Three years later, the members of the Council performed their sole recorded action by deciding which counties qualified for first-class status. Next year they disbanded themselves and passed the buck back, declaring that they were perfectly content to leave the decision on all matters to the MCC. In 1904 an advisory committee of the MCC took over the organization of the championship. As the counties still did not play the same number of games, the championship was decided for many years by a system of points and percentages which, compared with what we now endure, was simplicity itself.

Our Victorian grandparents lacked the advantage we enjoy of a lavish supply of doctoral dissertations on the philosophy, psychology and sociology of sport, but they had the root of the matter in them. They knew that it is the essence of any sport that while the contest is in progress, every participant should behave as if nothing in the world mattered except winning by fair means, but that the moment the match ends, nothing matters less than who won. So long as this paradoxical attitude is maintained, every player goes into a contest with the sole ambition to win; this was the spirit in which matches even at the top level were once played. As soon as the match is converted into one of a series by the intrusion of league points, cup competitions, Test rubbers and so on, the situation arises in which the prime consideration is to avoid losing, a very different thing. Every cricketer knows that a drawn match can be desperately exciting. Often in the last innings of a game the target of runs is unattainable in the time available, and the result turns on whether the fielding side can take the remaining wickets. A pair of tail-enders, hanging on by the skin of their teeth, can achieve a moment's glory to which their batting abilities rarely expose them, and the side robbed of victory in this way will readily admit that the game was far more enjoyable than an easy win. But in a league match, where a draw gains more points than a loss, many a team from the very start of a game aims first to avoid the zero score in points which defeat entails. Hence those dreary struggles for first-innings points in the championship not long ago, the phoney declarations, the waste of time and the other abuses which have brought three-day county cricket, for years the peak and crown of the game, to its present shabby condition.

The root of the problem, as of most problems in sport, lies in the attitude of the players. It seems incredible today that in the nineteenth century, of the first sixty-two matches between Oxford and Cambridge only three were drawn – all of them ruined by rain – in spite of the fact that the laws regulating declaration and follow-on, which between them removed the chief obstacles to achieving a decision in three days, did not exist until after 1880. County cricket did not quite equal this low proportion of drawn games, but until 1914 there was no reason to suppose that three days did not afford enough time for a first-class match. The extension beyond this limit came, like many another ruinous influence in the world of sport, not from the domestic but from the international scene.

One of the most dangerous of clichés is that 'international sport promotes friendship among nations', all the more dangerous because it contains a germ of truth. International sport started with the visits of teams to other countries, playing against clubs of their own level; as no external considerations were involved, these were friendly matches in the best sense of the term. From the beginning such exchanges have been and still are of great value, and clubs, schools and universities still send their teams abroad to play against their counterparts with the happiest results. But the moment one of these teams is held to 'represent' its country of origin, questions of national prestige arise and the whole scene changes. Today an unbiased observer has to admit that so-called international sport has become an evil, not in the least mitigated by the large amounts of money made out of it.

It is natural that cricket, the first team game to be organized, was also the first to promote international team sport, but in this field cricket shows a difference from other games developed in Britain. In football, for instance, the earliest international matches were 'domestic internationals', involving Scotland, Wales and Ireland. In these countries, cricket is less firmly rooted than in England. The reason for this is not any inferiority in cricketing skill or temperament among Celts, but is simply climatic. Rain spoils a game often enough in England, and much more rain falls on the Celtic fringe. In spite of this, good cricket is played there. For the last fifty years, Glamorgan, latest of the counties to be granted first-class status, have kept the banner of Welsh cricket flying in the highest circles and have twice won the championship; on the first occasion, in 1948, their team was composed almost entirely of Welshmen. But tradition decrees that an international cricket match is one played against a country outside Britain, and even when the team representing Britain includes Scots or Welshmen, it is always called England.

The first cricket team to go abroad went, not as we might expect to Australia, but to the United States and Canada; this was in 1859. Like all early tours it was a private venture, designed on the lines of Clarke's All England XI in this country, to make a little money for some professionals. It was organized by W. P. Pickering of Eton and Cambridge, who took twelve professionals across the Atlantic at the close of the English season. October is not the best month for cricket anywhere in the northern hemisphere, and it is not surprising that the final match ended in a snowstorm. This missionary effort did not encourage the game in North America as much as might have been hoped. Cricket is still played in Canada and the States, but in neither has it achieved popularity. Chance and fashion play a great part in the history of sport. Of the countries colonized mainly by the British, Australia, New Zealand and South Africa have taken cricket to their hearts, but not North America. Here and there in East and West Africa cricket is played by Africans, but their prowess does not compare with that of the descendants of the Africans who were taken across the Atlantic as slaves in the eighteenth century; these have put the West Indies among the great cricketing countries. Even more surprising is the persistence of the love of cricket in India and Pakistan a generation after the departure of the British Army, which took the game to those countries. Outside the former British Empire there are only two places where cricket has any great hold. The survival of the game in Corfu is explained by the fact that the island was a British naval base until 1864; it is not so easy to account for cricket in Holland. The solution of these problems must be left to ethnologists.

In 1861–2 the second touring team to leave this country went to Australia, as did all important tours until the end of the century. All were private ventures, and the players were mostly professionals. The matches played by these early teams were all against superior numbers, and it was not until 1877 that the first eleven-a-side game took place. Next year an Australian touring team came to England for the first time, and caused a sensation by beating a MCC XI at Lord's in a single day. The total of runs scored in the match was 105, so clearly the wicket was one of the kind on which anything can happen; later in the tour the Australians were defeated by Cambridge University. The third Australian team in 1882, after imitating its predecessor of 1878 by being beaten by Cambridge, retrieved its reputation by a victory over an England XI at the Oval in August. This evoked from the *Sporting Times* the delightful epitaph on the death of English cricket, with its famous postscript, 'N.B. The body will be cremated and the ashes taken to Australia.' The mythical Ashes thus created were given corporeal existence in the following winter, when a team led by the Hon. Ivo Bligh defeated Australia in two out of three games. At the end of the third match the stumps were burned and the ashes presented to Bligh by the Australian captain. The urn containing them is still to be seen at Lord's; it is a sad reflection that the health of cricket might be improved if this object were thrown into the middle of the Pacific and forgotten.

None of the teams in the nineteenth century 'represented' England or Australia in the sense in which we understand the term. The touring sides of both countries were the personal choice of the man who undertook financial reponsibility for the tour; in the winter of 1887–8 there were two 'England' teams touring Australia, one led by Lord Hawke, the other by the Nottinghamshire professional, Arthur Shrewsbury. In this country the 'England' sides for matches against the tourists were selected by the county on whose ground the game was played. (The earliest recorded date for the use of 'Test' for these matches is 1894.) The first touring side to be otherwise chosen was the Australian team of 1886, picked by the Melbourne Club. As late as 1901 the MCC refused to undertake the responsibility of sending the team to Australia, and the task was performed by A. C. Maclaren; at least the MCC cannot be accused of having grasped at power. Not until 1903–4 did the Club send out a tour in its name, and truly representative cricket may be said to date from this point.

At this time South Africa showed that she had become an important force in the cricket world. Touring teams under private auspices had exchanged visits since 1888. In 1905–6 the MCC for the first time sent out a team which lost the Test rubber by 1–4. The South Africans at this period owed much of their success to their exploitation of googly bowling, which had been invented in England by B. J. Bosanquet. (It is a linguistic curiosity that the term 'googly' was coined by Australians, but they soon abandoned it in favour of 'bosie', after its inventor, which they still use.)

In 1912 an interesting experiment was held in England – a triangular tournament between the three leading cricketing countries. It was unhappily not a success and has never been repeated. The summer was one of the wettest ever recorded, the South Africans were not strong enough, and the Australian team lacked several of its best players, who had quarrelled with their Board of Control about the money they were to receive from the tour – coming events casting their shadow before. These players, alas, included the incomparable Victor Trumper; the opportunity of another tour in England which he thus threw away was never to come again. By the time cricket was resumed after the First World War he was dead, one of many players who have died at the very height of their youthful powers, even before road accidents began to take their modern toll of sportsmen.

In spite of the small blemishes of 1912, it may fairly be claimed that international cricket before the First World War was wholly for the good of the game. The long sea voyages gave the players an opportunity to relax after the rigours of the domestic season and to renew their zest for cricket, and when fatigued at the end of a tour to rest before the next season at home. Not every summer had a visiting touring side, and so the event had a rarity value. Most important of all, Test rubbers and the Ashes had not yet become an obsession; each Test was treated on its merits and presented cricket at its highest degree of skill. Although no more than the three days of a county match were allotted to Tests in this country, surprisingly few matches were drawn.

The dwindling body of those who remember the world before 1914 know that the First World War, much more than the Second, brought the end of an era, and this is true of the small domain of sport. In cricket every effort was made after the war to get the game on its feet again. The county championship was resumed in 1919, with the curious experiment of two-day matches with extended hours of play. There were fewer drawn games than might have been expected, but spectators did not drop in to watch an evening's play as had been hoped, and the experiment has never been repeated. The season was brightened by a team drawn from the Australian Imperial Forces, who had been fighting on this side of the world, and this held out high promise for the future.

But the world was in too great a hurry in its attempt to return to pre-war normality. The MCC unwisely yielded to pressure, and sent a touring team to Australia in the winter of 1920–1; this was followed by an Australian tour of Britain in 1921 and another MCC visit to Australia in 1924–5. Of the fifteen Tests in these years, England lost twelve. This in itself did not matter in the least. To be beaten in any sport is no disgrace, and in this case there was every reason for England's lack of success; too many of the young men who should have been claiming places in her teams were lying in graves in France. The disturbing element was a new outlook on Test matches, due in large measure to an unfortunate Australian choice of captain. W. W. Armstrong was a great all-round performer, but as a captain he was a disaster. His conduct on the field was often objectionable, and Englishmen could be forgiven for thinking, 'Well, if that is what they want. . . .' His attitude to the tour of 1921 was all wrong. Nothing mattered except winning Tests: matches against counties, provided that the disgrace of defeat was avoided, were unimportant.

The vast superiority of the Australian team prevented some of the darker aspects of this new philosophy from showing themselves at once, but they emerged in the years following. Separate Tests did not matter in comparison with winning the rubber; a side which had secured a victory aimed at avoiding a defeat in the remainder of the series, even if this meant playing for a draw from the beginning of each match. No risks must ever be taken in a Test match: 'safety first', a slogan from wider walks of life at the time, was the watchword. So three days were too short, because the reasonable scoring rate and the sporting use of the declaration which a three-day match demands were unthinkable in a Test. In this development, England was as guilty as Australia. As Test after Test was lost, journalists filled the papers with headlines, 'What is wrong with English cricket?' and their answer was that England must copy Australian methods.

Unhappily it was not the best side of Australian cricket which they recommended for imitation. In 1921 C. G. Macartney scored a century before lunch in a Test, conduct which would be thought indecent today. In 1905 Warwick Armstrong hit the last ball of a day's play out of the ground. (Nowadays it is accepted that during the last half-hour a batsman must make no attempt to score, but simply try not to lose his wicket, although if a batsman cannot make runs off an attack exhausted by a day in the field, it is unlikely that he will do so next morning when the bowlers are fresh again.) No one suggested that this was the Australian approach to be adopted. The solution offered was that the ranks of English cricketers should be combed for those with the 'Test match temperament'; this meant that they must 'stay there and let the runs come' without ever taking the slightest risk. Young batsmen, naturally anxious to assert their claim to play for England, modelled their game on this philosophy when they were playing for their counties, and a grim utilitarianism crept into championship cricket from which it has never recovered.

There is one episode in the cricket of the inter-war period which the historian must take into account, if only because it involves a deep and still abiding injustice. Moreover it shows how the persistent refusal of the MCC to accept responsibility in the game had rendered the Club incapable of acting in a crisis with the necessary firmness. The tour of Australia in 1932–3 can only be understood against a historical background.

The history of many games, like that of warfare, is an account of the development of successive techniques of attack which triumph for a time until the appropriate defence is devised. Cricket presents a special case here, since each of its chief activities, batting and bowling, exhibits both of these opposite facets; there is attacking batting and defensive batting, attacking bowling and defensive bowling. Unhappily first-class cricket today has long become stereotyped, and has degenerated into a series of clichés, both in batting and bowling. No one now playing has experienced anything resembling the revolutions in the game in the years before 1914, with the invention of the googly by Bosanquet and the exploitation of the swerve by George Hirst, and in batting the enchantments of K. S. Ranjitsinhji, who brought to the English game qualities derived from an Eastern culture, summed up by a Yorkshire professional in a famous dictum, 'He never made a Christian stroke in his life'. Perhaps his most celebrated contribution to the art of batting was the leg glance off a fast ball on the leg stump. Writers on the game sometimes suggest that he was the only man who could perform the feat, but this is untrue. The stroke was found not to be difficult for those who had the courage to attempt it, and first-class batsmen quickly added it to their repertory, though doubtless none of them performed it with the grace and elegance of its begetter. So it soon became a fundamental tenet that for a fast bowler to aim at the leg stump was simply to offer easy runs to the batsman, and fast bowling was now directed exclusively to the offside of the wicket. For twenty years batsmen had few opportunities of dealing with the fast ball on the leg stump, and the technique was almost forgotten.

Australia won the Test series of 1930 in England largely through the astonishing batting skill of Donald Bradman; the English players came to the conclusion that if Bradman's batting could be contained, they had a very good chance of turning the tables in the coming tour. They had detected that if Bradman had a weakness it was on the leg stump; certainly they had had plenty of opportunity of studying his methods, for his Test innings in 1930 had included scores of 131, 254, 334 and 232. Douglas Jardine was appointed captain for the tour, possessor of perhaps the keenest intellect ever devoted to the game, and also, fortunately, of qualities of character to match these mental powers. He had at his disposal a quartet of fast bowlers, two of them outstanding for accuracy, and together the team worked out a plan based on attacking the leg stump.

Nothing could be more legitimate than this. A bowler's first aim is to hit the wicket; if the batsman's skill prevents this, the bowler tries to tempt or compel him to action which will result in his being caught or stumped. Leg theory, the attack on or outside the leg stump, had been exploited by slow bowlers for years – the Australian W. W. Armstrong had been one of its chief exponents. Now fast bowlers were to pose forgotten problems to batsmen. Since cricket began, it has never been disputed that a bowler may legitimately bowl as fast as he can. A few outstanding batsmen prefer fast bowling to slow because it conserves the batsman's energy; the speed which carries the ball to the boundary is provided by the bowler. But most of us ordinary mortals would confess to a certain trepidation when facing a fast man. On the best of wickets a ball may fly, and painful knocks are inevitable. Ten years before Jardine's tour, a pair of Australian fast bowlers, Gregory and Macdonald, had torn through English batting; an England batsman had lost his wicket in a Test match through being struck on the head by a ball from Gregory. But no one in this country dreamed of impugning their motives.

From the beginning of the tour in 1932, it became obvious that the new plan was successful and would continue to be so until the Australian players produced the technique to counter it. Instead of developing this skill, they tried to ruin the plan by instituting a malicious campaign of vituperation in the press, accusing the English bowlers of purposely trying to inflict injury on them. This press attack naturally inflamed the crowds, and some Australian batsmen added fuel to the flames by playing to the gallery, ducking extravagantly to balls which rose scarcely above stump high, and being very properly hit in the ribs for their pains. The stupidity of this outburst of insult is clear from the name which the Australians coined for the English leg-theory plan – 'bodyline' bowling. Any bowling directed at the wicket comes straight at the batsman's body, unless he has taken guard two feet outside the leg stump, which few players do. Moreover, every cricketer knows that the short ball bowled intentionally to kick up high enough to inflict serious injury is fairly easy to evade and the bowler soon tires of wasting his energy in this way. But in an outbreak of mass hysteria such as now followed, no rational considerations have any weight whatever. It was a situation demanding strong action from above, and that was conspicuously lacking.

Since the time of the ancient Olympic Games, the governing bodies of sport have rarely been notable for the wisdom of their decisions; on this occasion the Australian Board of Control broke all records of folly. Since its inception the Board has shown an uncanny facility for quarrelling with its leading players. One of these unseemly squabbles occurred just before the English tourists arrived in 1932, the point at issue being whether Australian Test players should be permitted to write for the press about games in progress. For a time it looked as if the events of 1912 would be repeated, and the Australians would take the field without some of their best performers.

The difference was patched up, but members of the Board were on edge, and when the 'bodyline' trouble blew up, they felt it necessary to placate those whom a few weeks before they had regarded as potential rebels. Disregarding the suggestions of Jardine and Pelham Warner, the English manager, for a discussion on the spot, the Board took the extraordinary step of sending a cable to the MCC, implying that the English team were attempting to cause injury, and including the words, 'In our opinion it is unsportsmanlike'. The MCC reply to this was too long and wordy. It opened properly with a complete rejection of the charge, but then meandered off into verbiage and ended, 'If you consider it desirable to cancel the remainder of the programme, we would consent with great reluctance.' This was mistaken feebleness. There should have been a clear statement that unless the Board made a complete retraction and took steps to stop the vicious compaign of press and spectators against the English team, it would be recalled immediately. Even the hint of possible cancellation alarmed the Board with the thought of the loss of gate money from the remaining Tests.

(Above left) A Royal Tennis court, 1632.
(Above right) The layout of a Lawn Tennis court as illustrated in the first edition of Major Wingfield's *Rules of Sphairistike or Lawn Tennis*, 1873.
Lawn Tennis, a social as well as sporting occasion, 1882. (*Punch*, George du Maurier)

THE country Swaines, at footeball heere are ſeene,
Which each gapes after, for to get a blow,
The while ſome one, away runnes with it cleane,
It meetes another, at the goale below
Who never ſtirrd, one catcheth heere a fall,
And there one's maimd, who never ſaw the ball.

(Above) Football, from Henry Peacham, *Minerva Brittana*, 1612. *(British Museum)*
A Robert Cruikshank cartoon (1827) showing the rough and tumble of contemporary football.

Their reply virtually repeated the accusation of their first cable, but ended, 'We do not consider it necessary to cancel remainder of programme.' The MCC response to this was even feebler than the first. 'We note with pleasure that you do not consider it necessary to cancel the remainder of the programme. May we accept this as a clear indication that the good sportsmanship of our team is not in question?' This evoked the amazing reply, 'We do not regard the sportsmanship of your team as being in question.' In view of the direct accusation of the first cable, this was monstrous. It was neither retraction nor apology. The tourists agreed, perhaps unwisely, to accept it as if it were, and the tour staggered with undiminished bitterness to its end, the MCC winning the rubber by 4–1.

The one bright feature on the English side was the unswerving loyalty of the players to their captain, a loyalty which he would certainly not have commanded had there been anything even remotely unsportsmanlike in his conduct. It is pleasant also to remember the one Australian batsman, S. J. McCabe, who found the proper reply to the bowling with the bat, and those other Australian players who dissociated themselves from the malignant attacks, among them that king of wicketkeepers, W. A. Oldfield.

The whole venom of the Australian abuse had been directed against Jardine personally, and he was to find that if enough mud is thrown, some of it sticks. A few veteran English batsmen at home, unwilling to face the task of discovering a new technique in the evening of their careers, unhappily marred their reputations by allying themselves with the Australians. The MCC showed by its action that the spirit of appeasing the wrongdoer, which was to prove so disastrous in the political sphere during the near future, was already strong in Britain. It is true that they appointed Jardine captain of England against the West Indies and India in the next year, and so gave him the opportunity of demonstrating by a superb century in a Test match against fast leg theory that McCabe was not the only batsman to find the proper solution to the problem. But then the Club made an inexcusable mistake. The Australians had demanded a new law to deal with the imaginary abuse; in a letter of classic good sense the MCC had demolished the arguments for it. The law proposed by the Australians had read:

> Any ball delivered which, in the opinion of the umpire at the bowler's end, is bowled with the intent of intimidating the batsman or injuring him, shall be considered unfair, and 'no ball' shall be called. The bowler shall be notified of the reason. If the offence be repeated by the same bowler in the same innings, he shall be instructed by the umpire to cease bowling, and the over shall be regarded as completed. The bowler shall not be permitted to bowl again during the innings.

The letter of the MCC in reply included the passage:

> The new law recommended by the Australian Board of Control does not appear to the committee to be practicable. Firstly, it would place an impossible task on the umpire, and secondly, it would place in the hands of the umpire a power over the game which would be more than dangerous, and which any umpire might well fear to exercise.

Then underground forces must have got to work. Suddenly the MCC collapsed, yielded to Australian pressure and adopted the law which still disfigures the book. As their letter had pointed out, it requires from umpires the ability to know the hearts of men, a prerogative reserved to God. Far more important was the fact that the surrender inevitably suggested to the world at large that the MCC accepted the Australian criticism of the tourists. Small wonder that Jardine, thoroughly disillusioned, retired from the game at the height of his powers. Such is the force of evil propaganda that today young sports journalists, who were not born at the time of these events, write of him as if his name were a blot on cricket. There is another side to the picture. A few years ago, a book, *Great Cricket Captains*, contained a warm-hearted tribute to his old leader from the Yorkshire bowler W. A. Bowes, who was a member of the 1932 team and so in an unequalled position to know what really happened.

Unhappily it came too late; when it appeared, Jardine had been dead for some years. We shall not look upon his like again. Cricket is an unforgiving game, and English cricket deserves the retribution that has befallen it for its treatment of Jardine. Since his day, England has had respectable captains, but never one above the second rank.

After the sole important contribution to bowling tactics since the First World War had been defeated in this way by scurrility rather than batting skill, it was not surprising that bowlers lost heart. Australia won the next two Test series, and so the object of the campaign was achieved. Runs acquired easily and unadventurously multiplied in Test and county cricket. The farce might have seemed to have reached its zenith in 1938, when in the final Test at the Oval England scored 903 for seven wickets. But even this was surpassed in the following year, when in the last Test in South Africa the two teams remained locked in combat over a period of twelve days, and even then the match was left unfinished, because the England players had to run away to catch the boat home. In such a grotesque situation, some action would surely have been taken, but the war came.

When peace returned, first-class cricket was resumed, as in 1919, with apparently very little changed. But we can now see that there were fundamental differences. In the immediate post-war years there was plenty of money circulating in the country, but very little to buy with it. As a result, cricket, like all other games, attracted large numbers of spectators, with a consequent increase in the revenue of the clubs. Even county matches were well supported, and Tests became an obsession. There were now six countries besides England of Test status, Australia, New Zealand, the West Indies, India, Pakistan and – until the pathetic cessation of matches in this country – South Africa; this meant that every season saw at least one Test series in England. The money which these crowds brought into the game changed the whole aspect of county cricket.

Until 1939 many of the counties still valued the special qualities which the amateur brought to their teams. In a good year, at least half a dozen men who played in the University Match went straight into county sides for the rest of the summer. A few weeks later, the end of term released the schoolmasters in the same way. An August match between, for instance, Sussex and Somerset, even though it had no bearing whatever on the destination of the championship, presented cricket at its highest level as still a game; this meant sheer enjoyment for the players and therefore for spectators. But the amateur, being his own master and at liberty to refuse an invitation to play, presents a problem to club secretaries, and after the war, when there was plenty of money to pay professionals, he came to be looked on as a nuisance. No one who would not sign a contract was welcome. The convention that the captain of a county side must be an amateur persisted for some years after the war, but the accident that the first county to appoint a professional captain, Warwickshire, won the championship that summer for the first time for many years killed the custom stone dead. There was a handful of university players of such skill that they provided the best English batsmen of the period, and these could obviously not be disregarded by the counties; unfortunately, charming men as most of them were, none possessed the forcefulness of personality to influence the development of the game's organization. In 1963, to the accompaniment of whoops of joy from every sporting journalist, the distinction between amateur and professional was abolished. Now every player in first-class cricket is a hireling. The Gentlemen v. Players matches, which for 150 years had provided some of the finest cricket ever seen, inevitably ceased.

Any levelling which resulted from this change was a levelling down, especially in standards of conduct on the field of play. The high wages paid to these gladiators have attracted some undesirable characters into the game. T. A. Graveney, seeing the situation as an ex-professional, writes in his *On Cricket* (1965), 'I know one old professional of international fame who is prepared to swear that the game is overloaded with slackers who prefer playing cricket to working harder on another job.' One may suspect that the 'old professional' is a Mrs 'Arris, but the verdict is no less impressive for being Graveney's own. E. R. Dexter, whose view is that of a one-time amateur, has expressed the same misgivings about the quality and motives of some aspirants to the county game. It is significant that players nowadays cannot be relied on to satisfy the spectators unless they are offered bribes of money or champagne for 'brighter cricket', or threatened with fines if their laziness permits the 'over rate' to drop too far.

The financial euphoria of the post-war years did not last. The listless cricket provided by the hired lackeys caused spectators to stay away from three-day county matches in increasing numbers. Faced with this problem, the counties prevailed on the MCC to abolish all effective rules of qualification, so that they could buy players of established reputation from Commonwealth teams, in the belief that they would lure back the crowds. This has had two unfortunate but foreseeable results. Young English cricketers, ready to make their mark in the game, see these stars brought in over their heads and are naturally disheartened at this frustration of their hopes. Moreover, the presence of these outsiders diminishes the attractiveness of visiting tours. Fifty years ago, an Australian team coming to this country brought back old favourites who had not been seen for four years and some newcomers who had not been seen at all. Today, some Test teams of overseas countries include a majority of players who can be seen any day of every season playing for county sides here, and all zest of novelty is lost.

These efforts to revivify the championship have not succeeded, and nowadays only a team well in the running for the title can attract gates that are anything but derisory. For a time, financial disaster was postponed by the share-out of the profits of Test matches. The label 'Test' applied to a match has curious effects. In English batsmen it produces instant palsy. Some touring teams have been shown by their results to be not above the standard of an average county side, but in Tests their very moderate bowling reduces the cream of English batsmanship to a terrified timidity. Yet although this often makes the opening days of a Test match even drearier than an ordinary county game, the crowds still flock to see them. National honour is at stake. For some years this gate money kept the counties on their feet, but steady inflation made it inadequate. County clubs, having undertaken commitments to large staffs of professionals, faced bankruptcy. To escape this they imitated other sports by appealing for 'sponsorship', a mealy-mouthed euphemism for exploitation by advertising interests.

Financial support from outside for sport and sporting events is no new phenomenon; it was widely practised in the ancient world. In both Greece and Rome the wildly unequal distribution of wealth was slightly mitigated by the readiness of rich men to improve the lot of their humbler fellow-citizens by great endowments to the public life of the city. The building of temples, theatres, gymnasia and stadia was largely paid for in this way, as were the productions of plays and other contributions to the cultural life of the time. In Rome, chariot racing and gladiatorial games were presented by the wealthy, often by aspirants to political power, who bought votes in this way, and in Imperial times by the Emperors, who regarded these entertainments as a convenient means of keeping down discontent among the proletariat of Rome and other large cities. In Greece the big money prizes offered at most athletic meetings were put up by wealthy citizens who accepted the position of President of the Games. The four great 'Crown' Games were connected with religious centres, and the expenses for the athletics appear to have been met from the general offerings to the temples. Only one instance of sponsorship of the ancient Olympics is attested. Shortly before the Christian era, Herod I of Judaea was in Greece in an Olympic year and found the festival in financial difficulties; in return for being made President of the Games, he endowed the Olympics in perpetuity. Today he is better remembered for his murder of babies in his attempt to liquidate Jesus, usually called the Slaughter of the Holy Innocents. He hardly affords a very admirable precedent for sponsorship.

Every intrusion of outside money into sport is bad for sport, none more so than the subsidies of commercial advertisers. It encourages the setting up of a structure on a completely insecure foundation; when a slump comes or a more promising field for advertising is opened to the industrialists, the sponsorship may be withdrawn. The man who pays the piper calls the tune, and to satisfy the demands of advertisers the shape of a sport may be changed for reasons which have nothing to do with the well-being of the sport itself. Cricket is a perfect example of this. Advertisers would not spend money to prop up the moribund county championship; crowds were too small and matches too long drawn out. So new competitions were devised for one-day games, and these show every sign of completely monopolizing public interest.

There is no ideal duration for a cricket match. Much depends on the skill of the players concerned. All the most enjoyable cricket today is played in one-day or half-day games, a time allowance excellently suited to ordinary levels of ability. But the experience of more than a century has shown that for first-class players the three-day match is best. The two innings do something to reduce the impact of sheer chance on the result, full scope is given to the skill of players in adapting the scoring rate to the state of the game, and the judgement of captains is called upon in timing declarations. These vanish in the one-day game played by cricketers of county standard; the bowling is reduced to negative defensive stuff designed solely to keep down the runs scored off the limited number of overs, and there is no place in these encounters for the subtleties of the slow spinner.

There are other and graver considerations. The commodities advertised by cricket matches are chiefly razor blades and cigarettes. Even the tenderest conscience could hardly find any objections to promoting the sale of razor blades, though the appearance of some young cricketers suggests that they have little enthusiasm for the product. But cigarettes are a different matter. Many thoughtful young men have no wish to encourage the spread of lung cancer; today it is impossible to play first-class cricket without doing so. What sponsorship can do to demean the game was shown clearly enough a few years ago, when a South African tour to this country was cancelled at the last minute. Faced with the loss of gate money from the Test matches, the MCC hastily discovered a sponsor and arranged a series of matches against teams scraped up from here and there under the name of 'The Rest of the World'. The title 'Test match', hallowed by long association with the great figures of the past who had engaged in Homeric contest on behalf of their countries, Grace and Noble, Gregory and Tate, Jessop and Woolley and many another, was bestowed on exhibition games by twenty-two hirelings advertising stout.

With county championship matches still occupying six days of most summer weeks, the new one-day competitions made it necessary for Sundays to be used as well. Only the most rigid Sabbatarians object to the playing of any games on Sunday, but there is probably an underlying good sense in the illogical British resistance to the commercial exploitation of so-called sport on that day. Apart from such considerations, cricketers are now confronted with a seven-day week. Championship matches still start on Saturday, and often a team is whisked away in the middle to play a Sunday game in another competition many miles away. The cricket pages in Monday morning's newspapers now resemble an intelligence test. Not many years ago, several young cricketers played soccer professionally in the winter and so kept alive their zest for both games. With the extension of the football season this has become impossible; in 1973 Carlisle United Football Club suspended a player who failed to report for training at the beginning of August because he was playing cricket for Leicestershire. To earn his living in the winter a cricketer is nowadays conveyed to the other side of the world on a tour or a coaching engagement, and steps straight out of the aeroplane on to the cricket field. Small wonder that county cricketers appear as bored with their job as any factory worker, and that the impression produced on the spectators at many championship games is that all on the field are praying for rain so that they can retire to the pavilion and play cards.

A few years after the Second World War there occurred a revival of an old controversy, which showed how unstable was the control of the game. The point at issue was throwing by bowlers. Every cricketer who has ever swung his arm knows perfectly well whether he is bowling or throwing, but it is impossible to frame in words an exact definition of the difference. A slow bowler can secure extra spin by a jerk of the wrist; the throw of a fast bowler is really dangerous to the batsman, and it is round fast throwers that controversy has from time to time boiled up. There was one outbreak at the end of the nineteenth century so threatening that some counties broke off fixtures with others because they fielded players whose actions were regarded as unfair. K. S. Ranjitsinjhi in his *Jubilee Book of Cricket* (1897) dealt with the problem at some length, pointing out that theoretically there is no difficulty; the law directs that an umpire shall call 'no ball' 'unless he is absolutely satisfied of the fairness of the delivery'. But umpires are old players, and no one likes to appear to be accusing a cricketer of unfairness on mere suspicion. However, the controversy subsided at that time, because counties ceased to employ bowlers of suspect action; and anyone whose active cricket career fell within the first half of this century regarded the whole matter as belonging to ancient history. But in the 1950s some bowlers emerged in English county cricket who were patently throwing.

One of the finest of our umpires, the late Sydney Buller, prevented the authorities from conveniently shutting their eyes to the problem by courageously acting on the law and no-balling the offenders. The MCC showed the same half-hearted shilly-shallying as with the Australian attack on Jardine. In duty bound they deprecated throwing, but there was much talk of 'mere suspicion' and 'ruining the careers of promising youngsters'; the cricketing Establishment certainly contrived to give the impression that they regarded Buller as an officious busybody. By a curious but fortunate coincidence, there were outbreaks of the same trouble at the same time both in the West Indies and in Australia. In 1897 Ranji had written, 'For some reason the Australian conscience is more tender than ours upon this question of cricket morality. This is one of the many grand examples in cricket conduct that Australia has given us, and we would do well to follow it.' Now the Australians came to our help again. The Board of Control took a strong line, and acting on their behalf Bradman put some much needed backbone into the MCC. But Buller died, as Jardine died, with the totally undeserved shadow of a cloud still hanging over him.

The attempt to distinguish between bowling and throwing is a reminder that the word 'bowl' itself presents two interesting features. One is purely phonological. By every law of sound change, the word should be pronounced to rhyme with 'howl'; but well before 1900 this was regarded as a solecism, though at the turn of the century there was a President of the MCC, a noble lord, who always pronounced it thus, and corrected anyone who used the new-fangled 'bole' in his presence. It has been conjectured that our Victorian grandparents modified the pronunciation in order to avoid any embarrassing confusion with 'bowel'.

The other curiosity is that the same word should be used for bowling in cricket and for the very different action seen on bowling greens and ten-pin alleys. The explanation, of course, is that they were originally the same, projection by a pendulum swing of the arm. This underarm bowling was the only kind permitted in the early days of cricket, but some bowlers invented interesting variations of it. Among the Hambledon men was David Harris, whose speed was regarded by his contemporaries as terrifying. Nyren describes his action thus:

> His mode of delivering the ball was very singular. He would bring it from under the arm by a twist, and nearly as high as his arm-pit, and with this action *push* it, as it were, from him. How it was that the balls acquired the velocity they did by this mode of delivery, I never could comprehend.

Most of us will share his puzzlement.

The next modification to underarm bowling was the introduction of the round-arm technique in the early years of the nineteenth century. This met with some opposition, and Nyren regarded it as throwing. But it made its way, and in 1835 a MCC law clarified the position by banning the raising of the bowler's arm above shoulder level. This prohibition, which must always have posed problems to umpires, was abolished in 1862; then the modern overarm style became legal and is now universal. For fast bowlers it is obviously the only technique – in spite of the stories about David Harris – but slow underarm lobs permit a ferocious degree of spin which is quite unattainable with an overarm delivery. Such bowling was last used in a Test match in 1910, when Simpson-Hayward achieved much success against South Africa. In cricket books of fifty years ago, schoolboys were constantly urged to practise this kind of bowling, but they always dreaded the prospect of being called 'cissy'. In the inter-war period Surrey experimented briefly with a lob bowler, and he might have found imitators had not the war come. Since then no underarm bowling has been seen in first-class cricket, and there are probably no cricketers now playing in any class of the game who have ever been called upon to face it. It is a sobering thought that if anyone tried it in county cricket today, there would be a clamour from our stereotyped batsmen to have it made illegal.

At one time a pleasant story used to be told about the invention of round-arm bowling. At the beginning of the nineteenth century a cricketer named John Willes had a sister who used to bowl to him in the nets – or wherever practice was done in those days. The voluminous hooped skirts then fashionable made it impossible for her to use the normal underarm delivery, and she was compelled to raise her arm considerably towards the horizontal. Her brother found her bowling, coming at him thus from an unfamiliar angle, so difficult to cope with that he practised it himself and employed it with great success in matches. Sad to say, we are now told that this picturesque legend must be abandoned; there are difficulties about the dates. But the story reminds us of the part which women have played in cricket. The evidence for the early period is to be found chiefly in the picture gallery of the pavilion at Lord's. There is a mezzotint by John Collet, dated 1778, entitled 'Miss Wicket and Miss Trigger', depicting one lady with a shotgun and the other with a bat. The caption runs:

Miss Trigger, you see, is an excellent shot,
And forty five notches Miss Wicket's just got.

More charming is a watercolour, signed 'T.H. 1779', of the Countess of Derby and her friends playing cricket in the grounds of 'The Oaks', Lord Derby's country seat from which the horse race takes its name. The most valuable evidence is the caption of a well-known engraving attributed to Rowlandson:

> On Wednesday October 3rd 1811 a Singular Cricket Match took place at Balls Pond, Newington. The Players on both sides were 22 Women, 11 Hampshire against 11 Surrey. The Match was made between two Amateur Noblemen of the respective Counties for 500 guineas each. The Performers in the Contest were all Ages and Sizes.

The picture is frankly a caricature, and the word 'Singular' shows that such a game was not a normal feature of life at the time, but a stunt conjured up by the 'Amateur Noblemen'. ('Amateur' here means 'sport-loving'; it has nothing to do with the modern use as antithesis to 'professional'.) Richard Daft mentions in *Kings of Cricket* that about 1850 a Notts village team regularly had a lady playing for them; with true Victorian reticence she is named as Miss D——. Such mixed cricket continued at that level well into the twentieth century and probably still survives here and there.

The organization of women's cricket arose from the introduction of the game into girls' boarding schools, where it was found to be a useful alternative to tennis in the summer term. This led to women's clubs and international tours and Test matches. Here we can see the part played by chance and fashion in the world of sport. Women's tennis is news, women's swimming and athletics are news, the feats of women skaters and skiers and players of badminton and table tennis are recorded in our papers, but women's cricket is not news. Where it is recorded at all, it is in very small print indeed. Among men who follow cricket keenly probably not one in a hundred could say who were England's opponents in the last women's Test series, and still fewer know who were the winners.

In 1963 the Reverend David Sheppard, now a Bishop, made the last of a number of distinguished appearances in England's Test team, a reminder of the considerable part the clergy have played in the game. We have seen that in 1743 the 'British Champion' denounced cricket because it caused clergymen to associate with the lower orders. Happily they have never taken any notice of him. Today there are enough of them playing to have a competition of their own for the *Church Times* Inter-diocesan Cup. In village and club cricket they mingle with the laity, and most players have happy memories of cricketing clerics with whom they have shared their enjoyment of the game, and would agree that the association is good for Church and cricket alike. On occasions they have been known to set a good example in other than purely moral ways. It is recorded that in 1911 the Clergy of Somerset in a one-day match declared at 453 for 9, made in 215 minutes. Lest the parsons should be guilty of the mortal sin of pride, the Somerset Stragglers replied with 454 for 1 in 122 minutes. Those were the days.

Some of these clerics have achieved first-class status. The Church would probably prefer to forget that Lord Frederick Beauclerk was a parson, but there have been worthier examples. The most remarkable of them was perhaps the Rev. J. R. Napier. In 1888 he appeared for the first time for Lancashire in two games, the Roses match against Yorkshire and that against the touring Australian XI. (One can imagine the outcry today if a Lancashire selection committee picked a neophyte parson for these two matches.) The experiment was triumphantly justified. Both matches were won, and Napier, a fast bowler, made a decisive contribution to both victories with the bat as well as the ball; he was top scorer for his side in one innings against the Australians. Then he vanished from the first-class scene for ever.

Lancashire were perhaps moved in their decision to play Napier by the achievements of another parson, the Rev. Vernon Royle, who had played regularly for the county between 1873 and 1881. Many still living will remember with pleasure J. H. Parsons, a Warwickshire professional before the First World War. He joined up in 1914, had a fine army career, and after the war took Holy Orders. Thereafter, when he could escape from parochial duties, he played for the county as an amateur. Since then a handful of other clergymen have achieved the same distinction, but only Bishop Sheppard attained Test rank. The year of his retirement saw also the abolition of the distinction between amateur and professional, and the establishment of the present set-up in first-class cricket, a set-up which makes it impossible for any clergyman to play in those circles. It is certain that Bishop Sheppard will never have a successor; perhaps that is the saddest comment on the present state of affairs.

Apart from the defects of internal organization, the greatest threat to top-level cricket today comes from the behaviour of crowds at important matches. This is no new problem. A crowd riot at a match in Sydney in 1879 between New South Wales and Lord Harris' XI stopped play for the day, and similar scenes occurred at Sydney in the first Test against Warner's team in 1903. Both these riots were set off by umpires' decisions against Australian batsmen, and in each case it was suspected that heavy gambling was the root cause of the crowd's anger. Actual interference with play by spectators was not seen for many years after that, and recurred only in recent times, first in the West Indies and Pakistan; here too betting is suspected to be a prime motive, along with chauvinism and heavy drinking. Sometimes, it is said, the rioting is set off by political considerations which have nothing whatever to do with cricket. Recently, however, the behaviour of players in the middle has exacerbated crowd violence, even if it has not caused it.

Cricket in England, long free from any such dangers, has at last succumbed. Spectators of the baser kind appear to have been attracted from football to the new one-day matches, and there have been ominous incidents both at these competitions, and at Test matches. Journalists and after-dinner speakers try to drown them in soothing syrup, and express pious hopes that this is only a passing phase; unhappily there is every indication that matters will become worse. Those in control of the game will soon have to ask themselves whether they are prepared to have cricket played, like football in South America, inside barbed wire enclosures.

Fortunately there is still much good and enjoyable cricket played by thousands at the level of school and village, college and club, but this sound substructure now lacks what it enjoyed for a century, a peak of excellence at the top to command admiration and inspire imitation and emulation. It is idle to pretend that this is not so. When a cricketer as admirable as Brian Statham can write in his autobiography, 'I am not altogether sorry to be leaving the game which has given me so much', the confession tells its own tale. Even sadder are the words of Sir Neville Cardus:

> It is pretty certain that if I were young today, I wouldn't become devoted to first-class cricket and wish to write about it. . . . Since round about 1960, cricket, in the organised form in which it is presented to the public, has been changed so much that W. G. Grace would not know it was cricket at all.

Any detached observer has reluctantly to admit that most of what passes for top-level cricket today is the wrong kind of cricket played by the wrong kind of cricketer to titillate the wrong kind of spectator. No one would wish any aspiring youngster to imitate it.

6
Rowing and other Aquatic Sports

Most games have their origin in the spare-time activities of a leisured class. Rowing as a sport, on the other hand, arises at least partly from a very utilitarian occupation. Small boats have always played a significant part in the harbour life of coastal towns and on the rivers of great cities, acting as tenders to large ships and ferries where bridges were few. They were invaluable in London, where for centuries they fulfilled the functions now performed by buses and cabs; already in the sixteenth century their fares, like those of taxis today, were regulated by the civic authority. It was among the watermen who manned these craft that boat racing started. The oldest event with an unbroken record in the history of British sport is the sculling race for Doggett's Coat and Badge, founded in 1715 by an actor, who endowed a prize for an annual contest on the Tideway for six young watermen just out of their apprenticeship. With some inevitable modifications, the race continues to this day.

Water transport was even more important in Venice than in London, and from early in the seventeenth century, travellers were bringing to this country accounts of the regattas held in that city by the gondoliers, events where the spectators contributed as much to the splendour of the spectacle as did the competitors, In the next century the institution was brought to England, and the Venetian word *regatta* was imported to describe it. The first one known took place on the Thames in London on 23 June 1775, all the events being for watermen. Dr Johnson was in Lichfield at the time, and so unable to attend, but he sent a letter to Mrs Thrale in which he envied her the treat and gave some characteristically sententious advice:

> I have just had your sweet letter, and am glad that you are to be at the regatta. . . . Every new scene impresses new ideas, enriches the imagination, and enlarges the power of reason, by new topicks of comparison. You that have seen the regatta will have images which we who miss it must want, and no intellectual images are without use. But when you are in this scene of splendour and gaiety, do not let one of your fits of negligence steal upon you. *Hoc age* is the great rule, whether you are serious or merry; whether you are stating the expenses of your family, learning science or duty from a folio, or floating on the Thames in a fancied dress.

Mrs Thrale, 'floating on the Thames in a fancied dress', points forward to the social glories of Henley in its greatest days.

The watermen borrowed the idea of a championship from other professional sports of the time, and the title changed hands in the same way, a match being arranged when a challenger could find sufficient financial backing to make the contest attractive to the holder. Races have never been frequent. In 1876 the title was won by an Australian, and since then most contests have been held in Australia or Canada; the event arouses little interest in Britain.

In 1830 Henry C. Wingfield gave a prize for a sculling race 'for gentlemen', to be rowed at half flood from Westminster to Putney annually on 10 August; after the first few years it was to be organized by a committee of past winners. The winner of the race assumed the title 'Champion of the Thames', and until well into this century the contest was run on the lines of championships in other sports. A preliminary race was held among the challengers, and the winner of this then sculled against the holder. The race has always taken place on the Tideway, but it was transferred from Westminster to the Boat Race course from Putney to Mortlake. The 'gentlemen' of the early days were still far from modern notions of amateurism; challengers for the Wingfields used to put up stakes or 'entry fees' of £5 a head, and the winner took all.

While the sport of rowing has one root in the races of professional watermen, it owes a great deal to the contribution of pleasure boating. This has long been a pursuit of leisure hours. Pliny has a charming picture of holiday crowds enjoying swimming and boating from the sandy beach of Hippo in North Africa in the first century of the Christian era, and in

Sport in the universities: an inter-university hurdle race in 1871. *(A. Lockwood)*

(Above) The finish of the 1877 Oxford-Cambridge boat race – the only dead heat on record. *(Illustrated London News)*
The boat race was declared void in 1912 when both boats were waterlogged in rough conditions. This picture shows the Cambridge crew sinking. *(Syndication International)*

another letter he describes rowing and punting on the shady reaches of the river Clitumnus in Italy, with a hint that the boaters had a swim in the stream as well. In Britain pleasure boating was well established by the eighteenth century, and has remained popular ever since, somewhat spoiled recently by the intrusion of the internal combustion engine. It has various delights; it is cool in hot weather, it affords good exercise, and it gives the opportunity to acquire skills in the neat management of small boats. Moreover rowing produces a special aesthetic satisfaction, paralleled only in dancing and musical performance, of a group of people performing a rhythmic action simultaneously. It was in order to make this possible that boat-builders began to turn out pleasure craft for six, eight or ten oarsmen. We read of these many years before there is any evidence of racing in them. Boating at Eton is first attested in 1793; by 1812 a Captain of Boats was being elected there, and the College owned a ten-oar and three eights. Westminster School were rowing in a six-oar a year later. In 1818 the Leander Club was formed by the fusion of two groups named after the boats they used, Star and Arrow.

Perhaps the decisive step in the establishment of rowing as a sport was taken in 1829, when Charles Wordsworth arranged the first Oxford and Cambridge Boat Race, just two years after he had performed the same service for cricket. It was probably an accident, and a lucky one, that the Universities chose eights for this event. Eton's ten-oar Monarch has remained a curiosity to this day, but six-oared boats were well established at the universities and might well have been selected. Six-oar rowing long persisted in coastal clubs in this country, and much early rowing in American Universities was done in these boats; in 1875 thirteen college crews competed in a race for coxless sixes, won by Cornell. There are still races for 'best boat' sixes across the Atlantic.

The eights chosen for the first Boat Race are particularly convenient, because the crews can be divided into two fours. Those who like their sports to be rooted deep in the remote past can point to the story in the chronicler Florence of Worcester that King Eadgar of England at his coronation in 973 was rowed down the river Dee by eight kings, but it would be difficult to trace an unbroken record of rowing in eights since that time.

The challenge to the Boat Race of 1829 shows that there was already racing in eights at Oxford and Cambridge. It was in the form of those bumping races which have been the backbone of rowing there ever since, a contest suited to the narrow and twisting rivers available; the traditional dates for their beginning are 1822 at Oxford and 1826 at Cambridge. We possess for Oxford an account of 'The Eights about 1827', written by W. S. Cole in 1893.

> The boats were started in those days in a primitive way. I do not know how many boats existed then on the river, but I can only remember three – Christ Church, Brasenose and Jesus; there might have been another. Iffley lock would not hold more than four, and the process was this. The boats were stationed in the lock, and the stroke of the first boat went forward into the bows as far as he could, so as to leave room for the bow oars. He then placed his hands against the brickwork at the side of the lock and shoved the boat along, gradually going astern himself, and as he went, bow got his oar into the water and began to pull; shortly number 2 did the same, and by the time stroke got to his place, two or three oars were at work. On taking his seat he began to row, and as quickly as possible all the oars got into play. The same process was observed by the succeeding boats. I believe that not one of the boats then in use belonged to any College. I may be wrong, but I believe all were hired. I remember that St John's had a four-oar, and Wadham and, I think, Trinity; but I do not remember any others. The crews were not very strictly members of a College. Christ Church had a waterman to row for them, and also Jesus.

This account bears obvious traces of the failing memory of old age – Cole must have been ninety when he wrote it – but the description of the start from the lock is very circumstantial. No one in his senses would invent from scratch this method of starting a bumping race, especially with its limitation to four crews. We can, however, trace in it the vestigial survival of a natural procedure. Boatloads of undergraduates used to go down in the afternoon for a pleasant excursion to Sandford or Nuneham. On their return early in the evening they went into Iffley lock, and the lockkeeper, anxious after the manner of his kind to save himself unnecessary work, waited until his lock was full of boats. Meanwhile the earliest arrivals at the upper end of the lock, eager for their evening meal, fretted with growing impatience, and when the gates were at last opened scrambled out one by one and set off home, each in hot pursuit of the boat in front. Here is the *Ur* Bumping Race.

There is a description of Eights as an established feature of Oxford life a few years later in *Tom Brown at Oxford*. This was published in 1861, but the picture it presents is that of twenty years earlier when the author was in residence at Oriel. As a work of literature the book is inferior to the *Schooldays*, but to the historian of sport it is no less valuable. Tom went up in January to St Ambrose (a fictitious college, unlike the Rugby of the *Schooldays*). The college was going through a bad period, having fallen into the hands of a fast set, amusing themselves in the fashion of the previous century: 'They drove tandems in all directions.' At the only two important inter-collegiate sports of the time, rowing and cricket, St Ambrose was making a poor show: 'Their boat lost place after place on the river: the eleven got beaten in all their matches.'

The universities had not yet taken to football, so in spite of his prowess at the game at Rugby, Tom took up rowing. 'Pulling looked a simple thing enough – much easier than tennis; and he had made a capital start at the latter game and been highly complimented by the marker after his first hour in the little court.' There was a shortage of rowingmen at St Ambrose and 'The crew had to be filled up from the torpid or by watermen.' So Tom secured his place without difficulty. The bumping races were not then concentrated into six or four days, but took place twice a week over a period of three weeks. There is a fearsome picture of training methods: 'The current theory of training at that time was – as much meat as you could eat, the more underdone the better, and the smallest amount of drink upon which you could manage to live: two pints in the twenty-four hours was all that most boats' crews were allowed.'

The first University Boat Race was held at Henley, which was also the scene of other matches in the next few years. In 1831 there was a race between Oxford and Leander. In 1837 Lady Margaret Boat Club, head of the river at Cambridge, rowed there against Queen's, head at Oxford. Next year there was a race between Cambridge and Leander; both crews were steered by watermen, and there was so much fouling that the umpire declared 'No race'. (Generally our great-grandfathers had a more robust attitude to collisions than ours; for a race between Eton and Westminster in 1835 'an agreement was made that there should be no fouling until the first half-mile was over'.)

The citizens of Henley found that their town was profiting so much from these events that in 1839 they instituted a regatta. At first it was a modest affair, with a Grand Challenge cup for eights open to all, and a Town Cup for the fours of local clubs. The programme was steadily extended, and Henley became and remained for many years the focus of the sport of rowing for the whole world. The University Boat Race in its early history did not take place every year, and several times the Grand at Henley offered the opportunity for Oxford to meet Cambridge, but from 1856 the Boat Race became an annual event on the Tideway; for many years this race and Henley Regatta were the two chief events in the rowing calendar, and between them they exercised an enormous influence on the development of the sport in all its aspects.

Rowing is expensive in money and time; it is not surprising that the older universities, whose undergraduates enjoyed a disproportionate share of these advantages, played so great a part in its growth. There was a long tradition that afternoons were free for recreation and sport. Unkind critics have said that violent exercise was necessary at Cambridge in order to keep warm, and at Oxford in order to keep awake. Undeniably college crews had the opportunity for daily practice all the year round in a way not easily possible for less fortunate clubs. Naturally therefore Henley for many years was dominated by Oxford and Cambridge. But there were other centres of rowing. The first recorded regatta at Durham was in 1834, five years earlier than the first Henley; it was organized by the university. Chester can claim the credit for having commissioned the first racing eight to be constructed of bent wood rather than clinker-built of strakes, the earliest 'best boat'. The Thames at London had long seen rowing by oarsmen from the universities and public schools; Tideway rowing began to assume a position of importance with the foundation of London Rowing Club in 1856 and Thames R. C. in 1870. London first won the Grand at Henley in 1857; Thames had to wait until 1876 for that achievement.

The popularity of rowing grew steadily; new clubs were formed, schools took up the sport in increasing numbers, and regattas were organized all over the country. Oarsmen from overseas began to enter for Henley from 1872, and won their first victory there in 1878. This invasion reached its first culminating point in 1906, when a Belgian eight won the Grand. This was a salutary shock to British rowing, which had grown complacent. It was so effective that at the Olympic regatta of 1912, in which each country was allowed to enter two eights, Britain took the first two places with Leander and New College.

The Stewards who administer Henley Regatta have always been a completely autonomous body, self-elected and self-perpetuating, like the MCC in cricket. They lay down conditions for all races at their regatta, and can accept or reject entries at will. Like the MCC they acquired without aiming at it a position of power in the rowing world. As the sport grew, it was thought advisable that there should be a central authority for it on the same lines as the governing bodies which were being appointed for other games, and in 1882 the Amateur Rowing Association (ARA) was formed. Its leading figures were naturally drawn from the same sources as the Henley Stewards, and relations between the two bodies have been good; there had not yet been in rowing anything resembling the disastrous dyarchy of Football Association and Football League. The first duty of the new body was to define the qualification for taking part in amateur regattas, and the Stewards were glad to share responsibility in this field, especially when they had to consider the entries of overseas crews. Unhappily the ARA arrived at a definition of amateur which was to bedevil the rowing scene for more than half a century.

In the early days of university rowing, undergraduate oarsmen, taking their cue from cricket, had mingled freely with watermen, who coached, steered and rowed in college crews. Rowing at this time resembled contemporary cricket in another respect, the heavy stake money involved. About 1820 there was a ten-mile race on the Tideway between the Arrow crew and the Guards' Amateurs for £1000. The match at Henley in 1831 between Oxford University and Leander was said to have been for £200 a side, though the story was subsequently denied by the Oxford crew, many of whom had become respectable parsons. By mid-century the change in moral climate had begun to affect rowing as it had cricket, and in the anxiety to free the sport from any possible taint of gambling there was a movement to break away decisively from the professional rowing of watermen, in which money was always at stake. Shortly after 1850 the Oxford and Cambridge captains agreed not to employ watermen as coaches.

The 1880s were a difficult time for deciding amateur qualifications. The welcome spread of games into new social classes was bringing problems. The Football Association and Rugby Union were faced with the question of 'broken time' payments to working-class players, and were preparing to take their very different ways. Unhappily the ARA far outdid even the Rugby Union in the rigidity of the amateur definition they adopted. To exclude watermen was reasonable enough, but the ARA added 'anyone who is a mechanic, artisan or labourer or engaged in any menial duty, or is a member of a boat or rowing club containing anyone liable to disqualification under the above rules'.

One of the difficulties about law-making in any sport is that the committees responsible always include a preponderance of veterans with vivid memories of conditions forty years before but an imperfect realization of how the situation has changed in the meantime. In the early days undergraduates had obviously been at a disadvantage compared with watermen who spent much of their working life at the oar. In *Tom Brown at Oxford* a significant remark is put into the mouth of a college captain, 'We don't often get a university crew which can beat the watermen.' The heavy boats used before the introduction of outriggers had put the sheer muscular strength of any manual worker at a premium compared with the ordinary young man of leisure. The social prejudices embodied in the definition were normal at the time. What is reprehensible in the ARA is not so much that they laid down the definition as that they clung to it long after it had become completely untenable. The sad result of the law was that many of the newly-formed clubs found that they had members not qualified as amateurs, whom rightly they were not prepared to expel. In 1890 these clubs formed themselves into a National Amateur Rowing Association (NARA), and organized their own regattas. There were now two kinds of amateur.

The controversy was never the plain embattled struggle of black against white which it appears today. Many members of

ARA clubs resented the rule, and did everything in their power to encourage and help the NARA cause. R. C. Bourne, when Member of Parliament for Oxford City, used year after year to umpire at the local NARA regatta. There were many attempts to heal the breach. At one of the earliest of these, in 1891, the committee of enquiry received a letter which shows all too clearly how complex the problem was, and how diverse were the attitudes of those concerned. A representative of the NARA wrote, 'I do not ask the ARA to alter their amateur definition in regard to the exclusion of mechanics, because I am open-minded enough to understand and appreciate the object of some such classes being barred: the condition of athletics and football form arguments which only those who are wilfully blind cannot see.' With much goodwill on both sides a compromise should have been reached, but the diehards of the ARA constantly took fright at what was happening in other sports, regardless of the fact that rowing differs from most other sports in one important respect; it is difficult to imagine any circumstances in which an oarsman could make much money by rowing in an eight. At last, in 1937, NARA crews were admitted to ARA regattas, but even then vested interests lingered on, and not until 1956 was amalgamation of the two associations finally achieved.

Henley and the Boat Race afforded the opportunity to test many innovations in rowing equipment. The most important of these was the outrigger, which about 1845 reduced the beam of the racing boat and greatly increased its speed. Next came sliding seats. Here the prime movers were some oarsmen who wore leather shorts, greased their fixed thwarts and slid on them. London R.C. in 1872 were the first crew to appear at Henley with seats on wheels. This was the beginning of the end for one of the oldest of mankind's jokes, the wear and tear on the human skin caused by rowing on fixed seats. The jest is first found in Aristophanes, and it recurs constantly in the light verse which adorned academic journals a hundred years ago. Sir Arthur Quiller-Couch's parody of Poe is typical:

See the freshers as they row
To and fro,
Up and down the Lower river for an afternoon or so –

(For the deft manipulation
Of the never-resting oar,
Though it lead to approbation,
Will induce excoriation) –
They are infinitely sore,
Keeping time, time, time
In a sort of Runic rhyme
Up and down the way to Iffley in an afternoon or so;
(Which is slow).

An even neater allusion comes in his description of autumn twilight in Oxford, after Cowper:

The boating man returns,
His rawness growing with experience –
Strange union!

Rowing men are conservative, and for many years it was thought that before a man could race on a slide, he must serve a long apprenticeship on fixed seats, just as it was thought that a man who was to command a steamship must be trained in sail. In 1898 it was suggested that the Thames Cup at Henley should be rowed for on fixed seats; the proposal found no seconder. But at the Peace Regatta in 1919 racing for the Public Schools Cup was on fixed seats, and for many years after the First World War the same was true of Torpids at Oxford and Lents at Cambridge; the consequent discomfort is a lively memory to many of the older generation. No doubt there is no case today for such racing, but many beginners might well be kept on fixed seats for a few more days to master the basic problems of getting the oar usefully in and out of the water before being confronted with the additional difficulties of controlling a slide.

The innate conservatism of English rowing is further illustrated by the time needed to establish the use of swivel rowlocks. They were invented in America about 1880, and soon adopted for sculling in this country, but there was a strong resistance to them for rowing, especially at the universities, where the fixed thole and sill survived until well after the Second World War. The great virtue of the older equipment was that the machine-gun rattle of a ragged finish quickly made a crew aware of that particular failing. Conservatism too was responsible for the rejection of some promising experiments in the shape of oar-blades. Eton in 1885 won the Ladies with Dr

Warre's 'coffin' oars with the greatest width at the inboard end of the blades. In 1890 Oxford won the Boat Race using 'barrel' blades with the greatest breadth just inboard of the tip; neither pattern caught on, and most crews still use oars substantially the same as those of a hundred years ago. It will be interesting to see if 'spade' blades are any longer lived.

In the 1950s an intriguing experiment was carried out by some members of London R.C. It was based on the theory that the intermittent thrust of a crew rowing in unison must be less efficient than pressure constantly maintained. The method depended on the duration of the stroke being exactly half as long as the swing forward. Three pairs of oarsmen embarked in an eight. As one pair finished their stroke, the second pair took their beginning, while the third were in the middle of their forward swing. The boat travelled smoothly enough, but it was soon realized that accurate time-keeping would be impossible to maintain in a race as the crew tired.

More important was the 'Battle of the Styles' in the inter-war period. For years coaching methods in this country had relied on principles enunciated in the 1880s by Dr Warre, headmaster of Eton. These were based on the postulate, 'Your muscles may tire, but your weight is always with you.' Coaches tended to concentrate on the movements of the oarsman's body and to regard the legs as primarily useful to direct the body weight on to the loom of the oar. Shortly after the First World War a picturesque figure reappeared at Cambridge, the Australian Steve Fairbairn, who had rowed in four university crews forty years earlier, and was now able to devote his time and abundant energy to coaching. He attacked orthodoxy at almost every point. He declared that a crew using its leg muscles properly would have any orthodox crew hopelessly beaten long before its own muscles tired. The coach should not worry about the oarsman's body. All that mattered was what the blade was doing, and Fairbairn aimed his coaching at the blade, especially at the beginning of the stroke, urging oarsmen to 'listen for the bell note'. He denied any utility to the quick body recovery at the finish, beloved of the orthodox, and told his crews to 'lie back till the cows come home'. The combination of these methods and Fairbairn's forceful personality produced outstanding results from the crews he coached, at Cambridge those of his old college, Jesus, and Thames R. C. on the Tideway. Although orthodox and Fairbairn oarsmen looked very different in the early stages of their training, they came to resemble one another in maturity, and rowing men of the two schools had little difficulty in combining in the Cambridge crews of the period which maintained what appeared to be a never-ending superiority over Oxford.

Oxford's counterpart to Fairbairn was Dr G. C. Bourne, head of a famous rowing family. In 1882 and 1883 he and Fairbairn had been in opposing crews in the Boat Race; a product of Eton and New College, he belonged to the purest orthodox tradition. As a coach he was not the equal of Fairbairn; his contribution to rowing was very different. Shortly after the First World War he designed an eight of revolutionary pattern, based on an interesting theory. As a boat moves through the water, it throws off two waves on each side, a side wave from the point of the widest beam, and a bow wave; the production of these waves causes skin friction which slows the pace of the boat. Bourne in his eight took the side wave forward by placing the greatest beam between numbers 2 and 3, instead of between 4 and 5 as usual. The extra buoyancy which this gave to the front end of the boat allowed the entry to be made so fine that six or seven feet of the bows rode out of the water, and the bow wave was brought that much aft. As a result of these modifications, the trough of the bow wave coincided with the crest of the side wave, and so one wave was eliminated, with consequent reduction of skin friction. The eight was designed on strict mathematical principles, but its lines were found to be identical with those of the fastest fish that swims (Dr Bourne was Professor of Zoology and an authority on marine biology). It had a brief career of success; anyone who saw New College at the head of the river in 1922 and 1923 will remember the remarkable phenomenon of their boat leaving behind eight puddles and a thin wake, but otherwise hardly a ripple on the water.

The design was adopted by the Oxford crew of 1924 for the Boat Race, which it was confidently expected to win, but lost. Like many another losing crew, they looked round for a scapegoat, and pitched on the Bourne boat. The design immediately went out of fashion. A contributory factor in its failure to establish itself was no doubt that the quarters of the stern oars were uncomfortably cramped compared with those in an orthodox craft; the boat club officials who are responsible for ordering new boats are commonly found among the stern oars. Certainly the Bourne eight never had a fair trial. Now that English rowing has fallen on evil days, there is every reason for giving it another chance.

Bourne's other contribution to the art of rowing was equally characteristic. Like Fairbairn he attacked the problem of the movement of the oar blade in the water, but whereas the Cambridge approach was pragmatic, the Oxonian was theoretical. The Professor published a learned work, *The Turning Point of the Oar*, of such scientific profundity that very few oarsmen or coaches could understand it, much less make any use of it; today it seems to have vanished even from the bibliographies of books on rowing.

Since 1946 the chief development at Henley has been the steady increase in the successes of crews from overseas, until nowadays a home victory in the principal events is a rarity. One reason is that in most countries the best talent is concentrated in a limited number of clubs, and the finest of them, those which come to Henley, are naturally in a class by themselves. In this country the talent is widely spread over a large number of small clubs and colleges, with the result that we have fewer outstanding crews; but the loyalty which keeps good oarsmen faithful to the clubs which have fostered them is a quality not to be despised. Of recent years, too, Henley has had to face another problem. Since the inception of the regatta, schools and colleges have supplied a large proportion of the entry. Today the ever-widening sprawl of examination timetables both for degrees and for A Levels means that many potential members of Henley crews are simply not available for training. The number of entries from Oxford and Cambridge colleges has fallen steeply, and the quality has certainly not improved; after an unbroken link of more than a hundred years, Eton has withdrawn from Henley.

The constant failure of home crews to match the invaders has led to a call for measures to restore the balance, and the movement has been given additional force by the growing importance of Olympic and other international regattas, at which Britain has recently not been conspicuously successful. It is natural to wish to see national teams victorious in any sport, but one need not be a diehard antiquarian to realize that not all in the international scene is lovely, and that success in it may be dearly bought.

Until 1868, all fours in races at Henley and other regattas had been coxed. In that year, W. B. Woodgate, captain of the Brasenose four in the Stewards' Cup, thinking a steersman unnecessary on a course as straight as Henley, ordered the cox to jump overboard at the start of the race; the crew won but was disqualified. The regatta Stewards, however, saw the point. Next year there was a race for coxless fours, and after 1873 all fours at Henley and other first-class regattas were coxless, as pairs always had been. But outside Britain, races for coxed fours and pairs were part of the rowing scene, and because Britain must compete here as elsewhere, a race for coxed fours has reappeared at Henley and will no doubt soon be followed by one for coxed pairs; if logic is to be our guide, the Diamonds will have to be duplicated, with a race for coxed scullers. Yet it remains true that an oarsman who needs a steersman in a pair or four has no place whatever in a first-class regatta. The situation is even more deplorable now that the cox has been transferred from the stern to the bows, and compelled to assume a contorted posture which is an affront to human dignity. He is completely unnecessary; but a man, or boy, can acquire an Olympic medal by carrying out a function which could equally well be performed by a lump of lead.

One motive in this multiplication of categories in international games has been to make the possibilities of acquiring medals by rowing equal to those in other sports. In the past, regattas in this country have contrived a full programme by having several races for each kind of boat at different levels of ability. Sometimes the entries are regulated by division into senior, junior and maiden classes. At Henley, where all oarsmen are assumed to be seniors, it is left to the crews to decide which races to enter, the standards of the different events being fixed by tradition. In representative international regattas this is clearly impossible. But there is a well-tried method of producing additional classes, far better than loading boats with useless coxes.

For many years men of different weights used to row together in the same crews; indeed it was long considered essential to have a lightweight stroke to give liveliness to the heavies behind him. Now, however, the importance of size and muscular power has become obvious; no first-class crew today can afford the luxury of lightweights, and the smaller man is in danger of being crowded out of rowing. (In the final of the Grand at Henley in 1840, a Leander crew averaging 10 stone 7½ pounds beat Trinity, Cambridge, whose average weight was 10 stone 7 pounds. In view of the heavy boats of those days, these figures are remarkable.) In other sports where size matters, such as boxing and wrestling, division into classes by weight has long been established. In university rowing in America the principle has been tried, and it should be followed everywhere. Three classes defined by average weight would be ample, light, middle and heavy. This would enable the ridiculous coxed classes to be discarded, and would open top-level rowing to everyone.

Since this chapter was written, the International Rowing Federation (FISA) has recognized light-weight rowing, fixing the standard at under 11 stone average, with no member over 11 stone 5½ pounds.

The Henley course has always been regarded as one of the finest in the world, and in 1948 it was the scene of a memorable and enjoyable Olympic regatta. But two or three times in a century, exceptionally wet weather in June produces a very strong current down the course which is much more unfavourable to one of the two stations than to the other. An occurrence of this phenomenon at regatta time a few years ago lent extra urgency to the demand for a six-lane course in Britain to equal those used for international regattas elsewhere, and to serve as a centre for producing British crews to rival other national teams. This has now been provided in gravel pits at Holme Pierrepont, six lanes of dead water, deadly dull for oarsmen compared with the lively water of a river or the Tideway. A national squad under a national coach has been established to turn out the splendid crews which will bring back Britain's rowing glories.

It is early days yet, but already the project has thrown down a whole tree-full of apples of discord. Some Tideway oarsmen selected for the national squad see no reason why they should waste time in travelling to the wilds of the Midlands for their rowing. At Oxford and Cambridge, where there was already tension between college and university clubs over men who grasped at a Blue but would not row in their college eights, a new trouble has arisen with some who turn their backs on the university boat and aspire to the national squad. After the outcry over the unequal stations at Henley, the cynic may well smile at the complaint about Holme Pierrepont, and about similar courses at Moscow and Munich, that in the prevailing wind two of the lanes are so disadvantaged that victory in them is impossible. In 1973 Holme Pierrepont was used for trials to select the British crews for the European Junior championships. Eton, chosen in one category, found themselves faced with an application to the courts from a rival club, City Orient, for an injunction to have the selection declared null and void, on the ground that City Orient had drawn one of the inferior lanes. Such is the world of modern sport. Eton may well have wished that they had remained loyal to Henley.

The establishment of the national squad may have a good effect on rowing. Because the sport had its origin partly in pleasure boating, many of our best regattas, including Henley, have always preserved something of the happy atmosphere of a family picnic. This is in danger of being lost. But if the humourless galley slaves who are prepared to sacrifice anything for an international medal can be siphoned off to Holme Pierrepont, the situation may yet be saved for those who want rowing to remain enjoyable. There are plenty who do, as is shown by the growth in numbers of those taking part who certainly do not aim at international honours. Oxford and Cambridge no longer dominate the rowing world; there is nothing regrettable in the fact that the London University crew is often superior to both. The pre-1914 glories of Eights and May weeks as social events have departed, but the bumping races have never been so popular. Nine divisions are now necessary, and even these cannot accommodate all who wish to row; preliminary 'getting-on' races are held to keep the numbers down. At each university a thousand men take part each summer. Except for a few crews at the top, the standard of the first two divisions is clearly not what it was fifty years ago, and at the lower levels the rowing is phantasmagorical; the oarsmen appear to be suffering the tortures of the damned as they catch their hideous crabs and endure ignominious overbumps. Yet over all is an Arcadian hilarity, and even the crustiest old curmudgeon cannot deny that here at least the true spirit of sport still lives. Rowing wiseacres frown on bumping races because they are not the best way of producing Olympic oarsmen, but few forms of sport afford more fun to spectators and participants alike.

Towards the end of his life the novelist V. C. Clinton Baddeley ventured into a new realm by writing a handful of old-fashioned detective stories with the traditional amateur detective, and for this rôle he created an old-fashioned Cambridge don, Dr Davie. Nothing does more to establish this character than the brief scene in which we see him on the towing path, and no one has ever come nearer to putting into words the strange *mystique* of the bumping race.

When the Lent bumping races came on, Davie was down on the tow-path, wrapped up to the ears, following the fortunes of the St Nicholas's crews.

Never in his life had he pulled that sort of oar, but as a spectator he found the occasion irresistible. He loved that curiously Victorian scene, like some lightly coloured sporting print – the river bank backed with pollard willows, and the view of the village church on the rising ground beyond the water; and that most amiable of crowds, cheering and laughing, the young men with their girls, the older men without their girls, addicts of the river. And the coaches on bicycles, miraculously weaving along the narrow tow-path, bawling strange exhortations through megaphones. And the boats, so graceful as they paddled to the starting point – but then, transformed, so formidable in pursuit.

If you have planted yourself at the right station on the bank, the excitement of this multiple involvement can be excruciating, for each pursuer is itself pursued, and victory does not come at the winning post, as in a horse race; it comes anywhere – anywhere the pursuing boat can claim a bump, or, conversely, anywhere that the intended victim can make certain of escape. And victory or defeat may be a matter of inches – fluctuating, agonising inches. Davie, heart in mouth, saw St Nicholas's second boat make a bump, and it made him feel very ill indeed, which, as he told himself on the way home, was highly absurd, because he was not remotely interested in rowing; only in the anxiety of winning by inches.

(*To study a Long Silence*, Gollancz, 1972.)

Punting and Canoeing

The most striking difference between Eights week today and forty years ago is the disappearance of punts from the scene. A lady visiting Oxford for the races in those days expected to view them from a punt, and usually found that her escort had a fair degree of skill with a punt pole. The college watermen showed themselves masters of the art, as they took their ferry punts back and forth across the river; some of the younger ones used to enter for the professional championship of the Thames – which was in effect the championship of the world. All undergraduates had the opportunity of seeing punting well done, and a few of them took the trouble to get a waterman to coach them. There were plenty of punts for hire, trim and well maintained, varnish shining and cushions immaculate.

Today all is changed. There are still plenty of pleasure punts at Oxford, but they are dirtier and shabbier than the ferry punts of former days. Lord Peter Wimsey was shocked at what he found on a return visit to his old university when he took his Harriet on the Cherwell in a punt; now he would refuse to allow her to set foot in a punt at all. Once upon a time, punts in Eights week were marshalled six deep under the bank as the time for each race approached. Today there is hardly a punt to be seen. The one gain is that the strain on coxes is reduced as the crews make their way down to the start; the worst managed cabin cruiser is slightly less unpredictable than a punt in unskilled hands. Few young people of this generation have ever seen punting of any reasonable standard of competence, and when they embark on their first experiments with a pole, they do not even know what they ought to be doing.

Punting has never been a widely spread sport, being largely confined to Oxford, Cambridge, and the boating centres on the Thames between Oxford and Teddington. Its heyday was the end of last century and the beginning of this, when many regattas included punting races in their programme, and special racing punts were built for them. Truth to tell, it was not a very satisfactory medium for racing. The punter is too much at the mercy of the depth of the water and the state of the river bed, and these can vary almost from yard to yard. It is difficult to find a course on which two punts side by side enjoy identical conditions. So punting has dwindled, and when the present generation of boats fall to pieces, which will not be long, it is possible that they will never be replaced.

The place of the punt has been taken by the canoe, not so much the Canadian canoe popular in the great days of punting as the other version, which at that time was called the Rob Roy

(Above) A bumping race at Oxford, 1969. *(B. Harris)*
The start of the Bath–London bicycle race, 1874. *(A. Lockwood)*

(Above) Tom Cribb, Champion of England, carried a number of considerable wagers when he fought the American Negro Tom Molineaux in 1811. 20,000 spectators watched Cribb batter the American into submission with a broken jaw in the 11th round. *(A. Lockwood)*

Harry Angelo's fencing academy, depicted by Rowlandson in 1791. He later shared his rooms in Bond Street with the school of pugilism run by 'Gentleman' John Jackson. *(British Museum)* and is now the kayak. These boats were already popular pleasure craft in the opening years of the nineteenth century. In his *Espriella* (1807) Robert Southey gives a pleasant picture of canoeing at Oxford:

> Many of the smaller boats had only a single person in each; and in some of these he sat face forward, leaning back as in a chair, and plying with both hands a double-bladed oar in alternate strokes, so that his motion was like the path of a serpent. One of these canoes is, I am assured, so exceedingly light that a man can carry it; but few persons are skilful or venturous enough to use it.

Rightly this sport has an enormous appeal for the young. There is no better way of acquiring the basic skills needed for the management of small boats. Those who have no desire to race find the canoe an invaluable and inexpensive form of transport for camping holidays, while as a competitive sport it offers races, some needing primarily speed in calm waters, others demanding control in rough conditions. The sport has achieved Olympic status, and has a great future before it.

Sailing

The earliest sailing races in this country, like the earliest rowing races, made use of ships and boats constructed for utilitarian purposes. Increasing enthusiasm for such races at the end of the eighteenth century led to the building of craft designed especially for racing, so that in its origins modern yachting was a rich man's sport, and it partly remains so today.

A race for ocean-going yachts can be of any duration, but a one-day regatta must have a base, and when it includes classes for boats of various sizes, the smaller ones need waters which are not too exposed. These requirements are admirably met in the seas round the Isle of Wight, and when the first yacht club was founded in 1815, Cowes was a natural choice for its headquarters, and Cowes has since been to sailing what Lord's is to cricket. The earliest racing yachts were large vessels needing crews of working sailors, who could easily be found in Portsmouth and Southampton. The club was granted the title Royal in 1820, and in 1833 it changed its name to the Royal Yacht Squadron. In 1867 the Squadron appointed a Sailing Committee to codify the rules of racing, and this in turn became the Yacht Racing Association, having much the same relation to the Squadron as the ARA has to the Henley Stewards.

In 1851 a yacht from the USA, the *America*, won a race at Cowes. The cup which she took home as a result was offered twenty years later as a challenge trophy, and the attempts to bring the America's Cup back across the Atlantic have had a considerable influence on the subsequent development of the sport. In this century Sir Thomas Lipton commissioned a series of Shamrocks which crossed the seas in unsuccessful quest of the elusive trophy. Between the two wars, the last of these, *Shamrock V*, was one of a class of large yachts which graced our coastal regattas, among them *Westward*, *White Heather*, and, loveliest of all, *Britannia*, built in 1892 for Edward, Prince of Wales, and sailed until the end of his life by that keen yachtsman, King George V; the sight of those boats in competition is a thrilling memory for all who saw it. But the King died and the war came. After 1946 such yachts were an economic impossibility, and we shall not see such a class again. Rich men's sailing continues; a challenger for the America's Cup is now such a laboratory of computerized gadgetry that only a syndicate can afford to build it. There are smaller but still sizeable yachts which can be crewed by amateurs with a minimum of professional assistance, but even these are within the reach only of the wealthy.

Happily there is another side to the yachting world – small boat sailing, and the expansion of this is as welcome as the growth of canoeing. Much can be done to hold down the cost. Equipment is kept simple, and clubs are formed to buy and maintain boats for the members; the fibreglass hull will help in this direction. There are problems for these small boats too. They need more sheltered waters than their bigger sisters – estuaries, gravel pits and rivers. Unfortunately such places are also eagerly sought after for power boats, those horrors which spoil the enjoyment of everyone except their occupants.

When these small sailing boats race, handicapping is a difficulty, as it has been for all classes of yachts since the sport began. Multiplicity of design makes the problem more acute, but too much standardization would be an undesirable check on experiment and innovation. A recent addition to the programme of regattas, races for teams of two or three boats, has interesting possibilities, and will protect the sport of sailing against any possible accusation of spotlighting the individual too much. Fortunately too, racing is not essential to make sailing enjoyable. Many keen young sailors are perfectly content simply to face the endless problems presented by the elemental challenge of wind and water.

Swimming

It used to be said that man is the only animal which needs to be taught to swim. This view is probably the result of anxious parents in an urbanized society keeping their children out of danger by keeping them out of water. Left to themselves, tiny children seem to take to swimming as easily and as early as they take to walking. Most peoples, unless hindered by some religious or social taboo, have liked to cool themselves in hot weather by plunging into sea or river, and swimming is a welcome concomitant to this. Rather strangely the Greeks were an exception. A seafaring people, they regarded swimming as a necessity. Their phrase for the rudiments of schooling was 'the ABC and swimming', the equivalent of our 'three Rs'. But apart from one casual reference to swimming races, in a way which suggests that they were unusual, there is no mention in Greek literature of swimming for pleasure, and Greek medical writers deprecate sea bathing on the ground that it is liable to cause a chill. The Romans, on the other hand, were enthusiastic swimmers in sea and river. Both Greeks and Romans delighted in baths, but for hygienic and social rather than sporting motives.

In Britain, Shakespeare's mention of 'Little wanton boys that swim on bladders' gives a clue to the situation in his time. Certainty is impossible, but most children probably picked up swimming as they played with their companions in stream or sea. This was easy enough so long as the bulk of the populace lived in the countryside or in small cities, but when they crowded into large towns, and rivers were befouled by industrial pollution, it was no longer possible. The first attempt to provide a solution was made in Liverpool, where in 1828 the civic authorities opened a public swimming bath; London followed in 1846, and soon such baths became commonplace. Their heated water made indoor swimming pleasant in the winter months, and in the British climate this is a great advantage for those weaker mortals who cannot emulate the hardy souls who break the ice to maintain their all-the-year-round outdoor record. Today the demand for pools of Olympic standard has caused swimming to be regarded as an indoor activity. This is regrettable, for the sport belongs essentially to sunshine and the outdoors. But we have to admit that it is increasingly difficult to find any stretch of lake, river or sea beach where the water is not filthy with industrial waste or oil or sewage.

In the second half of the nineteenth century there was a movement in Britain for founding associations to organize various sports and physical activities. Swimming shared in this, and the Amateur Swimming Association was formed in 1869. Its primary object was to bring home to people the importance of learning to swim, and to encourage and assist the provision of facilities and instructors; later it undertook the organization of racing, and in 1884 it recognized water polo, the only game based on swimming which has so far been developed.

Swimming races, arranged in a somewhat ramshackle fashion in the harbour of the Peiraeus, were held at the celebration of the first modern Olympic Games in 1896, and have remained part of the Olympic programme. The scramble by swimming associations to secure a larger share of the medals for their sport has had results as undesirable as those in rowing. Races and categories have been multiplied, until Olympic swimming medals are now ten a penny. The multiplication has been without rhyme or reason. The object of a race is to determine superior speed, and a competitor is entitled to choose his own method. There is no case for races with artificially imposed limitations on the method used. The breast stroke and back stroke are both useful in their own spheres, but neither would be chosen by anyone wishing to swim fast. Still less defensible is the butterfly stroke. This unnatural movement was invented shortly before the Second World War for use in breast stroke races, from which it was not then excluded by the existing definition of the breast stroke. In order to increase categories, the butterfly was made illegal in breast stroke races and granted events in its own right. It has no merits; it is slower than free style and more exhausting than breast or back stroke. And it is hideously ugly. To hop backwards is a difficult and strenuous exercise, but no one in his senses would demand races on the track for it as part of the Olympic athletics programme. The butterfly has no better claim.

The improvement of techniques in women's swimming has had one strange and disturbing effect, not confined to swimming but most clearly evident in that sport. A twelve-year-old girl is better streamlined for swimming than she will be in four or five years' time. As this truth has gradually sunk home, the age of swimming medallists has gone down and down, and now a girl may be past her best long before her eighteenth birthday. Younger and younger girls are being cajoled and compelled by ambitious and unscrupulous parents to undertake the régime of training for many hours a day, year after year, which is essential for success at the highest level. This routine makes impossible the all-round experience and enjoyment of life in all its aspects which is surely childhood's birthright. The public see on their television screens the juvenile winner in her hour of triumph; she always declares, of course, that the sacrifice has been worth while. They do not see the hundreds who have failed to make the grade, and who for no reward have lost part of their life which they can never recover. Nor is the later effect on the winner yet sufficiently established. Everyone who plays games has to face the moment when he realizes that he is past his peak and going downhill. It is part of the process of achieving maturity. Normally it happens in the twenties or early thirties, when the victim has acquired some experience of life and is able to put his sport into the proper relationship to his other activities. If he is wise and lucky, he goes on playing his games at a level suited to his diminishing capacities. The sixteen-year-old medallist is in a far different position. She has been conditioned to regard her sport as the be-all and end-all of existence. Now while still emotionally a child, she has reached the utmost pinnacle that life has to offer her, and there is nothing beyond it to achieve. Sport is a valuable aid to a happy, full and balanced life. When it becomes an obstacle to achieving that end, the time has come for some new and serious thinking.

7
Football

The size of a ball largely determines the nature of the games played with it. For more than three thousand years the small hand ball has been used in games which depend on throwing and catching or hitting the ball with a club. The larger ball, generally the inflated bladder of a pig or ox, was also known in antiquity. Galen, a Greek medical writer of the second century A.D., tells us that in his day children used to try to make the bladder spherical by warming it in hot ashes and rubbing it, singing as they did so a traditional song. Unhappily he does not record the words of the song, but he does say that it was an appeal to the bladder to grow rounder.

We do not know at what date a bladder was first enclosed in a stronger case; the earliest mention seems to be in Shakespeare's *Comedy of Errors*:

> Am I so round with you as you with me,
> That like a football you do spurn me thus?
> You spurn me hence, and he will spurn me hither;
> If I last in this service, you must case me in leather.

Until this was done, the bladder cannot have been used for any very violent game, as it would have burst; whatever use the Greeks and Romans may have put it to, there is not the slightest evidence that they played any game based on kicking. (For a full discussion see H. A. Harris, *Sport in Greece and Rome*, p. 103 ff.) The inflated bladder was much less likely to cause damage than the hard hand-ball with its tight stuffing. In the Statutes of Galway (1527), after the usual prohibition of most sports except archery, the citizens are told that they must not indulge in 'horling of the littl ball with hockie sticks or staves . . . nor use no hande ball to play without the walles, but only the great foote balle'.

The ultimate origin of football may be left to the anthropologists. It appears to be basically a struggle between two groups to secure possession of some trophy, such as the head of a sacrificed animal, and carry it off to a safe place. In the Middle Ages the trophy was represented by a large ball or small cask, the groups were often neighbouring villages, and the place of security was the porch of the village church. When the game started midway between the villages, the members of each squad naturally positioned themselves between the ball and their opponents' porch, and tried to drive the ball forward towards their own church, using every available method including kicking. So when today we see this contest in the stylized form of a soccer match between, for example, Chelsea and Arsenal, what we call the Chelsea goal, guarded by the Chelsea goalkeeper, is in fact the Arsenal church porch, in which the Arsenal players are anxious to lodge the ball.

The medieval tussles were generally part of Shrove Tuesday celebrations, and they have survived or been revived in some parts of the country. They were not confined to villages; similar struggles took place in towns, where they caused much damage. It was during one such game that the young St Hugh of Lincoln kicked a ball through the window of a Jew's house, a feat which resulted in his assassination. Violence on these occasions was unlimited. Not surprisingly most of the early references to football in Britain deal with attempts to suppress the game.

The first efforts to reduce the mad scramble through streets and over fields to a formalized game were made not in this country but in Italy in the sixteenth century. We are fortunate enough to possess two accounts of this, one by Scaino, whom we have already encountered as an authority on Royal Tennis, the other by Giovanni de' Bardi. The latter is particularly valuable because it has an illustration of a game about to start in the Piazza di Santa Croce in Florence. Some features of this scene are surprisingly modern, such as the covered stand and the railing to keep the playing area clear of spectators, while the tents with their open doors remind us of the origin of football goals. Most remarkable of all is the arrangement of the teams, exactly the same as that in the famous football match in *Tom Brown's Schooldays*. Scaino gives us the names of the groups, the forwards (*antiguardia*, Tom Brown's 'bulldogs'), the 'quarters' (*gagliardi*) and the goalkeepers (*retroguardia*). The game was played by twenty, thirty or forty players, which presumably points to teams of ten to twenty on each side, far different from the masses involved in Tom Brown's first game at Rugby.

It is probable that news of this civilized version of football was brought to Britain at the time and did something to shape the game here, especially in the schools. The term scrummage or scrimmage may embody a vestigial trace of this Italian ancestry; it is a variant of skirmish, the Italian *scaramuccia*. In general, Renaissance writers on education in England deprecate the game on the ground of its violence and hooliganism, but there is an exception. Richard Mulcaster was headmaster of Merchant Taylors' and then of St Pauls'. In his *Positions* of 1581, he defends football and pleads that 'the abuse of it is a sufficient argument that it hath a right use'. He reveals its popularity in his day when he argues that 'it would not have groune to the greatnes that it is now at, if it had not had great helpes, both to health and strength'. He advocates the appointment of 'trayning maisters' in schools, and 'a smaller number of players sorted into sides and standings, not meeting with their bodies so boisterously to trie their strength'. The phrase 'a smaller number of players sorted into sides and standings' certainly suggests that Mulcaster knew something of the orderly Italian game; his advice to appoint sports masters in schools had to wait 300 years before it was acted upon.

We have an account of a game played in Cornwall in Elizabethan times, which is highly relevant to the history of football; it is found in Carew's *Survey of Cornwall*, 1602. Carew describes two games called hurling. The first, 'hurling to the country', is the usual scramble between two villages three or four miles apart. The other, 'hurling to goales', is much more interesting. Like the Italian game, it is played by teams of fifteen, twenty or thirty players 'more or less':

> They join hands in ranke one against another; out of these rankes they match themselves by payres, one embracing another, and so passe away, every of which couple are especially to watch one another during the play; after this they pitch two bushes in the ground, some 8 or 10 feet asunder, and directly against them, 10 or 12 score paces off, other twain in like distance, which they term goales, where some indifferent person throweth up a ball, the which

whosoever can catch and carry through his adversaries goale, hath wonne the game; but herein consisteth one of Hercules his labours, for he that is once possessed of the ball, hath his contrary mate waiting at inches and assaying to lay hold upon him, the other thrusteth him in the breast with his closed fist to keep him off, which they call *butting*. . . . They must hurle man to man, and not two set upon one man at once. The hurler against the ball must not *but* nor *hand-fast* under the girdle, he who hath the ball must *but* only in the other's breast, and deal no fore ball, that is, he may not throw it to any of his mates standing nearer the goale than himself.

Few historians of football have accorded this passage the attention it deserves, partly no doubt because 'hurling' suggests Irish hockey, and partly because it nowhere mentions kicking. But the Cornish game, with its close marking, its hand-off, its tackling, and its passing, with forward passes barred, resembles modern Rugby football far more closely than does the game in *Tom Brown's Schooldays*. The ban on the hand-fast below the waist shows why tackling at rugger used to be called collaring, a term now rarely heard, though it aptly describes much that passes for tackling today.

The popularity of football in Elizabeth's reign which Mulcaster records suffered in common with other games from puritan repression; James I's *Book of Sports* (1618) does not even mention it. Yet Oliver Cromwell is said to have been a keen footballer in his youth. Attempts were made to play the game at the universities; Sir Thomas Overbury in his *Characters* (1614) says of 'A meere Scholar': 'The antiquity of his University is his creed, and the excellency of his Colledge (though but for a match at foot-ball) an article of his faith.'

But the game was frowned upon by the university authorities. In 1580 matches between colleges were forbidden at Cambridge, and at Oxford the Laudian statutes of 1636 proscribed the game altogether. The ban was not always observed. The great Oxford antiquary, Anthony à Wood, quotes an extract from the Proctors' Black Book of 1666, recording in stately Latin that Robert Duke, Scholar of All Souls, no less, was sent down for a year for playing football (*quia lusus pilae-pedalis convictus fuerat*). In the same year the same penalty was inflicted on a man from Queen's College and two from Exeter College, one of them a B.A. Seeing that on the previous page Wood records a violent fight between Queen's and Exeter, it is tempting to conjecture, in the light of the earlier prohibition of such matches at Cambridge, that the riot at Oxford started in a football game between the two colleges. In part extenuation of these scandalous proceedings, Wood tells us that at the time 'Exeter College was much debauched by a drunken governor'. A few years later we hear of a tradition of playing football at Michaelmas at Magdalene College, Cambridge; the college authorities grudgingly permitted an allowance of beer for those rendered thirsty by the exercise.

If the game gained little ground in the universities in the seventeenth and eighteenth centuries, we can find an explanation in a chance statement about sport in Trinity College, Dublin in 1780. Football was played every evening in the College park, but only by pensioners or commoners, not by wealthy fellow-commoners. Such authorities as mention the game in the eighteenth century all insist that it was a pursuit of the 'common people'. This is confirmed by J. Strutt in his *Sports and Pastimes of the people of England* (1801), our best authority for the early history of sport. Of football he writes:

> It was formerly much in vogue among the common people of England, though of late years it seems to have fallen into disrepute and is but little practised . . . When a match at football is made, two parties, each containing an equal number of competitors, take the field and stand between two goals, at the distance of 80 or 100 yards the one from the other; the ball, which is commonly made of a blown bladder and cased with leather, is delivered in the midst of the ground, and the object of either party is to drive it through the goal of their antagonists, which being achieved the game is won.

In a footnote he adds, 'The goal is usually made with two sticks driven into the ground, about two or three feet apart.' At first sight, 'feet' looks like a slip for 'yards', but as the game ended with the scoring of the first goal, there was every inducement not to make this feat too easy.

Even if the game was falling in popularity in the country generally at the beginning of the nineteenth century, it was widely played in schools, and this was the root from which the modern forms of football were to grow. Matches between schools were unknown, so every school developed its own kind of game, largely shaped by local conditions, with unwritten laws laid down by tradition. Some of these survive to this day, or have done until living memory. Eton has two such traditional games of her own, Field and Wall; Harrow, Winchester and Edinburgh Academy play others.

In 1850 there were still only two major sports with any considerable following at Oxford and Cambridge, cricket and rowing, at which the universities had been competing against one another for a quarter of a century. Now the new social trend among undergraduates was to produce an explosion of enthusiasm for other games, destined to spread remarkably quickly to all classes of the community, and the field in which this movement first appeared was football.

Credit for this must go primarily to Cambridge. In a surviving letter H. C. Malden writes, 'I went up to Trinity in 1848. In the following year an attempt was made to get up some football in preference to the hockey then in vogue.' Difficulties immediately arose because of the various origins of the players. 'I remember how the Eton men howled at the Rugby men for handling the ball.' So a meeting was held, attended by two representatives from each of Eton, Harrow, Rugby, Winchester and Shrewsbury, and two from non-public schools, of whom Malden was one. 'Every man brought a copy of his school rules, or knew them by heart.' A code of laws was agreed on and printed as the 'Cambridge Rules'; copies were distributed and posted up on Parker's Piece. Unhappily no copy has survived. It is important to notice that, while Rugby was one of the schools represented, there is no evidence for the statement of Morris Marples, one of the best of football's historians, that the meeting was called to agree on rules for *Rugby* football; the representatives of the other schools would have seen to that. The meeting agreed on laws for *Cambridge* football; their code was printed as the Cambridge Rules.

In the next few years, football clubs were founded in many parts of the country, and they followed the rules known to their founders. The very influential Sheffield Club, for example, was founded in 1855 by Harrovians. Rugbeians founded Blackheath in 1858, and Richmond and Harlequins, using the same rules, followed a year later. Uncertainty about the laws must have been a constant difficulty, especially when we remember that there were no umpires or referees; disputes were settled on the spot or after the match by the captains.

The decisive year for the history of modern football was 1863. At Cambridge the 1848 code was either forgotten or no longer adequate, and early in October 1863 a meeting was held there which produced a new set of laws. In the same month, representatives of a number of clubs met in London, apparently in ignorance of the Cambridge proceedings, and formed the Football Association. The first few meetings were concerned with organization, and it was not until the fourth, held in November, that the laws came under consideration; by this time, members had heard of the new Cambridge code, and they decided to discuss it at their next gathering. This meeting, on 8 December 1863, settled the future of football. The Association suggested laws which allowed running with the ball, tripping and hacking (deliberately kicking an opponent's shins), 'but no player shall be held and hacked at the same time'. The Cambridge laws allowed charging, but banned tripping and hacking; they contained no mention of running with the ball. The meeting adopted the Cambridge code.

We know practically nothing of the discussions at these meetings, but there are several obvious points of difference in the traditions of the various schools which must have come under consideration when they were arriving at a compromise, among them the shape of the ball, handling and running with it, and whether or not the ball must be kicked over a cross-bar in order to score a goal. We could have understood a representative taking a final stand on any one of these as an essential. Yet when F. W. Campbell, champion of the Rugby tradition, left the meeting, and his club, Blackheath, withdrew from the Association, it was on none of these grounds. The reason was that the laws banned tripping and hacking. Campbell declared that the laws now adopted entirely destroyed the game and took away all interest in it; tripping and hacking made just the difference between baseball and football. (The dragging in of baseball suggests an appeal to anti-American prejudice.) It is the final irony that when the Rugby Union was formed eight years later, Campbell himself proposed that hacking should be forbidden. Churchill called the War of 1939–45 'The Unnecessary War'; the split in the football world of 1863 was equally unnecessary. Far more often than some historians are willing to admit, human events have been directed by accident and the idiosyncrasies of a few individuals. It is fascinating though perhaps unprofitable to dream of what the shape of football would be today if Campbell had been a less stupid man.

Association Football

In many countries this is simply 'football'; in others, where several codes are played, the clumsy title is conveniently abbreviated to soccer, a word which enshrines a curious piece of linguistic and social history. Among Oxford undergraduates in the period before 1914, there was a fashion for mutilating words by replacing the final syllables by –er, preferably preceded by a guttural or dental stop. Thus exercise became ekkers and Torpids became Toggers. The fashion is said to have originated at Harrow, and certainly the earliest known example, footer for football, is recorded from there. The trend died with the First World War, and today no man proposing to attend a lecture after breakfast would think of saying, as his great-grandfather might have done, that he was going to a lekker after brekker. The few examples which survive are mostly connected with sport – rugger, soccer and the convenient Cuppers for inter-collegiate cup-ties. There is one notable exception to the general rule that such coinings were confined to Oxford before the First World War; in rugger circles Lord Wakefield is often referred to as Wakers, and this name must have been conferred on him at Cambridge just after that war, when he was a tower of strength to the university and England packs.

The first football played under the new Association's laws must have been closer to rugby than to modern soccer. True, the teams numbered eleven a side – the number was probably taken from cricket – but they were marshalled as nine forwards, one half-back and one back. The use of the hands was allowed for stopping the ball, but not for catching, hitting or holding it. If the ball went over a side-line, the first player to touch it had to throw it in one-handed at right angles to the line, as in rugby. The goals had no cross-bar. Hacking and tripping were banned, but shoulder charging was permitted. A touch-down behind the opponent's goal-line entitled the player to a kick at goal from 15 yards out. To be on-side a player had to be behind the ball.

These laws were accepted in the South, but in the North the Sheffield Club had formed another Association of clubs in that area. Happily any difficulties which this might have caused were removed when in 1866 a match was arranged between representative teams of the two Associations. Sheffield agreed to play under the London rules with a few additions. The ground was to be 120×80 yards, the ball to be 'Lillywhite's No. 5', and the duration of play one hour and a half; the colours to be worn by the two teams were also agreed. In such ways standardization was being achieved in the early days, and modifications and alterations to the laws came steadily. In 1865 the goalkeeper is mentioned for the first time, and by 1871 he is the only one allowed to handle. In 1867 a player was on-side provided there were three opponents between him and their goal-line. About the same time, a cord between the goal-posts was introduced, under which the ball had to pass for a goal to be valid; this was soon replaced by a solid cross-bar. The corner kick came in 1871. From 1880 the throw-in could be in any direction, and in 1882 the two-handed throw over the head was introduced. The touch-down over side-line or goal-line had vanished.

Well before the turn of the century the game had taken the shape with which we are familiar today. Since then the only important change in the rules – as distinct from the interpretation of rules – was made in 1925, when the number of opponents required to put a player on-side was reduced from three to two. Those of us who played under both rules would probably agree unanimously that the change was a great improvement; it certainly made the referee's task easier.

If the laws of the game have changed little, its tactics have developed out of all recognition. In the early days of nine forwards, there was little more than kicking ahead and following up. But the subtler skills began to show themselves. At some schools, notably Charterhouse which was then in London, the boys had to play their football on a small paved area. Under these conditions, heavy body-charging was out of the question; the aim was to beat the immediate opponent by skilled foot-work, ball control and body feinting, such as can be seen today whenever a group of boys start to kick a ball about informally in street or playground. Soon the kick-and-rush game was enriched by passing the ball and running with it under close control; the word 'dribbling' for this is still used by the old-fashioned.

By 1885 the tactical formation of the XI was standardized which was to hold the field for half a century – goalkeeper, two full-backs, three half-backs and five forwards – and until recently players kept closely to their appointed positions. For many years there was a difference between amateur and professional teams in the tactical functions of the positions. In both, the centre half looked after the opposing centre forward. In the amateur game, wing forwards were marked by wing halves. Inside forwards were marked by their opposite numbers in mid-field, but when they were near their opponents' goal, the duty was taken over by the full-backs. In the professional game, full backs marked wing forwards, while wing halves looked after inside forwards. For some curious reason of tradition, West Bromwich Albion followed the amateur practice long after it had been abandoned by all other professional clubs.

In 1871 the Association offered a Cup for annual competition among its constituent clubs, and thus took the first step towards producing the opinion widely held today that no game is worth playing simply for its own sake. Of fifty member clubs, fifteen took part in the first competition. Early winners included the Old Etonians, the Royal Engineers, Oxford University and the Wanderers, a team of old public school boys; this was natural, for these clubs were drawn from the social class which had recently brought the game into being.

In fairness to that social class at that time – a fairness now always denied them – we must remember that with the passion for social justice which was a mark of the Victorians, these young men were making every effort to extend the enjoyment of sport to the less privileged. In those years a considerable proportion of graduates took Holy Orders, and when they went out into their parishes they encouraged and helped boys and young men to form their own football clubs. Many of the most famous clubs in the soccer world today trace their ancestry to one of these parish teams, Southampton to St Mary's, Queen's Park Rangers to St Jude's, Fulham to St Andrew's, Bolton to Christ Church, Blackpool to St John's. These working-class clubs soon claimed a position of importance in the game. In 1882 the Old Etonians beat Blackburn Rovers in the Cup Final. Next year Blackburn Olympic defeated the Etonians in the final, and for the three following years the winners were Blackburn Rovers; the supremacy of the public schools and universities had ended. But the nation-wide competition for the Cup had already revealed financial problems. One year the Old

Etonians visited Lancashire to play Darwen in one of the early rounds. The result was a draw, but Darwen were unable to travel to London for the replay. The Etonians offered to pay their fares, but the Darwen players simply could not afford the loss of wages which the journey would entail. Clearly the question of payment for 'broken time' had to be faced.

It was a period of difficult decisions. In every sport, great efforts were being made to escape from the effects of betting and the corruption which inevitably goes with it, and to the great advantage of British sport in the next seventy or eighty years, these efforts were succeeding. Many felt that this movement would be endangered by any payment being made to footballers, and there was a possibility that the FA might follow the same disastrous line as the rowing authorities. On the other hand, they had before them the example of the cricket world; most of them were cricketers themselves. Cricket had freed itself from the abuses which had disgraced it at the beginning of the century, and amateur and professional were enjoying the game together in harmony. In 1885 soccer took its decision, and payment for broken time was legalized. Steps were taken to guard against possible harm to the game which might result. To prevent poaching of players by wealthy clubs, it was enacted that 'Professionals shall be allowed to compete in all Cups, provided they qualify as follows: in Cup matches, by birth or residence for two years past within six miles of the ground or headquarters of the Club for which they play.'

The influence of the example of cricket is obvious here. Unhappily this qualification was not long maintained, but another provision with the same intention, the maximum wage, lasted until after the Second World War. Only in very recent years has it been possible for a professional footballer to make anything more out of the game than a decent living; the principle long survived that the sole purpose of allowing payment was to make it possible for men of all social classes to enjoy top-level football, and amateur and professional played together as in cricket. At the beginning of this century the professionals of Wolverhampton Wanderers after a home match used to drop in at the vicarage for tea; the vicar's son, also a parson, the Reverend K. R. G. Hunt, was a regular member of the team, and played for them when Wolves won the Cup in 1908.

Such a happy relationship inevitably had its effect on the

standards of sportsmanship of the time. In an elementary school team from a working-class district before 1914 – *experto crede* – the behaviour on the field was considerably better than that of many university sides today. Any player showing the slightest dissent from a referee's decision was very quickly told by his fellows to play to the whistle. The scorer of a goal was not kissed by his team-mates; the most he could expect was a 'Good shot, John'. This was partly due to the excellent precept and example of our masters, but it owed even more to that remarkable pair, the *Magnet* and *Gem*. To suit the tastes of the bulk of their readers, Greyfriars was a soccer school. The feats of Harry Wharton and Bob Cherry on the football field may sometimes have passed beyond the improbable into the impossible, but their sportsmanship was always impeccable, and that was our exemplar. (These two periodicals elicited from George Orwell one of the silliest critical essays ever written, a glorious example of the readiness of the left-wing intellectual to detect a Bloated Capitalist under every bed. Perhaps one better qualified to judge them than an Old Etonian could possibly be may suggest that at worst they were harmless and at best highly entertaining and beneficial.) That standards of conduct were high in the early days is indicated by the fact that the penalty kick was not introduced until 1891. Even then amateurs felt it unnecessary. The Arthur Dunn Cup competition for Old Boy teams of public schools would not acknowledge its existence until quite recently.

The growing gap in ability between amateur and professional led to the provision of events confined to amateurs, starting with the Amateur Cup in 1893. Before this, an important step had been taken in promoting the amateur conception of sport by the foundation in 1882 of the Corinthian F.C. The moving spirit in this Club, which drew its members mainly but not exclusively from Oxford and Cambridge, was an Oxford don, N. L. Jackson. He was one of a number of senior academics who made a great contribution to the development of sport in the older Universities and consequently in the whole country. The undergraduates of those days, who could recognize a good thing when they saw it, gladly availed themselves of the experience and advice of these figures in the coaching of college teams and crews, and even more in the acquiring of playing fields for the universities and colleges. Sad to say, this seldom happens now. Few of the younger dons have any qualities which would fit them for offering advice, and today's undergraduates, who know it all, would reject any such help as savouring of paternalism.

Jackson showed one remarkable piece of prescience. Professionalism had not yet been legalized, and in any case the amateurism of Corinth would have been taken for granted. He realized that an even more insidious threat than money to the true spirit of sport lay in such competitions as the FA Cup. One of the original rules of the Corinthians was, 'The Club shall not compete for any challenge cup or any prizes of any description whatever'. Although it was to be a long time before the Corinthians entered a competition for the first time, for many years until 1907 they used to play the winners of the FA Cup, the cream of professional soccer, and almost always beat them. Twice in the 1890s Corinth supplied the whole of the England team in a full international match.

In 1888 a second competition was founded – not by the Association – destined to have even more influence than the Cup on the future of the game. Twelve clubs from the Midlands and North formed a league. Their first motive was to facilitate the arrangement of fixtures and to ensure a full season's programme, but from the start there was a competitive element. *Whitaker's Almanack* for 1889 reported, 'These clubs play a sort of American Tournament for the league championship.' This has since been imitated in almost every branch of sport. A knock-out cup competition has its own attraction, arising from the 'sudden death' principle in every match, but the league championship is a better test of the all-round ability and staying power of a team. (It is noteworthy that attempts to combine the two principles – league and knock-out – in the same event, as in international cup competitions for clubs with home-and-away ties, and in the World Cup of 1974, have all demonstrated that they encourage tactics against the true interests of the game.)

However, the growth of the League and its management has brought a threat to the football world. The League, whose policy is that of the wealthy clubs which form it, has become far more powerful than the Football Association itself and is able to dictate to it; the relationship between the two bodies resembles that between the Trades Union Congress and the government of the day. A game, like a country, which has two governing bodies is not in a healthy condition.

The happy partnership of amateur and professional in soccer received a set-back in 1907, when a body of amateurs, alarmed by some developments in the professional game, set up an Amateur Football Association (AFA; since 1934 the second A has stood for Alliance). The FA unwisely took offence at this and proscribed AFA clubs, so that they could no longer enter for the FA Cup. Happily the breach did not survive the First World War, and shortly after that war the Corinthians, hoping to bring back to soccer the same friendliness between amateur and professional which still existed in cricket, broke with their foundation principle and in 1922 entered for the FA Cup. They were accorded the same exemption from the early rounds as the senior league clubs, and in the first few years they justified that privilege. A victory in 1925 over Blackburn Rovers recalled the earliest years of Cup history, and this was followed in 1927 by a glorious defeat at the hands of Newcastle United, then, like Blackburn Rovers, one of the most eminent clubs in the First Division. But in the succeeding years it became clear that even Corinth could not match the skill and fitness of full-time professionals. They withdrew from the Cup, and formally united with the Casuals, who had long been virtually their second XI and were members of the Isthmian League, the senior amateur competition of the London area. In those days the Isthmian clubs were genuinely amateur, and really did represent the places whose names they bore. Corinthian-Casuals remained a first-class club for several years, and as recently as 1956 reached the final of the Amateur cup. But most of the Isthmian clubs gradually descended into a sleazy shamateurism. The league accepted money for advertising cigarettes, and used it to bribe players not to be guilty of dirty play. Corinthian-Casuals sank to the bottom of the league.

> Men are we and must grieve when even the shade
> Of that which once was great has passed away.

Soon after the Second World War, a group of players conceived an ambition to restore the former glories of amateur football; like the founders of the Corinthians, they included a strong element from Oxford and Cambridge. It would have been logical had they directed their energies to a revival of Corinth. Unhappily the post-war generation developed a contempt for tradition and for the knowledge and experience of their predecessors. 'We are the people, and Wisdom was born with us.' So a new club was inaugurated, Pegasus. Like a meteor it shot to the top, and in 1951 won the Amateur Cup. Then, as suddenly as it had appeared, it vanished. Those who know the inside story are probably reluctant to reveal it, but in the interests of future historians of sport it should be written. It will make sad reading.

In the decade after the institution of the FA Cup came the first matches between England, Scotland, Wales and Ireland, which mark the beginning of representative international sport. Incidentally, this explains why there has never been a 'Great Britain' team, except in the Olympic Games, and why in the International Federation (FIFA) Britain is still represented by four Associations, a circumstance which arouses fury in other nations.

The game spread slowly into Europe, and in 1896 an England team played against Germany, Austria and Bohemia. The spread was signalized in 1904 by the foundation of FIFA. The British attitude towards these international organizations in their early days was something less than enthusiastic. The FA were naturally foundation members of FIFA, but they resigned in 1919, rejoined in 1924, resigned again in 1928 over the definition of an amateur, and returned again in 1946. England won the football competition in the Olympic Games on the first occasion when it was held, at the Fourth Olympiad in 1908, and again in 1912. In 1920 they were knocked out by Norway in the first round, and did not enter in 1924 and 1928. Since then the event in the Games has been farcical, because of the different interpretations put on 'amateur' by different nations; Britain, which has tried to be honest in this matter, has not had the remotest chance of success. When the World Cup was instituted, Britain held aloof, and when at last she did enter, regarded it somewhat lightly. This led to the extraordinary defeat in 1950 at the hands of the USA, in whose sporting world soccer has never been more than a fringe activity. Not until the year of victory, 1966, did Britain take the competition seriously.

The blame for this casual attitude must be laid at the door of the leading English clubs. Their managers, conscious of the vast sums of money they have expended on their stars, have no wish to see them endangered in the ferocious realm of international matches. The clubs are naturally supported in this by the Football League, which represents their interests, and this causes difficulties for the FA, which is responsible for selecting and managing the international teams. But though the clubs may be reluctant to have their players injured when playing for their country, they have no compunction about exposing them to the even greater perils of international cup competitions for clubs. These proliferating organizations have introduced a melancholy phenomenon into football, the two-leg cup-tie with home and away matches. The visiting side usually makes no attempt to score goals; their sole aim is to avoid defeat, in the hope of clinching victory in the home leg, when at least they can be sure of having the referee on their side because of his fear of what might happen to him at the hands of the crowd if he were not. The dreary tactics thus engendered have to be seen to be believed.

The spread of soccer into almost every part of the world has inevitably produced some changes in the game itself. Football grew up as a game to be played in the English winter on soft English mud and turf, on which the violent contact of body and body was rarely dangerous. The laws still mirror this conception of the game. They define a fair charge – shoulder to shoulder – and are content to lay down circumstances in which this must not be used. But there is another law penalizing dangerous play. When we watch international matches on our television screens, we see playing fields in other countries as green as our own, and we are apt to forget that these are the arenas of wealthy clubs which can afford the extensive watering necessary to maintain this excellence. Anyone who has travelled in warmer climates and kept his eyes open knows that most of the football in the world today is played on stretches of sun-baked gravel and native rock, compared with which the paved area on which Charterhouse boys used to play was smoothness personified. It is small wonder that referees who controlled matches on such surfaces took the view that any charging on them was dangerous. In early games abroad, English players used to be bewildered when they were penalized for tackles which under the interpretation of the laws current in this country were perfectly legitimate. But now our referees have conformed to the continental pattern. Body-to-body contact has been replaced by leg-to-leg, which is far more dangerous.

The movement to eliminate all physical contact has had one

very undesirable result in the absurd immunity it has conferred on goalkeepers. The law still states that the goalkeeper must not be charged unless he is holding the ball. If that does not mean that he may be charged if he is holding the ball, the English language has ceased to have any meaning. As recently as 1958 in the Cup Final, Bolton Wanderers' centre forward scored a goal by charging Manchester United's goalkeeper into the net with the ball in his arms. Nowadays the moment a goalkeeper lays a finger on the ball, all players of both teams run away from him, or perhaps a foolish opponent stands a foot away making faces at him. This flagrantly contradicts a fundamental principle of the game, that while the ball is in play it is legitimate for any player not off-side to play it. It also gives too many opportunities for time-wasting. Clearly the abuse cannot now be cured by a return to the old-fashioned charging; the law must be rescinded and replaced by another. It should be made illegal for the goalkeeper to catch, hold or lie on the ball; his use of his hands should be limited to punching or pushing the ball away, and the other offences should incur a penalty kick. This would have the additional advantage of increasing the number of goals scored.

The present withholding of the ball from the other side by the goalkeeper is in effect a form of obstruction, as is also much of the 'screening' of the ball by a player about to be tackled. Our grandfathers were more liberally minded than we are on this point. There is a delightful picture of their practice in *The Complete Association Footballer* of 1912. The book was written by two Cambridge Blues, so we can be sure that we have here the pure milk of the amateur tradition.

> Another thing which the full-back must be prepared to do at all times is to hold off an on-rushing forward, and prevent him tackling or reaching another of the defence in possession of the ball, in order to allow the latter to have a clear kick. . . . This holding off need not be done roughly; a heavy charge is quite out of place, but one's object can be achieved by shouldering the man gently or even falling back slowly in such a way that the forward cannot get past; at times, of course, one has to charge the forward heavily to attain this purpose, but in these cases it will generally be the forward's fault if he is seriously inconvenienced, for the back will be quite content with gentle obstruction.

There were giants in the land in those days. 'Seriously inconvenienced' is superb. We are reminded of the famous reply of an Etonian's mother to a friend who warned her of the danger her son ran from playing so rough a game: 'If anyone gets his leg broken, it won't be Arthur.'

The spread of the game into new regions after the Second World War brought more changes. Some countries, notably the Hungarians and South Americans, introduced fresh skills and tactics, which did much to give new life to the game. For a time, until our players had mastered these techniques, Britain lost her old supremacy, but she was able to re-establish her position by England's victory in the World Cup in 1966. Less happy were the developments in the financial organization of the game. When soccer came to these new countries, it was as a spectator sport. They had no tradition of the game played simply for the enjoyment of the players, such as had shaped its early stages in Britain and was still inherent in it. The considerations, for instance, which had led to the fixing of a maximum wage for professionals, were completely unintelligible to them. Soon after the war, wealthy Italian capitalists found that the success of a local football team helped greatly in the avoidance of industrial unrest in their factories, and so they poured money into the game. Italian clubs offered high wages to the star players of other countries, and several British players were tempted to seek their fortunes abroad. It is true that most of them found that the money did not compensate for the drawbacks and returned home unhappy; moreover the football authorities of most countries soon restricted the number of expatriate players a club could employ. But before the threat of a drain of top talent had diminished in this way, Britain had abandoned the maximum wage, and British clubs were plunged into the financial jungle in which they now struggle. Players bargained for higher and higher wages, transfer fees mounted to ridiculous heights, and the clubs started to snivel at the threat of the bankruptcy which they were bringing on themselves by their own folly.

The dangers which involvement with these huge sums of money brings to the game are so recent that their full effects are only now beginning to be seen. The sudden wealth of a stardom which cannot last more than a few years sets problems to young players which not all of them are capable of solving. This is not peculiar to football; it extends to the whole world of entertainment. Far more important is the risk of bribery and corruption which always waits on wealth. When football was first organized, the governing bodies had 2000 years of human experience to guide them. They were fortunate compared with the administrators of other sports in that there was no strong tradition of betting on football to guard against, as there was in cricket, rowing and athletics. On the whole, the authorities in those sports, zealous for the new ideals of amateurism in their day, were remarkably successful in channelling organized gambling into horse racing. Even so, as early as 1892 the FA found it necessary to introduce a law forbidding betting on football by players and club officials, and making clubs responsible for preventing betting among spectators. It was more than half a century later that the first threat to the integrity of the game from this source appeared. In the meantime, the steady increase of taxation on earnings lawfully acquired had made gambling much more attractive, and a vast betting industry had come into being, anxious to extend its activities over ever-widening fields.

There is only one safe way of making money by gambling – never to bet except on a certainty. From time immemorial professional gamblers have tried to achieve this position by 'fixing' matches. In this respect soccer is fortunate, since most betting on it is done through the pools, and even the largest syndicate could hardly bribe sufficient players to ensure a winning coupon. But an increasing number of bets are laid on single matches which can be fixed, and a real danger exists here. Two notorious law cases in 1963 and 1965 revealed that players in League teams had accepted bribes to 'throw' a match.

Great as is the risk of bribery based on betting, there is a much more insidious form of corruption in top soccer circles, suspected though not yet proven in Britain but recently revealed in Germany. The financial status of a club depends to a great extent on the division of the league to which it belongs, so that promotion and relegation concern other things besides pride. Towards the end of the season, there are in each division a few clubs at the top with hopes of championship or promotion, and a few at the bottom trying to avoid relegation. Between them are a body of clubs for whom hope and fear alike are dead for that season, and both players and managers are merely going through the motions. There is a temptation for the clubs at the top or bottom to take advantage of the situation. A player from a middle club is approached in a bar by a stranger with) 'Here's £10 for you now and £100 if you lose next Saturday.' The cost to the hopeful or threatened club is trifling compared with the financial results of a change of division. The player approached sees no great harm in making a little easy money; at the end of an exhausting season he probably did not intend to try very hard next Saturday anyway. This can work in another way. At the end of the 1971–2 season a club faced with relegation revealed in the press that it had been approached by four of its players with a demand for extra money as an inducement to keep the club in the First Division. Three of the players were named, and no libel action followed, so the facts may be assumed to be unassailable. What the players would do if their demands were not met was not stated; it was obvious enough. Naturally they were placed on the transfer list; more surprisingly another club paid a large fee for one of them. In the world of commercialized sport there is no limit to human folly.

Rugby Football

When the withdrawal of Blackheath from the meeting in 1863 made it certain that there would thenceforth be two codes of football in Britain, all the advantages seemed to be on the side of the Rugbeians. They already had a set of laws embodying the experience of half a century. The soccer players had to arrive at a compromise code drawn from several traditions and needing some years of experiment to get over its teething troubles. Yet by 1871, the year in which the Rugby Union was founded, the Association game had assumed a disciplined shape which we should recognize today. Many years were to pass before the same could be said of rugby. The reason is easy to see. The Association, because of its heterogeneous origins, had to think out the basic principles on which their game was to be founded and try to express them clearly in laws. The Union were dealing with a game with a single tradition, which had been played for generations without any written laws, and in which the accepted practice of the players has, until very recent times, always been more powerful than any written rules. An example of the precedence of practice over law is to be found in that curious feature of the game, the field goal, scored by a fly kick at a loose ball. A goal was scored in this way by Oxford in the first University Match, in 1872, but it was disputed by Cambridge on the ground that one of their players had touched the ball in flight. Oxford did not press their claim, because they had won without it. The field goal was not abolished until 1905, yet it rarely figures in the score of any important match. Although lawful, it was regarded with contempt by the players.

The reliance on tradition transmitted on the field of play is no doubt partly the reason why there is no satisfactory history of rugby football. There appears to be a lack of written evidence, but an even greater obstacle has been the myth of W. W. Ellis. Set in a wall at Rugby School is a stone with this inscription: 'This stone commemorates the exploit of William Webb Ellis, who, with a fine disregard for the rules of Football as played in his time, first took the ball in his arms and ran with it, thus originating the distinctive feature of the Rugby Game. A.D. 1823.' This is the result of the efforts of a committee of Old Rugbeians appointed in 1895 to investigate the early history of the game. They had before them an article written in 1880 by M. H. Bloxham, who had been at the school from 1813 to 1820 and so had overlapped Ellis (1816–25). Bloxham did not see the incident; he related it on the authority of someone whom he did not name. This is as flimsy as evidence well can be; still, it would be impossible to prove that the incident did not take place. Where the committee went wrong was in jumping to the conclusion that the incident was unique, that it was an important innovation which changed the nature of the game, and that from it there was an unbroken development until their own day. The story provided them with a name, beloved of mythologists in all ages, and this made them disregard or distort the abundant evidence to the contrary.

They had the description of the game in *Tom Brown's Schooldays*, incomparably the finest piece of evidence for the early history of any modern sport. Although the account was written some years later, the game can be accurately dated to 1834, its author's first year at Rugby, a decade after Ellis' exploit. In this there is no running with the ball; a player catching it immediately kicked it with a drop. Moreover, when the committee met, the author, Thomas Hughes, was still alive, and in a letter to the committee he made it clear that 'running in' was a development of his own day (1834–42). He wrote:

> The question remained debatable when I was captain of Bigside in 1841–2, when we settled it (as we believed) for all time. 'Running in' was made lawful with these limitations. (1) The ball must be caught on the rebound. (2) That the catcher was not 'off his side'. (3) That there should be no 'handing on', but the catcher must carry the ball on and 'touch down' himself.

Even more conclusive was another letter sent to the committee by a younger contemporary of Ellis at Rugby, T. Harris. He left school three years after Ellis, and so his school football was played in the years immediately following Ellis' feat, when its effect on the game, if it had had any, would have been most obvious. He wrote:

> I remember W. W. Ellis perfectly. He was an admirable cricketer, but was generally regarded as inclined to take unfair advantages at football. I should not quote him in any way as an authority. . . . [In my day] Picking up and running with the ball in hand was distinctly forbidden. If a player caught the ball on a rebound from the ground or from a stroke of the hand, he was allowed to take a few steps to give effect to a 'drop kick' but no more. . . . All laying hands upon and holding a player was strictly forbidden under any circumstances.

Running with the ball would have made nonsense of this last prohibition. The picture of the game suggested by Harris' notes conforms exactly with the description in *Tom Brown*.

This so completely shattered the Ellis legend that the committee, with a fine disregard for the rules of historical inquiry at any time, asked Harris 'to mitigate his strictures upon Ellis'. Such tampering with witnesses is hardly likely to promote truth; small wonder that the writing of the history of sport is so arduous a task. It is easy to see why Bloxham's anonymous informant remembered the incident. Ellis was a day boy, and day boys are generally not highly regarded at boarding schools; moreover, as Harris makes clear, there were good reasons for his being not much liked. Most schoolboys commit some breach of school tradition in games or elsewhere and it is quickly forgotten. When the unpopular day boy was guilty of a gaffe, it was gleefully remembered against him by one of his fellows all his life. When I was in my school soccer team, we used to play against a private lunatic asylum, as we called such institutions in the coarse language of the day. The asylum team was composed mainly of staff, with such patients as could suitably be admitted. One year these included an undergraduate who had suffered a mental breakdown, a circumstance much rarer then than now. He was a rugger man, but it was thought that his experience of handling a ball qualified him to keep goal. Unfortunately he was inadequately briefed in the differences between the two codes. The first time the ball came near him he seized it and set off at full pelt towards the opposite goal-line. The other players stopped dead in their tracks, and even the referee was so taken aback that the flying figure had passed the half-way line before the whistle sounded. This was more than fifty years ago, but many details of the scene are as clear in my memory as if it had happened yesterday, just as Ellis' impropriety remained in the memory of Bloxham's nameless friend. It had not the slightest effect on the laws of soccer. There is no reason whatever for supposing that Ellis' blunder had any greater effect on those of rugger. It would be kinder to Ellis if we remembered him for the one undoubted sporting achievement which stands to his credit, that in 1827 he played for Oxford in the first University Cricket Match.

Today both rugger and soccer have their problems, but they are entirely different. In soccer they arise mainly from financial abuses; even the harshest critic can point to very little in the game itself which calls for reform. With rugby the financial threat is only beginning to appear; the problems are in the game and its laws. Its most passionate *aficionado* can hardly pretend that a game in which every season a greater proportion of the points scored comes from penalty goals is in a healthy condition. Analysis suggests that the difference arises largely from the fact that the Association decided from the start that football was a game for the feet, while the Union has never resolved the conflicting claims of feet and hands.

In the primitive rugby of *Tom Brown's Schooldays* the object was to drive the ball forward through the opposing mass of players and then carry it on by a foot rush. If by accident the ball came out behind the scrum, the 'quarters' tried to kick an 'up and under' in the hope that the forwards, following up, would arrive at the same time as the ball and the scrum would be resumed. In the first Badminton book on football (1887), the hacking of the pre-1870 game is half-heartedly defended on the ground that it was the only way of breaking up a tight scrum. Apart from the banning of this hacking, this was still the state of the game when the Union was founded in 1870. The one important change was that, instead of unlimited numbers of players taking part in a match, teams were now restricted to twenty. The earliest Oxford and Cambridge games were played with teams of this size, but the number was reduced to fifteen in 1875. International matches, which like those in soccer were played from 1871 onwards, followed suit in 1871.

In the early days only goals counted; later, points were awarded for a try. In the 1890s a try was called a 'minor' as opposed to the 'major' goal. In Wales, however, if the scores were equal, victory was decided, at least unofficially, by the number of defensive touch-downs conceded by each side, and the name 'minor' was applied to these; the older spectators on Welsh grounds can still be heard using the word in that sense. There is a similar tendency in soccer today to consider the number of corners conceded by each side as significant.

Because the game has always relied so heavily on traditional practice handed on by each generation of players to newcomers, it is very difficult to trace the development which has transformed the game since 1870. Even today a reading of the laws gives a very imperfect picture of what actually happens on the field of play, and the further we go back in time, the truer this is. The change which revolutionized rugby and made it what it is now was the admission of passing the ball from hand to hand, so rigorously banned by Tom Hughes' laws at Rugby in 1841. Yet no historian of the game appears to have been able to give even an approximate date for this. When the Union was founded, there were clearly still great restrictions on handling; it was not until 1874 that picking up a rolling ball was legalized in Bigside laws at Rugby School.

The 1880s saw some developments in tactics. One device was adopted for getting the ball through the opponents' scrum. A small forward would manoeuvre himself into the position now occupied by the hooker, and get down on all fours with the ball between his feet. Then, thrust from behind by his colleagues, he would try to insinuate himself between the legs of the other team, hoicking the ball along behind him, in the hope of emerging on the far side and leading a rush. (My authority for this is my father, who performed this unenviable function in those years.)

From the same period there is evidence of new tactics. In the season 1880–1, St Edward's School, Oxford, having been defeated by Magdalen College School by a goal and two touch-downs, appealed to the Rugby Union against the result on the grounds that 'heeling the ball out of the scrummage' was illegal. The Secretary replied that 'he was sorry to say that it was allowed'. (The Establishment was clearly not enthusiastic about innovation.) This deliberate giving of the ball to the backs suggests that the latter were now playing a more important part in the game. Yet in that same year a new conception of forward play was being worked out by H. Vassall, captain of Oxford University RFC and an England international. When he was at Marlborough, the school authorities as the result of an accident had imposed a rule forbidding forwards to handle the ball. Vassall, taking a tip from soccer, coached his forwards to control the ball and hold it closely in foot rushes, and even to kick long passes to one another across the field. This inaugurated a technique of forward play which is now lost; many still living can remember the fearsome sight of a disciplined forward rush accompanied by cries of 'Feet! Feet!' which could be halted only by dropping on the ball. Forwards found this much more enjoyable than spending most of the match packed in a never-ending scrummage, especially when they developed the further trick of wheeling the scrum and coming away in a rush with the ball. Here we can see the beginnings of a tension between forwards and backs which has persisted until very recent times. The experience of Magdalen College School showed that victory could be achieved by giving the ball out to the backs, but the pack could have much better fun by keeping it to themselves. Moreover they could always point to those many occasions, especially on wet days, when the backs, given the ball, failed to advance as far as the line of the scrum before the attack broke down. The backs, anxious to share the enjoyment, used to enjoin on the forwards the principle, 'Take the ball on until you are stopped and then heel it', hoping to secure what is called in modern jargon 'second phase possession'. But in the exhilaration of a rush the pack were rarely willing to admit that they had been stopped. Even today in those happy circles of C, D, and 'Extra D' fifteens, where enjoyment is the aim and the result is not regarded as over-important, forwards still tend to look on backs as second-class citizens.

After these refinements in forward play had been developed, a similar improvement in the tactics of back play was effected by such remarkable men as Conway Rees, Gwyn Nichol and Ronnie Poulton. Sport has few sights to offer more thrilling than rugby backs, supplied with plenty of the ball by their forwards, moving at speed in the fashion fathered by these players. But two further developments since the Second World War are making the spectacle rarer and rarer. One, inspired mainly by French example, has been the increase of handling by the forwards. One can hardly call it passing, for they tend rather to snatch the ball out of one another's arms, but the result is that the ball reaches the backs less and less often. Another is the technique of 'ten-man Rugby', a gift from South Africa. Aggressive defence has become so tight that it is found unprofitable to let the ball out to the three-quarters; as soon as it emerges from the scrum, one of the halves or a back-row forward kicks ahead in the hope of a lucky bounce. A wing today can play match after match without receiving a single useful pass. At times we seem to be back in the days of *Tom Brown's Schooldays*.

These tactical changes have been partly conditioned by developments in the social organization of the game. In the early days of the Union its constituent clubs, like those of the Association, were drawn from all classes of society, and in the 1880s the Union, like the Association, had to face the question of payment for broken time to players who otherwise would be unable to take part in the game at top level. The result is an outstanding example of how much human affairs are directed by accident and by the idiosyncrasies of character of a few individuals. The governing bodies of Union and Association were drawn from exactly the same background – the public schools and universities – and might have been expected, when faced with the same problem, to arrive at similar solutions. In fact they took exactly opposite lines. The Association, taking its cue from cricket, permitted payment to those who needed it, and amateur and professional mingled in the game for many years. The Union recoiled in horror from any such solution, and in 1895 completely proscribed any form of payment.

A large group of working-class clubs in the industrial North broke away, founded their own Northern Union, and developed a modified form of the game, now generally called Rugby League Football. The hard-headed northerners who shaped the game, faced with the necessity of raising money to pay the players, had to make it attractive to spectators, and they were well aware that what spectators appreciate most is passing movements by the backs. They also wanted it to be clearly regulated by rules and therefore easier for the referee to control. The older men among them knew how much rugby had been improved by reducing the team from twenty to fifteen; they took the logical step of cutting it down further to thirteen. This makes it easier for the referee to see what is happening in the mêlée, and the ball comes more quickly out of the smaller set scrum. The line-out had already become a mess, so they replaced it, and reduced kicking to touch by imposing salutary restrictions on it. Realizing the inherent possibilities of foul play in a loose maul and the insoluble problems which it presents to a referee, they substituted a simple method of bringing the ball back into play after a tackle.

The Rugby Union has always suffered from the weakness that in framing its policy it has paid less attention to reaching the best solution of a difficulty than to the negative aim of not doing the same as its rivals. When the question of payment arose, the rivals were the Association; they accepted payment, so the Union rejected it. Since 1895, in any discussion about improved laws, the first consideration has been that the Union must on no account follow the example of the Rugby League. This was made clear in 1895, when the Union decreed that it was an act of professionalism 'to play on any ground where gate money is taken in any match or contest where it is previously agreed that less than fifteen players on each side shall take part'. This had amusing repercussions many years later, when the organizers of the first seven-a-side tournament found that they were inviting players to become professionals, and they had to hasten to seek a special dispensation. For years many a rugger match was ruined for players and spectators alike by a dreary plague of kicking to touch, but not until 1965 could the Union bring itself to follow the League practice and restrict it. Not even the most diehard veteran now denies that this has brought a great improvement. But the automatic

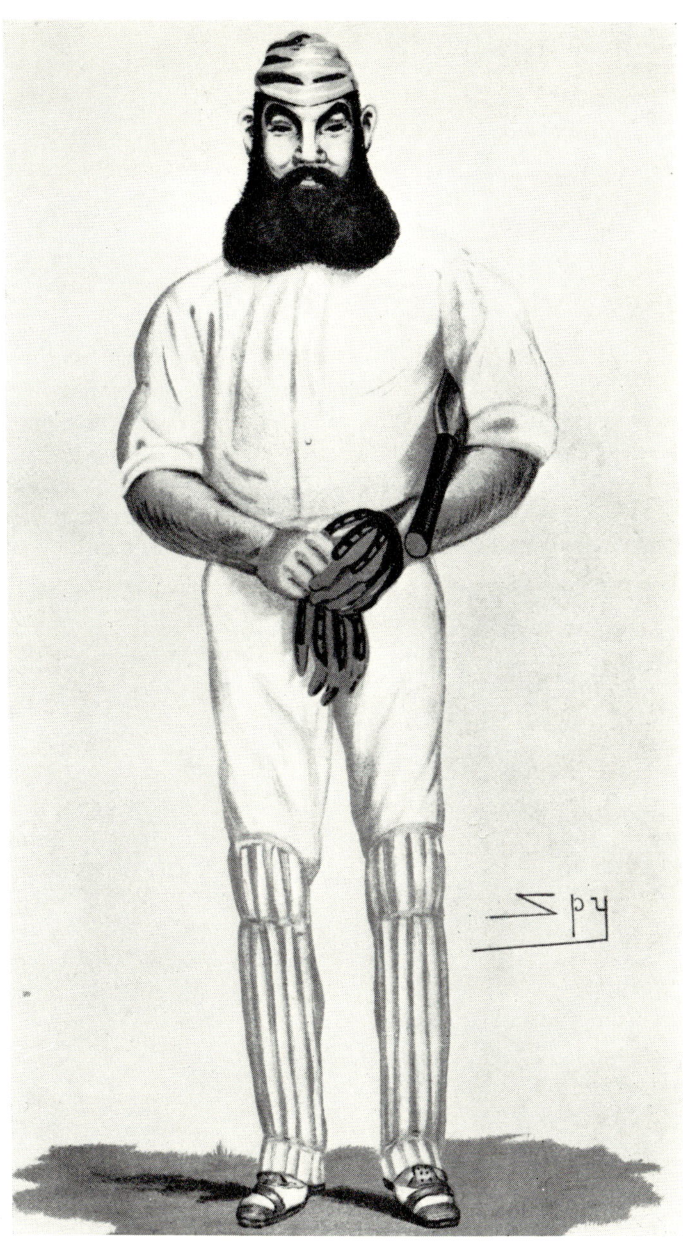

Dr W. G. Grace as drawn in a 'Spy' cartoon from *Vanity Fair* 9 June 1877.

(Above) Golf near Edinburgh Castle, 1745, from a water-colour by Paul Sandby. *(British Museum)*
A family playing at croquet in 1865. *(Curtis Museum, Alton)*

rejection of anything connected with the League has prevented many other desirable reforms in Rugby.

As was inevitable in any game which had been played for generations without a referee, the earliest compilers of written laws for football of both codes assumed that players were trying to observe the traditional laws. It was not until 1891 that both soccer and rugger punished deliberate breaches of the laws with penalty kicks which could result in the scoring of a goal. In both games there was resistance to the innovation from amateurs who loathed the implied reflection on the sportsmanship of players. The University Rugby Match was almost half a century old when, in 1919, the first penalty goal in its history was recorded. The young of today must find it incredible that in the 1920s, in the arguments between rugger and soccer men on the merits of their games, one of the points always hurled by rugger devotees against soccer was 'those dreadful penalty goals in your game'. And indeed in those days the number of offences in rugby for which the referee had no option under the laws but to award a kick was still small.

A referee at that time soon discovered that his first requirement was one blind eye, and that he need not always see perfectly clearly with the other. But in the efforts to clarify the rules, penalty kicks were imposed for more and more offences. In the 1950s a handful of prima-donna referees emerged who seemed to think that the game was played for their benefit, and that their excellence could be proved by the number of penalties they awarded. Nowadays much of a match consists of twenty-nine players standing shivering in the wind while a kicker makes his mud pies and then withdraws in spirit from those present in order to commune with Unseen Powers. This at least could easily be eliminated by adopting the oft-advocated suggestion that every penalty should be taken without delay by a drop-kick. Not the least unsatisfactory feature of these penalties is that they often depend on a completely idiosyncratic interpretation of the laws by a referee, and players, spectators and television commentators alike are left in bewilderment at the decisions. Many an old rugger player today when reading the sports pages disregards the score and looks to see if either side scored a try. Nor is it only the number of penalty goals that is disturbing. About twenty years ago the Rugby Union gave its blessing to a coaching film for use in schools. In it were exhibited sundry devices for luring opponents into committing offences which would win a penalty kick in a good position. Next to the soccer ploy of the melodramatic sprawl in the penalty area to deceive the referee, this is surely the most mean-minded trick in football; it is utterly contrary to the true spirit of the game.

Soccer shows how much a game gains by simplification. The proliferation of penalties in rugger arises from the ever-increasing complexity of the laws, and the growing ambition of players to break them undetected. The line-out affords a good example of this. It belongs to the earliest era of the game, for it figures in Tom Brown's match. But it gradually grew into such a hotbed of illegality, with each offence marked for penalizing by the rules, that in one notorious international match, of the first forty-three line-outs only three were not immediately greeted by the referee's whistle. Law after law has been tried to reduce the chaos to order. The most recent of these is typical. The rule now decrees that the two lines of forwards shall be two feet apart, and the players in each line shall be one yard from each other. To see whether forwards are fulfilling the first requirement, the referee must stand in line with the throw; for the second, he must place himself at right angles to it. Faced with this demand, a referee may well sympathize with Sam Weller:

> 'Have you a pair of eyes, Mr Weller?'
>
> 'Yes, I have a pair of eyes,' replied Sam, 'and that's just it. If they wos a pair o' patent double million magnifyin' gas microscopes of hextra power, p'raps I might be able to see through a flight o' stairs and a deal door; but bein' only eyes you see, my wision's limited.'

The irony of the situation is that the quick throw-in, still permitted by referees, makes nonsense of any requirements for a line-out. And long ago Lord Wakefield suggested a simple remedy for the whole difficulty, that the law should permit the ball to be thrown in any direction except forward towards the opponents' line.

The set scrum, another fruitful source of trouble and penalties, is less easily dealt with. Unlike the line-out, it played no part in the early history of the game, and it appeared for the first time in the laws in 1879–80: 'The ball shall be put down in a scrummage at the place where any breach of the law not otherwise dealt with has occurred, upon a claim being made to that effect by the opposite side.' The phrase 'put down' is significant. It suggests that the referee placed the ball on the ground and the players formed the scrum round it. This is supported by the old definition in the laws, 'A scrummage is formed by two or more players closing round the ball.' It is doubtful whether entrusting the task to the half-backs was a change for the better. It led to a crop of new offences in the scrum, and to the absurd specialization of forwards as loose-head props or blind-side back row men. Veterans who can remember the time when the Scots rejected all such notions, even a specialized hooker, and followed the principle of 'first up, first down', will wonder whether Scotland's forwards today are as formidable as those were. A return to the ball placed on the ground might be worth trying. As for rucks and mauls, which all too often produce unpleasant scenes of dirty play, sooner or later the Union will have to pocket its pride again and resort to a solution on the same lines of simplification as the Rugby League's.

In and near most towns today there are clubs for both codes of football. More thinly populated areas tend to follow one or the other. When the first clubs were being founded a century ago, the code adopted was a matter of chance, depending on the man who inspired a club's formation. But the problem of obtaining fixtures must gradually have put pressure on clubs to conform to the majority in the district. Soccer is now found everywhere in Britain. Rugger is still perhaps the majority game in Devon and Cornwall, in South Wales and in the Scots Border country. Elsewhere the effects of the expulsion of working-class clubs by the Union in 1895 are still apparent. It is interesting that in the northern counties, where the enthusiasm for professional soccer is unbounded, there is a growing tendency for Rugby League football to be played by amateur clubs, schools and universities.

The decision of the Union to expel working-class clubs had one particularly regrettable result; to use the jargon of our politicians, it made the game socially divisive. The idea that rugger is the more 'gentlemanly' game still persists in England, with the image of the rugger player as a white-collar man, just as the notion of soccer as the cloth cap game is not affected by the fact that it is played at Charterhouse, Malvern, Repton, Shrewsbury, Westminster, Winchester and many other public schools. Most deplorable of all was the tendency of headmasters of grammar schools, especially in the inter-war period, to encourage a change from soccer to rugger, in the hope of thereby improving their school's standing. There was a case for the authorities of boarding schools with compulsory games preferring the code which catered for thirty players to the one which allowed only twenty-two on a field of the same size; there was financial advantage in keeping down the number of pitches. This applied far less to grammar schools where games were optional and numbers consequently smaller. The greatest harm was done when a grammar school in a soccer-playing area changed to rugby. The scholarship boy in such a school was set apart from his brothers in a particularly sensitive sphere, sport, which should unite, not divide. One of the few arguments in favour of the vast comprehensive school is that its numbers allow it, at least in theory, to provide for a wide range of sports activities, including both codes of football.

One of the outstanding features of international rugby is the remarkable record of Wales, especially as the game is widely played only in the South – North Wales has always been predominantly a soccer area. There is an oral tradition about how the game came to Wales which deserves to be put on record. Llandovery College, a public school in Carmarthenshire, was founded in 1848, and in its early days a young master from Rugby encouraged the boys to take up the game. A number of them went on to St David's College, Lampeter, and took the game with them. The first rugger match ever played in Wales was between the two Colleges, in 1856. St David's College had been founded twenty years earlier than Llandovery with the primary aim of training clergy for the Anglican church in South Wales. These young men, like their counterparts in England, when they went out as curates into their parishes, induced boys and youths to form football clubs, and started that passionate enthusiasm for the game which is so strongly marked today.

When I joined the staff of St David's College in 1926, I was told this by William Davies, who had been the College Manciple for over forty years; he might well, therefore, in his younger days have talked with old members of the College who had played in that first match. In 1927, the year in which the College celebrated the centenary of its foundation, a professor died who had been appointed in the time of the first Principal; it would be difficult to imagine conditions more favourable for the preservation of oral tradition. The late Archdeacon R. J. Tree, who as a former Warden of Llandovery, a former Lampeter Professor and an old rugger player himself had a natural interest in the subject, searched for many years in journals and letters of the period for confirmation of the tradition, but at the time of his all too early death he had not succeeded in finding conclusive proof. But there is nothing improbable in the story. It fits the known facts and explains the present situation. Until further evidence is revealed, it deserves to be accepted.

It is a curious fact that the great devotion of Wales to Rugby football owes much to the unhappy sectarian bitterness which permeated Welsh life in the nineteenth century. The many nonconformist bodies differed from one another on theological grounds, but they were all heirs to the puritan tradition which distrusted enjoyment of all kinds, including games. Moreover, in all of them, total abstention was a fundamental article of faith. Teetotallers are by no means unknown among footballers, but no one could pretend that the creed is widely held in rugger clubs; many of them, indeed, maintain themselves very satisfactorily on their bar profits. Many a furious sermon was preached in the chapels, denouncing the game and its concomitant conviviality as a social evil and a threat to hopes of salvation. Young men being what they are, this acted as a great spur to church members and inspired in them a devoted loyalty to their game.

The young parsons were not content with merely encouraging others to play. Some of them achieved the highest honours in the game themselves. In Wales, two names are outstanding. J. Strand Jones, who played in five internationals in 1902–3, was the first of the modern attacking full-backs. W. T. Havard, capped in 1919, became Bishop of St Asaph and later of St Davids. In England the tally of clerical internationals is even more impressive, twenty-two in all, of whom two were capped after their ordination. It is noticeable that the supply dried up about thirty years ago. Whether this was due to a change in the character of ordinands or a change in the character of rugger only a sociologist could determine. He might then go on to investigate another strange phenomenon. Economic pressure has driven a steady stream of Welsh players north to join the professionals of the Rugby League, yet every attempt to establish the northern code in Wales itself has failed.

From its inception the Rugby Union set its face firmly against any form of competition; the game had to be played purely for its own sake. Whether this was merely another instinctive reaction against the Rugby League and the FA Cup, or whether the governing body was endowed with a remarkable prescience, it is impossible to say. Montague Sherman in his Badminton Library volume of 1887 set out the thinking of his time on the subject. 'The Rugby Union game, with its collaring and throwing to the ground, its scrimmaging and its collisions, is naturally so rough that not the least occasion should be given for allowing warm partisanship to lead to ill-temper, and ill-temper to brutality.'

The events of our day are showing how right he was. The decision of the Union had one delightful result. The rugger players of Oxford and Cambridge wanted to have an inter-collegiate cup competition to match those in every other sport. The Union reached a splendid compromise; there might be a cup competition, but there must be no cup. So every year, the winners of the competition, following the example of those in other games, used to present themselves at the college of the previous year's winners and demand the cup – there have never been any presentation ceremonies – only to find that that particular Snark was a Boojum. As recently as 1965 the Union was still holding out against competitions in the game proper but they have since capitulated, with results which are becoming only too apparent. A thousand years from now, sports historians will be solemnly debating the exact meaning of the term 'Knock-out' applied to the competition.

Before it yielded to the demand for a competition for regular sides, the Union had permitted seven-a-side tournaments, and these are proving more attractive to spectators than the traditional game. For financial reasons, to attract spectators has become the chief aim of the governing body of every sport. The world of sport is changing so rapidly that prediction is rash, but it is quite possible that in a few years' time there will be no cricket except one-day matches and timeless Tests, and no rugby except seven-a-side club competitions and fifteen-a-side international matches.

8
Athletics

The skills of running, jumping and throwing are fundamental to all human sport. Together with wrestling and boxing they were the events of the Funeral Games for Patroclus, the description of which in Homer's *Iliad* begins the literature of sport in Western civilization, and which inspired the programme of the ancient Olympic Games and of all Greek athletic meetings. No sporting events are easier to organize. The rules are few and obvious; competitors and spectators alike can see who are the leaders at different stages of the contests and who are the final winners. Such competitions have been practised in almost all human societies.

In Britain the earliest mention of athletic ability is found in the Venerable Bede, who records of the seventh-century saint, Cuthbert, that he excelled in jumping, running and wrestling (*sive saltu, sive cursu, sive luctatu*). Throughout the Middle Ages there are frequent but not very informative references to these activities, and it is clear that they were widely practised; this in turn implies contests, for competition is by definition the basis of athletics. Renaissance writers on the whole approve of these fundamental exercises. Roger Ascham, it is true, objects that 'Running, leaping and quoiting be too vile for scholars', but he is writing a book on archery and so is not altogether unbiased. Sir William Forest, who wrote in the reign of Henry VIII about the training of a prince, took a different view:

> To ride, run, leap or cast by violence
> Stone, bar or plummet or such other thing
> It not refuseth any prince or king.

James I thought the same about the education of his son Henry, Prince of Wales:

> The exercises that I would have you to use, although but moderately, not making a craft of them, are running, leaping, wrestling, fencing, dancing and playing at the caitch, or tennise, archerie, palle-malle and such-like other fair and pleasant field-games.

It was James I who authorized the first athletic meetings in this country of which we know. These were called by writers of the time 'Mr Robert Dover's Olimpick Games upon the Cotswold Hills'. They originated as Dover's protest against the puritanism of his day, and continued for forty years until three years after his death in 1641. The sports included wrestling, cudgel-playing, leaping, pitching the bar, throwing the sledge and tossing the pike. There was a brief revival of the 'Olimpicks' at the Restoration, and although it petered out, there is abundant evidence that the activities continued at local festivals all over the country. A delightful picture of the sports at such a 'Veast' is given in the early pages of *Tom Brown's Schooldays*.

An entry in Pepys' Diary gives us our first glimpse of an aspect of running which we have already encountered in other sports:

> [30 July 1663] The town talk this day is of nothing but the great foot-race run this day on Banstead Downs between Lee, the Duke of Richmond's footman, and a tiler, a famous runner. And Lee hath beat him; though the King and Duke of York and all men almost did bet three or four to one upon the tiler's head.

These running footmen were employed as messengers by the wealthy, who were as ready to back them in races of this kind as they were to back their horses. Such matches between two competitors became very popular at the end of the eighteenth century. Like the cricket matches at that time, they were often held in fields attached to inns; they were widely advertised and attracted large crowds, to the great profit of the innkeepers. The attraction must have been the betting, since as spectacles the contests were often dull; in the long-distance races one of the runners, finding himself outclassed, frequently dropped out, leaving the winner to finish alone.

When the running footmen raced, they were, like the Thames watermen in their contests, examples of 'job professionals'. 'Gentlemen amateurs' sometimes matched themselves against these professionals or against one another for appropriate stakes. The practice was especially common among army officers, and this lends some support to a tradition that athletic sports were being held at Sandhurst as early as 1812. School sports are attested at Eton in 1837, and by mid-century there was widespread but uncoordinated activity in athletics all over the country. As in many other games, the first steps in bringing some order to the scene were taken at Oxford and Cambridge, but whereas in football the impetus at the universities came from the schools, in athletics the first inspiration was from a very different source. There is much justification for assigning credit for initiating the movement to Exeter College, Oxford. In his 1887 Badminton volume, *Athletics and Football,* Montague Shearman relates the story on the authority of a man who had taken part in the events.

Although cricket and rowing were firmly established as fashionable sports for undergraduates by the middle of the century, the earlier tradition of sport based on the horse, such as hunting, was still strong, and each college held its annual point-to-point meeting or 'Grind'. On the evening of the Exeter Grind of 1850, some of those who had taken part were discussing the day's proceedings, and they agreed that owing to the poor quality of the hired hacks available the affair had been dull. One of them suggested that they could do better on their own legs. The others took up the idea, and a steeplechase was arranged and duly held in the fields near Binsey.

It was organized exactly as if the runners had been horses. The course was of two miles with twenty-four jumps. There were twenty-four competitors at an entry fee of £1 with a 10s. forfeit. A book was opened and odds quoted on eight runners, varying from 2–1 to 15–1; the eventual winner was at 8–1, while one of the two joint favourites at 2–1 finished second. The event was such a success that a few weeks later another meeting for shorter races was promoted by Exeter and held on Port Meadow on the other side of the Thames. Shearman reproduces in his book the printed programme of this gathering, the 'Exeter Autumn Meeting', which also treats the competitors as horses. It includes 'The Welcome Sweepstakes of a quarter of a mile' which attracted fourteen runners, 'The Bancalari Sweepstakes of 300 yards and a distance' with 10 entrants, 'The Jonathan Sweepstakes of 100 yards', 'A hurdle Race over 10 flights at 10 yards apart, 140 yards', 'Consolation Stakes for beaten horses' and a mile race. It is noteworthy that the division familiar from the Turf into flat, hurdles and steeplechasing is faithfully reproduced in these events.

Nine years before these Exeter sports, another event happened of a very different kind, destined to have almost as much influence on modern athletics. In 1848 a German classical scholar, J. H. Krause, published *Die Gymnastik and Agonistik der Hellenen*, the first examination in our time of the evidence for the athletics of ancient Greece. This book and his other works on allied subjects aroused much interest at Oxford and Cambridge, where the curriculum was still largely classical, and possibly did something to encourage the enthusiasm of the undergraduates for athletics. One firm piece of evidence for this is the fact that the Greek terms 'athlete' and 'athletics', unknown as English words to Dr Johnson when he compiled his dictionary, came into general use at this time and ousted the Latin 'pedestrian' and 'pedestrianism'. (The latter survived as terms for professional athletics. Until 1939 *The Times* used once a year to report the results of a professional meeting – the Powderhall in Edinburgh – always under the heading 'Pedestrianism'.) From now on, the horsy tradition embodied in the Exeter meetings began to be modified by the athletic practices of antiquity.

At Oxford the Exeter sports became an annual event, and other colleges quickly followed suit. The fashion spread to Cambridge, where St John's and Emmanuel held meetings in 1856. The universities were already competing against one another in four sports, cricket, rowing, rackets and Royal Tennis, and in 1864 athletics was added as a fifth. At Oxford in that year University Sports were held on 1 and 2 March to assist in selecting representatives to compete against Cambridge on 5 March, and a copy of the programme of the Oxford meeting has survived. The events included 100 yards, 440 yards, 1 mile, 120 yards hurdles (ten flights), high jump, long jump, putting the stone and throwing the cricket ball. There was also a 300 yards race for graduates, 'entries to be made on the ground'; as there were no post-graduate students in the modern sense of the term at that time, this event must have been aimed at the dons. The programme for the match against Cambridge was shorter: it included only running, hurdles, a steeplechase and the two jumps, with no throwing. The contest ended in a tie, each university winning four events.

The programme of the Oxford Sports shows that competitors chose their own colours – another pleasant link with horse-racing. Further light is thrown on the athletic costume of early days in a diary kept by two Victorian ladies, Emily and Ellen Hall. They attended a meeting between Sandhurst and Woolwich in October 1868: 'The Sandhurst men all wore – believe it! – silk stockings with white jackets and knickerbockers; the Woolwich men all ran in bare legs, which looked very bare indeed, and grey suits on their covered parts.'

While giving due credit to the Exeter undergraduates as prime movers in the development of modern athletics, we must remember that they did not start from a vacuum; there were centuries of contests in running and throwing behind them. Even in imitating the equestrian steeplechase they were not complete innovators. Shearman reports that in 1836 six medical students from Birmingham had held a similar race. We do not know the names of these pioneers; thinking that such a prank might be regarded as unseemly in aspirants to their chosen profession, they all ran under pseudonyms. But the Birmingham race had no immediate imitators. In another early effort, the Royal Military Academy, Woolwich, had held Sports in 1849 which continued annually until 1853 but were then abandoned. From the Exeter Sports of 1850 there is an unbroken line to our own day. The college has a more recent claim to distinction in the athletic world. Dr Roger Bannister, the first man to beat four minutes in the mile, is an Exeter man.

The events which made up these early meetings were already pointing towards the modern schedules in the Olympic Games and other international contests. Changes and modifications have taken place, and additions have been made, but already the three sources of inspiration are clear. The races, jumps and throws come from centuries of British tradition; hurdling and steeplechases were borrowed from horse racing. One detail is probably due to the example of antiquity, the strange absence of the half-mile from Oxford and Cambridge running. The ancient Olympic programme had no race at any distance between 400 yards (the *diaulos*) and the *dolichos*, the long-distance race of nearly three miles. The gap in the University Sports was not made good until shortly before the First World War, when the half-mile was at last included.

As with football, athletic activity at the universities quickly spread to London, where Mincing Lane AC was founded in 1863; it soon changed its name to London AC, which it still bears. Three years later the Amateur Athletic Club (AAC) was founded and gave a great impetus by acquiring a track at Lillie Bridge and starting championships. Keenness extended to the provinces; clubs were formed and meetings promoted all over the country.

Soon athletics was confronted with the same problem as all other sports at the time – the definition of 'amateur'. Football was fortunate here in having no tradition of professionalism or of matches played for high stakes. As we have seen, payment of players in this game was approached from a different angle. But in athletics, as in cricket, boxing and rowing, the whole early history of the sport had consisted of matches for stakes, and the distinction between professional and amateur had been purely one of social class. The difficulties of eliminating betting and its consequent corruption from the sport were enormous. The AAC wished to follow the example of the Henley Stewards and ban artisans and the working class generally from the ranks of amateurs. Other clubs, especially those in the Midlands and North, took a more liberal view. Hoping to end the controversy, the officials of Oxford University AC, of whom Montague Shearman was one, invited representatives of clubs to a meeting at Oxford in 1880, and there on 24 April the Amateur Athletic Association (AAA) was founded. It adopted a definition of amateur which excluded only those who had competed for money prizes; it also took over from the AAC the running of the championships.

Compared with cricket and football, athletics faces two great problems. In a society which depends fundamentally on corporate effort, team games have an obvious claim to superiority, and athletics, essentially a matter of individual excellence, can only with difficulty be turned into a team enterprise. Cricket and football allow players of considerably different standards of ability to play together, and the multiplicity of clubs enables the mediocre performer to find one to suit his level. This is difficult to achieve in athletics. The first problem found a solution in the universities, where inter-collegiate cup competitions and the Oxford and Cambridge Match made individual success a contribution to team victory. Elsewhere the problem was less easy to solve.

The difficulty of providing for the ordinary performer was even greater. For many years the AAA imitated the example of horse-racing and adopted a technique of handicapping. They did not follow the equestrian precedent quite as closely as the Exeter undergraduates in 1850. In that meeting, H. Wyatt, who had won one or two of the shorter races, was treated in the mile like a successful horse. Lacking saddle-flaps for the lead weights, he 'had to carry some pounds of shot in an old-fashioned shot-belt round his loins'. The AAA adopted the device of basing handicaps on recent performances, and necessarily this was nation-wide. A runner entering at a meeting filled up a standard form with particulars of his latest races. A novice entering for the first time was not generously treated by the handicappers, who were disinclined to take risks and assigned him a start which gave him little or no chance of winning. He would then embark on a process known as 'running for his mark', appearing at several meetings with no intention of exerting himself. Each failure added a few yards to his start. When he judged that he had attained a point where victory was possible, he began to train, and at a few meetings might carry off a clock or case of fish-knives – money prizes were of course taboo – until his successes had brought his mark back to an unprofitable level; he would then start the cycle again. This rather squalid procedure survived until the Second World War.

The liberal attitude of the AAA to the definition of amateur did not immediately meet with the reward it deserved. There was still too much undesirable money in the sport. From 1870 onwards, meetings were surprisingly popular, and promotion was a profitable enterprise. At the University Sports of 1876 at Lillie Bridge, when M. J. Brooks astonished the world with his high jump of 6 feet 2½ inches, the gate money reached £1100, a very considerable sum in those days. The prizes at ordinary meetings, though limited in value to ten guineas, could readily be converted into cash. All the efforts of the AAA to eliminate betting from the sport were proving unavailing, and corruption was widespread. Competitors of the baser sort, unable to win cash prizes, were ready enough to take a bribe from a bookmaker to lose a race; at times it seemed that only cross-country running was keeping alive the sporting spirit of athletics over the country as a whole. It is small wonder that university athletes took less and less part in the sport outside; there was enough domestic competition for them in their undergraduate days, especially after matches against American universities started at the end of the century.

The sport received a considerable impetus from the foundation of the modern Olympics in 1896. The instigator of the Games, Baron Pierre de Coubertin, was an idealist, with a romantic conception of what true sport might do for the modern world. He may have been too optimistic in the rosy view he took of the sportsmanship of the ancient Olympics, but there is no doubt that the Olympic Games which he inspired, until they turned sour, exerted an admirable influence on the whole of sport. The modern series had an uneasy start, but the London Olympiad of 1908 set it on a steady course, and naturally stimulated enthusiasm for athletics in this country. If nothing else, the Olympics gave support to the notion held from the beginning at the universities, that a medal was an adequate reward for athletic victory. Now university runners once again entered the main stream of national athletics.

The First World War interrupted but did not end this movement. After the war, Oxford and Cambridge produced a remarkable generation of athletes. In the three Olympiads from 1920 to 1928, H. M. Abrahams, Lord Burghley, G. M. Butler, D. G. A. Lowe, P. J. Noel-Baker, M. C. Nokes, A. E. Porritt, G. R. Renwick, B. G. D. Rudd and H. B. Stallard won medals, and T. C. Livingstone-Learmonth, C. E. W. Mackintosh, E. A. Montague, E. D. Mountain and G. C. Weightman-Smith reached the finals, a list which shows how the universities dominated British athletics at the time. Not only were these men outstanding performers, but they were also fired with enthusiasm for athletics and a deep desire to see it play a proper rôle in the world of sport.

To this end they founded the Achilles Club, in the hope that it would do for athletics what the Corinthians had done and were still doing for soccer. They aimed first to encourage athletics in the schools. London AC had long organized an annual meeting for public school boys; to this Achilles added a relay meeting for past and present members of schools, a happy event now unfortunately long since defunct. They took teams to compete against schools, with the seniors appropriately handicapped. They supported all attempts to organize team matches among the leading clubs. As a result of these efforts, athletics made great headway in schools of all kinds. Up to 1914, most schools had been content with an annual Sports Day. After the war, inter-school competitions were started, and county associations organized championship meetings for the schools in their area. There was still a gap in the field. A young man or woman of ordinary ability who did not go to a university found few opportunities to enjoy the sport after leaving school. In recent years this gap has been filled by the National Athletics League, one of the most encouraging developments in British sport today. It is still not out of the experimental stage. One of its best features, the inclusion of A and B level races in the same match, allows the mediocre preformer to make his contribution to the success of his team; much will depend on the willingness of clubs to play the game in their team selection, and it is to be hoped that this will always be forthcoming. In the meantime, Achilles, like Corinth, has suffered a decline, but we should never forget the debt which our athletics owes to the Club.

As swimming has produced one game based on it, water polo, so running gave rise to a team game, prisoners' base or bars. It was known to Shakespeare, who in *Cymbeline* describes the king's sons as

> Lads more like to run
> The country base than to commit such slaughter.

In Kent it survived as a game for adults into this century, under the name of goal-running (a term which has escaped the notice of the *Oxford Dictionary*, even in its latest supplement). I saw a goal-running match between two villages on Romney Marsh on the evening of the August day in 1914 on which war was declared. Unhappily it appears to be obsolete.

When a sport becomes international, one of the disadvantages is that reform and improvement become more difficult. The greater the number of interested parties to be consulted, the more likely it is that some opponent of a desirable change will emerge. Unwelcome practices become ingrained and harder and harder to eradicate. In athletics, few will cavil at the programme of races now accepted everywhere. Distances obviously have to be standardized, and not many will regret the virtual disappearance of races at 300 yards, 600 yards, 1000 yards and so on, though we have always to face the possibility that they will be revived by someone desperate for a record to break. The schedule of field events, on the other hand, is much more open to objection. These events have never achieved the popularity of races. The Greeks thought so little of them that throughout the thousand years of the ancient Olympics it was not possible to win a crown for victory in any of them singly. The three they practised – discus, javelin and long jump – were lumped with a race and wrestling in a pentathlon, with a single crown for victory. It was perhaps the same lack of interest which led to the programme of field events being inadequately scrutinized and improved in the early days of modern athletics, with the result that our present schedule, especially of throwing events, is completely unsatisfactory.

It is axiomatic that the pursuit of athletics should conduce to the utmost physical excellence, to beauty of movement and to the perfectly proportioned body, and it very often does. In the realm of art the human body had never been more superbly portrayed than in Greek sculpture, and the sculptors of that time had the daily experience of watching naked athletes on their training grounds, noting the ripple of muscles under sun-tanned skin and the rhythm of coordinated movement. Today little aesthetic satisfaction can be derived from watching our throwing events.

In the Oxford University Sports of 1864 there were two such events, 'putting the stone' and 'throwing the cricket ball'. It is much to be regretted that the latter skill never became part of the regular programme. (In deference to American susceptibilities it would have had to be called 'throwing the handball'.) The action required is the natural throw, which plays little or no part in our athletic throwing. No human action surpasses it in sheer beauty, as anyone can testify who has ever seen an Australian cricket team in the field. It is basic to two of the world's greatest games, cricket and baseball. And it is the least dangerous of all the throwing contests. To be hit by a thrown cricket ball is painful, but rarely fatal; and it would be easy to design a rubber ball for competition which would reduce the danger still further. Much would be gained if the event were promoted from school Sports Days to the adult programme.

The first match between Oxford and Cambridge had no throws. When they were introduced, the chosen two were the traditional British skills of putting the weight and throwing

Peter Oosterhuis, a modern British golf professional, seen in fine action. *(Peter Dazeley)*

(Above) Cambridge University versus New Zealand's 'All Blacks', 1972. The line-out, featured here, has been devalued by the modern style of play and often collapses into a disorganized shambles, thus disrupting the flow of the game. *(Press Association)* Soccer, the modern game: tense-faced defenders pack the goal-mouth in this 1975 FA Cup Semi-Final. There are fewer goals but huge crowds, and advertisements around the ground inject money into the massive soccer industry. *(Press Association)*

the hammer. Putting the stone is first recorded as a sport at the beginning of the fourteenth century and regularly from then onwards. A sentence in Urquhart's translation of Rabelais (1653), 'He did cast the dart, throw the bar, put the stone', shows that the distinctive action of the event – not a true throw – was used from the beginning. When the event was standardized in modern times, a 16-pound cannon ball was found to be a suitable missile, and the event is often called the shot, but there is no evidence that the action was ever used by artillery-men to 'pass the ammunition'.

As a sport it violates two fundamental principles. An athletic event should be open to everyone. The weight, like other throws, is in practice only for large men and women. And assuredly it does not conduce to producing beautiful human bodies, as a glance at the unattractive frames of its top practitioners will show, frames rendered still more bloated by the use of anabolic steroids. This is even more true of women. If a fairy godmother leaned over the cradle of a baby girl and promised her an Olympic gold medal for weight-putting, the child's mother, remembering the outlines of some victors from behind the Iron Curtain, might well swoon in horror. Two ways suggest themselves for dealing with this difficulty. One would be to divide the competitors into classes by weight, as in boxing and weight-lifting; but spectators would groan at the prospect of still more time being devoted to field events. The other would be to allot to each thrower a missile of a given fraction of his own weight. No doubt the biometrists could arrive at the percentage most likely to produce a well-proportioned body. There is a much simpler solution. Fifty years ago the Olympic Committee were ill-advised enough to admit a contest in throwing the 56-pound weight; they realized their mistake and abandoned it almost at once. They might well take the same course with the shot.

Throwing the hammer is also of respectable antiquity, recorded as early as 1622. The 'sledge' was only one of several odd objects which were thrown in competition, including bars, plummets and axle-trees; the Highland sport of tossing the caber perpetuates another of these. It was not until 1887 that the hammer proper with its wooden handle was superseded by the American version of ball and wire now universal. The event is open to the same criticisms as the shot, with two additions. It is much more dangerous, and it requires a much larger area for practice. Because of the danger, this area cannot be used for other purposes. In an age of food shortage, it is not reasonable to set aside land in our thickly populated areas for so limited a purpose.

The two other throwing events in the modern programme come straight from ancient Greece, but they are none the better for that. The discus is not an object which any man in his senses would choose to throw. The reason for its shape is that in Homer's *Iliad*, a work towards which the Greeks had a very reverential attitude, the weight-throwing contest used a missile which was also the prize, a useful ingot of iron. The mould used in the smelting process was a round hole in the ground, and this produced a lentil-shaped ingot. So conservative were the Greeks that they continued to throw this absurd missile for more than a thousand years. Skill, of course, is needed for the projection of the discus to ensure a steady flight, but it is a dead-end skill, leading nowhere in the wide world of sport.

Discus throwing was introduced into modern athletics at the first Olympiad in 1896. The Greeks, as the host country, were responsible; they regarded it as a symbolic link with ancient sport, which they were trying to revive, and they hoped by assiduous practice at the event, which was unknown outside Greece, to ensure at least one victory for themselves. In this they were disappointed, for the winner was R. S. Garrett of the USA, victor also in the weight, who saw a discus for the first time in his life a few weeks before the Games. By a curious coincidence, his winning throw, 95 feet 7¾ inches, was almost identical with the length of the only throw recorded from antiquity, 95 feet; but the latter was mentioned probably as the exceptionally poor performance of an otherwise fine athlete. In the early years of this century, an attempt was made to impose an imagined 'classical style' on throwers; in this the competitor was mounted on a small platform and was not allowed to advance the left foot beyond the right until the throw was completed. As the platform was based on an obviously corrupt reading in a bad manuscript of Philostratus' *Imagines*, and the other requirement on a bad reconstruction of Myron's Discobolus, the most famous but by no means the best representation of ancient throwing, it is hardly surprising that the style was an ugly caricature. It was admitted as an alternative event to the free style at the intercalated Games at Athens in 1906 and at the London Olympiad of 1908, after which it was fortunately dropped. No harm would be done if the free style followed it.

Discus throwing is a dangerous activity. The discus is a less lethal missile than hammer or javelin, but fatal accidents are by no means unknown. In legend the god Apollo accidentally killed his boy friend Hyacinthus while practising the event, and there are accounts from antiquity of the same fate being suffered by more historical figures. The danger is all the greater because of the unpredictable flight of the missile. Even the most skilled exponents are not always able to keep the discus within the fairly wide angle of the limit allowed them. All things considered, there is no good reason for retaining the event in the athletic programme.

In the ancient world, javelin throwing was in a very different category from the useless discus. In both Greek and Roman armies the thrown javelin was the regular secondary armament of the sword-and-shield infantrymen. A young man's life might depend on his ability to out-range his enemy in battle. As an athletic event, therefore, the javelin had an urgency which is totally lacking today. Nor can the modern event claim authentic descent from the ancient. Both in battle and in the stadium, Greeks and Romans threw the javelin with the help of a thong looped over two fingers of the throwing hand; this has not been followed in modern throwing. (It is worth noting, however, that William Fitzstephen, in his description of London, written in the twelfth century, states that among the sports which they practised, young Londoners threw javelins fitted with thongs for the purpose.) Rather strangely, the event was not included in the 1896 Olympics. The Scandinavians developed it, and it was introduced at the London Games of 1908.

In an endeavour to meet the objection that throwing events tend to a one-sided development of the body, a two-handed contest was held in the 1912 Olympiad at Stockholm, each competitor being assessed by the sum of the distances achieved with right and left hands. This logical and laudable enterprise proved still-born. Probably it was found that the throw with the weaker hand was less controlled and so even more dangerous than the other. For the javelin is more deadly than hammer or discus. Hardly a season passes without news of someone being killed by a javelin – often a schoolboy or girl – and anyone who spends much time on athletic grounds is constantly terrified by the sight of near misses. Some countries wisely ban the event from schools, and there is much to be said for dropping it altogether from athletics, along with the hammer and discus, on safety grounds.

The other field events are fundamentally justifiable, but recent developments in two of them are open to criticism. In the early days of high jumping there was a rule that the head must not cross the bar first. This was unfortunately abandoned half a century ago to allow the 'roll' techniques invented in America. These enabled considerably greater heights to be achieved, and so softer landing had to be provided at some expense. More recently came the 'Fosbury flop', in which the jumper goes head first over the bar and lands on the back of his neck. This should have been banned instantly by international action. The landing cushion now has to be still further built up, and this contravenes the principle that take-off and landing should be on the same level. A far more serious objection is the danger of the method. Youngsters are constantly admonished by television commentators and others not to attempt the flop except under conditions specially arranged for it, but everyone knows that it is useless to warn the young against taking risks, and the expensive landing cushion is not found everywhere. It can only be a matter of time before a boy or girl suffers a broken neck through attempting the technique. All the records in the world are not worth a single young life. A simple rule that a foot must touch the ground first on landing would solve all difficulties.

The recent development in pole-vaulting is equally regrettable. This activity is also of considerable antiquity and was utilitarian in origin. Greek vase-paintings of the fifth century B.C. show cavalrymen, who at that time had neither saddle nor stirrups, using their lances to help them to vault onto their horses. In low-lying parts of Britain, where the land was cut up by drainage dykes, farmers used to pole-jump across them when passing from field to field. It was early included in athletic programmes, no doubt because it is so spectacular, and was one of the events in the first Olympiad in 1896. At that time the pole was usually of ash or hickory; with these there was a danger that the pole might snap while the jumper was in mid-air, and he might be impaled on the sharp end. For this reason at the beginning of this century a change was made to bamboo, which may collapse but does not snap; in the decade after the Second World War, bamboo was generally superseded by light metal alloys. These were safer but made little difference to performance.

The same could certainly not be said of the fibreglass pole. The first experiments with this were made before 1950, and in a few years jumpers were attaining far greater heights with it. In an age when record-breaking is all that matters, this was enough, and in 1962 the International Federation (IAAF) legitimized the pole. It was an absurd decision. The fibreglass pole is a spring, and it would be equally logical to allow high and long jumpers to fit springs under their heels. Its use violates two basic principles of athletics, one that success should depend solely on a competitor's skill and not on an external manufacturer, the other that success should be open to all. Money alone cannot command victory in any game, but the lack of it can make success impossible in games where equipment is costly – and a fibreglass pole is very expensive. The fact that it makes vaulting more difficult is no argument for it. Dr Johnson had the right retort to that in another context: 'Difficult did you call it, Sir? I wish it were impossible.' If mere difficulty is required, the early technique of climbing up the pole hand over hand, banned from the event eighty years ago, might as well be restored. In the athletic stadium, pole-vaulting should be done with completely rigid poles of standard pattern, supplied by the management of every meeting in different lengths. The fibreglass pole should be left to performers in the circus ring. Almost incredibly, the IAAF, shortly after legalizing the spring pole, thought fit to object to extra spikes in sprinters' shoes.

Walking

Another activity which might well be dropped from the athletic programme is race walking, which has nothing to recommend it. It is illogical, for if a man wants to go fast afoot, he runs. It is grotesquely ugly, and it causes endless disputes about a fair action. Walking races for stakes are heard of in Britain in the first half of the nineteenth century, and the first squabbles about 'fair' walking occurred about 1860. The *Oxford Dictionary* records the earliest use of 'heel and toe' and 'toe and heel' in the 1860s. Walking has always figured in the AAA championships, but was not included in the Olympic Games until 1932. It has appealed to few countries – a standard history of 'Track and Field' in the USA does not even mention it. It is now threatened with explusion from the Olympics, and few will regret its departure.

Cross-country Running

In happy contrast to walking is cross-country running. This had its origin in the hare and hounds runs of schoolboys. *Tom Brown's Schooldays* shows that it was established at Rugby before 1840, and the records of 'the Royal Shrewsbury School Hunt' go back at least ten years earlier than that. In *David Copperfield* (1849–50) Dickens gives a pleasant glimpse of Mr Dick among the boys of Dr Strong's school: 'How often, at hare and hounds, have I seen him cheering the whole field on to action.' (The earliest use of 'paper-chase' recorded by the *Oxford Dictionary* is also from Dickens.) Like football, the sport was carried from school into adult life in mid-century.

The still flourishing club, Thames Hare and Hounds, traces its origin to some members of Thames Rowing Club who started paper-chasing in the winter of 1867 to keep themselves fit for the rowing season. A paper-chase was not a race, but a battle of wits between the hares and the hounds, calling for cooperation rather than competition among the latter. It afforded equal fun to all levels of ability; a slow pack was sometimes sent off in front of the tigers. Sadly but inevitably the sport of paper-chasing has died; intensive agriculture and campaigns against litter in the countryside have made it impossible today. Yet the formal cross-country races which have taken its place still preserve something of the old friendliness, and this sets them apart from track racing. Team races are the traditional form of competition across country, and so the mediocre performer can still play his part. If anyone doubts whether the true spirit of sport is still alive in our day, let him think of the runner finishing in 379th place in a field of 900 in a cross-country race and so helping his club to be twenty-third and not twenty-fourth in the final tally; his fears will surely be set at rest.

Races across country figured in the modern Olympic Games until 1912, but naturally courses could not be standardized, and so no world's records were possible. In an age in which it is every runner's ambition to beat the clock rather than the other runners, this is a fatal objection; the event was dropped from the 1920 Olympics and has never reappeared. Its place has been taken by a 3000m steeplechase over a stylized and standardized course, so the clock-watchers are happy.

Cross-country running pre-eminently belongs to the open air and can never be brought indoors, as is happening to all too many sports today. There is everything to be said for providing indoor training facilities for athletes, especially in those countries where the winter climate makes many outdoor activities impossible. Indoor athletic competition, however, is far more open to question. It is true that such meetings attract spectators, particularly in America, and promoters therefore find them a lucrative source of profit. But there are several objections to them.

Boards of varying degrees of springiness affect runners and especially jumpers differently, and make standardization impossible. The dimensions of even the largest indoor arena allow only absurdly short sprints, and the tight bends of the tracks make bumping and jostling unavoidable, even by the most sporting runners. Such jostling is unhappily becoming more frequent on the outdoor track, and the television camera is revealing how often it is deliberate fouling; it is at least as widespread in women's races as in men's. The authorities failed to take decisive action to stop it when it first appeared, and anyone who has followed on the screen the important Games of recent years could name more than one medal winner who should certainly have been disqualified. Glaring fouls go unpenalized, while an unfortunate sprinter who involuntarily beats the gun twice is dismissed from the race. (The latter *contretemps* could very easily be prevented. On our racecourses, the starting gate for horses, which Greeks and Romans used for their chariot races over 2000 years ago, has at last been adopted, to the great improvement of flat racing, but the governing bodies of our athletics steadily turn their backs on the similar gate for runners, which is of equal antiquity and would be equally efficacious.) Foul running is now so common that it has come to be accepted and even advocated. After the European Indoor Championships of 1973, a journalist of the *Sunday Telegraph* wrote, in language as inelegant as the tactics he was recommending: 'If more British middle-distance runners produced the panache of Browne and were not so afraid to use their elbows, rather than be elbowed, or push instead of being pushed, then standards would be completely different to what they are now.' Do we really wish to win races in this way?

Rough tactics on the track are likely to be encouraged by a recent phenomenon in the athletic world – the revival of professionalism. Since the great days of the decade after the Second World War, the numbers of spectators at athletics meetings have fallen steadily, and this has led promoters in the United States to believe that the crowds could be won back to the tracks by professional performers. If spectators were rational beings, this hope would certainly be disappointed. The attraction of races for the onlooker lies in keen competition and particularly in close finishes; these are not dependent on the eminence of the runners or the times of the races, and are just as likely to be seen at a good amateur meeting. But in these days spectators have become bemused by statistics and records. Some television commentators give the impression that for them the ideal race would consist of one runner and ten time-keepers. So it may be that a travelling circus of performers, who have made a reputation as amateurs in the Olympic Games and then turned professional, will be a commercial success, even though it is possible to predict with some confidence that it will not be long before all the races will be 'fixed', on the principle of 'Snooks's turn today'. Time alone will tell.

Cycling

In little more than a century, the bicycle has had a curiously varied history. It seems to have been invented in France but developed in Britain. In its early days its importance was social rather than sporting. By providing a means of transport cheaper than the horse – for after the initial outlay it does not require feeding – it extended enormously the outlook of the working classes, and it was perhaps the most powerful agent in the emancipation of women. The first cycling clubs, dating from about 1870, were social, but racing started even in the days of the 'penny-farthing'. The invention of the chain drive and of the 'safety' bicycle gave a great impetus to cycling.

Significantly the same year, 1878, saw the founding of the

Cyclists' Touring Club and of the National Cyclists' Union, the former fulfilling the functions suggested by its title, while the latter, in addition to safeguarding the interests of cyclists generally, made itself responsible for racing both on road and track. Until the end of the century, track racing drew large crowds of spectators, but suddenly its popularity waned. The meetings were mainly sponsored by manufacturers of bicycles in order to advertise their products, and our grandfathers were less impressed than are the present generation by this kind of thing. Shamateurism and corruption were widely suspected. Riders adopted the tactics, still often seen on cycle tracks, of a 'go slow' until the finish is in sight and then a wild scramble for the line. This did not produce a very thrilling spectacle.

A small body of enthusiasts has kept cycle racing alive in this country, and on the Continent it has never lost its appeal. The world of sport embraces many absurdities, but surely none more absurd than the five-day events for professional cyclists which constitute one of the silliest advertising rackets of our civilization. Attempts to introduce this preposterous activity into Britain do not appear to be meeting with any very favourable response. Somewhat less ridiculous is the endeavour to combine cycling with cross-country running in cyclo-cross; yet the sport remains a rather pathetic bastard, embodying the worst features of its parents and lacking the best. More to be regretted than the decline of cycle racing as a sport is the almost complete disappearance of the bicycle as a means of getting about the countryside, a purpose for which it is ideally suited and which it fulfilled admirably until about twenty years ago, when it was virtually driven from our roads by the growth of motor transport. Except Henry Ford, no one contributed more to this end, by the production of cheap cars, than William Morris, Lord Nuffield. It is a sad reflection that in his youth Morris was a keen racing cyclist.

9
Other Ball Games

Royal Tennis, as we have seen, was played mainly in covered courts, making it an all-weather game. Our ancestors, however, unlike the modern generation, preferred the open air for their sport where possible, and before the end of the eighteenth century had produced the mysterious 'Field Tennis', which in 1793, according to the *Sporting Magazine* of that year, threatened the popularity of cricket. This experiment appears to have been short-lived, and cricket continued undismayed.

The origin of the modern game is still a matter of dispute; the strongest claimant is Major Wingfield, who in 1873 published a book of rules for 'Sphairistikē or Lawn Tennis'. By choosing the name Sphairistikē, Wingfield clearly hoped to establish a link with the games played in the ball courts or *sphairisteria* of antiquity. Before publishing the book, he had experimented with the game for some years, helped by Lord Lansdowne and a group of young men, one of whom, the future Prime Minister A. J. Balfour, is said to have suggested the alternative name, Lawn Tennis. The game is now officially called Tennis, the older game being distinguished by the prefix Real or Royal (the words mean the same).

By taking out a patent for his game, Wingfield was able to make a commercial success of it by selling the necessary equipment. The game he offered differed little from the modern form. The court was wasp-waisted, the base-lines being longer than the net, which was higher than now, with a bigger drop in the middle. The method of scoring was as in rackets, by single points up to 15. In 1874 the rules of the game were referred to the Tennis and Rackets Committee of the MCC. Apart from recommending flannel-covered balls, they made no important change.

The game at once became popular; in 1875 the All-England Croquet Club, which had been founded seven years before and in 1869 had established its headquarters at Wimbledon, added lawn tennis to its activities and in 1877 organized the first championship, which is still the most highly prized title in the tennis world. For this, new rules were adopted. The court was now rectangular, but the net was 5 feet high at the ends and 3 feet 3 inches in the centre. (The modern height came in 1881.) For some odd reason the scoring up to 15 points was replaced by the Royal Tennis method, which still survives, though at the time of writing it is being abandoned in some of the rococo presentations of the game in America. Another feature of Royal Tennis which has persisted unnecessarily is the double service. The unpenalized first service remains a blot on the game.

One of the reasons for the rapid spread of the game was no doubt the fact that men and women could play it together. The Women's Singles championships at Wimbledon was started in 1884, and the Mixed Doubles in 1888. This epicene aspect of tennis perhaps explains why, although the Oxford and Cambridge Match dates from 1881, the universities and public schools played no part in the development of the game, as they had done in so many sports. Cricket was firmly established as the summer game, and the prestige of a school depended largely on the performance of its cricketers. Tennis was looked on as a rival which might deprive the XI of a potentially outstanding player. Moreover it was played with a soft ball, and therefore thought to be more appropriate to girls' schools. This attitude persisted in the universities, and at Oxford it was not until after the First World War that tennis was awarded the Full Blue which put it on a level with other major sports.

No game has played so great a part in the social life of the whole country as did tennis in the first third of the present century. Its heyday was in the decade after the First World War, when its popularity spread to all classes of the community. The exclusive clubs of pre-war days remained, now reinforced by many others for the middle classes, while for those who could not afford club subscriptions, local authorities provided courts in public parks which could be hired by anyone. The game was not without its snobbishness. Men in those days wore long white flannels for tennis; in one suburb there were two clubs, one familiarly known as 'Skimmed Milk', the other as 'Full Cream'.

In those years, every seaside hotel had to provide courts for its patrons, and on railway platforms in the holiday months almost every suitcase had a tennis racket strapped to it. Every householder with a garden of moderate size felt it incumbent on him to equip it with a court; these private courts were the scene of the tennis parties, the thought of which nowadays sends our young satirists into fits of merriment. In fact they were very pleasant functions. It is true that many of the ladies restricted themselves to an underarm service, but in retrospect they certainly appear to have been far more agreeable creatures than the hatchet-faced fairies of the Centre Court today. (Incidentally, one wonders how some of our much-admired experts would cope with a good underarm service; it would probably cause as much consternation as would underarm bowling on the cricket field).

During this period, tennis was becoming a world-wide game and was gaining ground as a spectator sport. This development owed much to two outstanding players, W. T. Tilden of the USA among the men, and Mlle Suzanne Lenglen of France among the women. Moreover, Wimbledon acquired great social prestige from Royal patronage. Queen Mary was regular in her attendance, as Princess Marina was to be in later years, and in his younger days King George VI was a player good enough to appear in the men's doubles in the championships. As a result, Wimbledon gradually usurped the position in the fashionable social events of the London Season formerly held by Henley Regatta and the University and Eton and Harrow Cricket Matches.

This growth in popularity as a spectator sport and the great improvement in skill of the leading players has strangely been accompanied by a steady decrease in the number of active participants in the game. Where fifty years ago the courts in our parks were crowded on any fine summer evening with young people happily playing tennis badly, they now stand deserted. Hotel courts have been converted into car parks, and the lawns of private houses have been dug up to accommodate swimming pools, the current status symbol. Apparently the youngsters of today, dismayed at not being able immediately to match the skill of the players they see on their television screens, abandon the game in despair. The same thing has happened in skating.

The steady rise in standards of skill meant that only those who could devote all their time all the year round to the game had any hope of attaining the highest level. All the leading championships in the world were theoretically for amateur players, but obviously no amateur in the proper sense of the term could hold his own in this company. For many years the pretence was maintained that the leading players were amateurs by the payment of 'expenses' which enabled them to live very luxurious lives. Some players not quite in the top rank turned professional and earned an honest living by coaching. In 1930 Tilden, still a champion, turned professional, in the hope that professional tournaments would lure the crowds away from the 'amateur' game. But he was approaching the end of his career, and few young players of outstanding ability followed his example at that time. There was little reason why they should; they were making just as much money as 'amateurs.' For a further thirty years the governing bodies of the great championships of the world continued to shut their eyes to the situation and to maintain the absurd pretence that their tournaments were amateur – the worst scandal of its kind in the whole history of sport.

Then in America a promoter saw the possibilities of a circus of performers of established reputation travelling the world and playing a series of exhibition tournaments as a commercial project, like the All-England cricket team of the nineteenth century, and he persuaded several leading players to abandon their amateur status and sign contracts with him; his project succeeded and naturally provoked rivalry. The 'amateur' meetings were faced with the loss of their crowd-drawing stars, and Wimbledon was driven to declare itself 'open'. For a time in the late 1960s the tennis world in Britain found itself in the situation from which rowing had escaped many years before – it had professionals and two kinds of amateurs. In order to attract the professionals, the management had to offer large money prizes, and because the professionals were all under contract to rival promoters, Wimbledon had to haggle with these promoters to secure the players' release. The whole tennis scene today is in a very nasty mess.

The confusion in organization has been accompanied by an

unhappy decline in standards of behaviour both on court and in the spectators' seats. Our sports journalists try to play this down by using a series of platitudinous euphemisms; we all know now, for instance, what is meant by the phrase 'an exuberant personality'. One thing is certain. In the world of commercialized sport, as elsewhere in commerce, demand creates supply. If spectators want to see players throwing their rackets at umpires, then rackets will be thrown at umpires. And if the trend now being set by the promoters of World Team Tennis in America follows the logical course, the game will soon be on a level with all-in wrestling.

Badminton

This game takes its name from the residence of the Dukes of Beaufort. One day in 1860, guests at a house party there were confined to the house by rain, and to amuse themselves they borrowed battledores and shuttlecocks from the nursery and devised for themselves a game on the lines of Royal Tennis which could be played in the Great Hall without any risk of doing damage. They took the net from tennis and the method of scoring from rackets. There was a door in the middle of each long side of the Hall, and in order to allow access to these while play was in progress, the net was made shorter than the baselines, producing the hour-glass shape of a court which was later to be adopted for Lawn Tennis in its early days; it lasted no longer in Badminton than in the younger game. Badminton is a valuable addition to our repertory of minor games, as it can be played in any large hall by daylight or artificial light and does not require a specially constructed court as squash does. In 1895 an Association was founded to organize and regulate the game, which has now become international.

Table Tennis

The *Daily Chronicle* of 2 May 1901 records: 'The inventor of Ping Pong has been discovered; it was Mr James Gibb, an old Cambridge athlete, now living at Croydon.' The game was thus one more British contribution in the latter half of the nineteenth century to the world of sport. The inventor appears to have called his game table tennis, but from the start the admirably onomatopoeic ping pong was also used. The *Daily Chronicle* of 16 December 1901 writes of 'a table tennis or "ping-pong" tournament'; the inverted commas are significant. The opening years of this century saw the outbreak of a craze for the game, like those for diabolo and yo-yo, and a Table Tennis Association and a Ping Pong Association were founded with almost identical rules. The craze died down, but the game lingered on, and in the years after the first war there was a revival. The name ping pong was officially dropped as being too frivolous for this now serious pursuit. The Table Tennis Association assumed sole control, and the game, rescued from youth clubs and wet afternoons in cricket pavilions, spread to other countries. It is an excellent amusement, but some may feel that its promotion to the status of international matches and other solemn occasions is mildly preposterous. The miniature has its place, but true sport needs the broad canvas.

Bowls

Games resembling bowls were played in the Middle Ages, but the modern game may be said to date from the invention of bias in the woods, first recorded in the sixteenth century; Shakespeare uses the word twelve times. Shakespeare is also the first recorded author to use the word 'jack' for the small ball aimed at in the game. It was in Shakespeare's lifetime too that Sir Francis Drake immortalized bowls by his refusal to leave his game unfinished when the Armada was sighted. The game was already played both in bowling alleys and, as today, on bowling greens. In Elizabethan times, matches were played for heavy stakes, and perhaps for this reason bowls lost ground in the puritan prime of the Commonwealth, but it is clear from the pages of Pepys that there was a revival at the Restoration.

The first organization of the modern game came in Scotland, where a committee was appointed in 1849 to standardize the rules. England was slower to do the same, largely because there were two irreconcilable forms of the game in the country. In the South, bowls is played on level greens, as in Scotland. In the northern counties, the crown green is used, which slopes away from the centre in all directions; this makes control of the woods more difficult and so calls for extra skill, but it is wasteful of space. In the early years of this century, several associations codified rules for their localities, and finally in 1905 the English Bowling Association was formed as the authority for the level green game all over the country. The game has grown so much in popularity that indoor rinks are now built to make play possible in the winter or in bad weather; it is much to be hoped that these will not lead to the abandonment of open-air greens.

Shakespeare makes it clear that women played bowls in his day. In his *Richard II* the Queen rejects a suggestion that she should play to relieve her boredom:

> 'Twill make me think the world is full of rubs,
> And that my fortune runs against the bias.

Pepys records that on 1 May 1661 he and a friend played bowls with their wives when they stopped for a meal at Petersfield; two years later he writes of a bowling alley in Whitehall Gardens 'where Lords and Ladies are now at bowls'. The game is very suitable for women, and it is a minor social curiosity that they were so slow to take part in the modern development of it. Even now, when women's bowling clubs are numerous, men and women for the most part play the game separately.

The term bowling has sometimes been applied to the game of knocking down skittles with balls in the alleys often annexed for the purpose to inns and public houses. This is now usually called skittles, but a few years ago the game of ten pin bowling was introduced into this country from America and promoted commercially with some vigour. For a time it showed signs of catching on, but now it appears to be losing its appeal in Britain.

Hockey

Club-and-ball games are of great antiquity and take various forms. Tennis and cricket have a long history among these games, but they are by no means the earliest. In the National Museum at Athens is a sculptured relief which can be assigned with certainty to a date before 478 B.C. It depicts two players with curved sticks engaged in what appears to be a hockey bully; unhappily nothing whatever is known about the game from any other source. In Britain, hockey under the name of hurling, shinty or bandy is attested first in Ireland. The Welsh game of *cnapan*, for which the sole authority is Owen's *Pem-*

(Above) Sport and broadcasting: Jimmy Hill and Brian Moore in the commentary position at Wembley during the 1970 FA Cup Final. *(London Weekend Television)*

Sport and art: L. S. Lowry's 'Going to the Match' shows Bolton Wanderers' ground. Northern industrial areas have generally provided the greatest following for soccer. *(The Guardian)*

(Above) Geoffrey Boycott (Yorkshire) and John Snow (Sussex): because of their uneven temperament,both players have often been ignored by Test selectors. *(P. Fagar)*

Squash. Jonah Barrington and Gogi Alauddin during the 1972 Open Championship at Sheffield. Barrington's influence as a professional player has done much to make squash one of Britain's fastest-growing sports. *(Sheffield Morning Telegraph) brokeshire* (1603), is sometimes adduced as an ancestor of hockey. It was played with a wooden ball, but while the players carried sticks, they appear to have used them to belabour their horses and their opponents, and not to hit the ball, which they propelled mainly by throwing.

By the middle of the nineteenth century, a game called hockey played with sticks was sufficiently well known in England for a writer in 1842 to be able to describe the unfamiliar polo as 'Hockey on Horseback', and we have seen that there was a vogue for it at Cambridge in 1848, until it was superseded by football. Clubs were being founded in London to play the game, and the need for the same standardization of rules which was happening in other sports led to the formation of two organizations. The Hockey Union followed the Rugby Union of the day in playing teams of fifteen, while the Hockey Association imitated the eleven-a-side game of the Football Association. In 1895 the Union adopted the Association's rules and disbanded itself. The modern game was thus born, and international matches started in the same year.

For hockey to be enjoyable it demands a smoother playing surface than football of either code, and the maintenance of this is costly. Perhaps because this meant a higher club subscription than rugby or soccer called for, hockey came to be looked upon as a more 'gentlemanly' game than football. This air of social distinction has been helped by the fact that it has never become an important spectator sport, and so its standards have not been endangered by professionalism; but it must sadly be admitted that in recent years some hockey players have shown a willingness to descend to the level of professional football at its worst, and generally conduct on the field has deteriorated. The decline is not likely to be halted by the decision taken in 1971 by the Hockey Association to accept money to advertise cigarettes.

Because it has always avoided violent personal contact in play, hockey has long been regarded as a suitable winter game for women, and it is widely played in girls' schools. From the enthusiasts at these schools women's international matches attract far larger crowds of spectators than are ever seen at men's hockey games. Moreover hockey is one of the few games in which matches between mixed teams of men and women are practicable.

Golf

Golf is unique among ball games in that it has become a matching of a single human being's skill against the forces of nature; any connection with anyone else doing the same thing at the same time is fortuitous and inessential. It is the only ball game which a man can legitimately play against himself.

Although there is abundant evidence that the game was played early in the Middle Ages in Holland, few Netherlanders would seriously dispute Scotland's claim to be the true home of golf. The term 'links' is still often used for a golf course, and this Scots word reveals that the game was developed among the links or sandhills near the sea, land useless for any agricultural purpose; no doubt a game which could be played in such places appealed to the thrifty nature of the Scots.

By the fifteenth century golf was so popular among all classes in Scotland that the law tried to suppress it as a threat to archery, after the pattern so familiar in connection with other sports in England. In March 1457 the Scots Parliament 'decreted and ordained . . . that the futeball and golf be utterly cryit doun and nocht usit'. Thirty-four years later the edict was repeated: 'It is statut and ordainit that in na place of the realme there be usit futeball, golfe or other sik unprofitabill sportis.' A century later still, in the heyday of puritanism, there were other attempts to suppress the game by law in Scotland, this time in the interests of the strict observance of the Sabbath. The kings were not bound by these restrictions, and most of the Stuarts played golf. The Scots who came to London with James I in 1603 were probably responsible for introducing the game into England; at any rate, in 1618 James thought it worth while to prohibit the import of golf balls from Holland, in order to encourage home production.

Strutt in his *Sports and Pastimes* (1801) relates a pleasant anecdote about James' son, Henry, Prince of Wales, at 'Goff'. On one occasion he was about to drive when he was warned that his schoolmaster, Newton, was in front. (These were the days when even tutors of princes did not spare the rod.) Henry replied, 'Had I hit him, I had but paid my debts.' Strutt adds some interesting facts about the game in his own day. The ball was made of leather stuffed hard with feathers.

When four persons play, two of them are sometimes partners and have but one ball, which they strike alternately, but every man has his own bandy. . . . . The handle of this instrument is straight, and usually made of ash, about 4 feet and ½ in length; the curvature is affixed to the bottom, faced with iron and backed with lead.

The game in England seems to have diminished in importance after the execution of Charles I, who was an enthusiastic player. Pepys, a keen observer of contemporary sport, does not mention it. But in Scotland it maintained its appeal, and in 1834 William IV gave it his approval by becoming Patron of St Andrew's Club, thus conferring on it the title Royal and Ancient. Soon after this, Scots resident in London are recorded as playing the game at Blackheath. The first golf club to be formed in England was the Royal North Devon, which opened its links at Westward Ho in 1864. Already in 1860 the first Open Championship had been held at Musselburgh; not until 1897 was this event allowed to go outside Scotland, though ten years before that the second Amateur Championship had taken place at Hoylake. The ladies' event was started in 1893.

The Open champions in the early years were all professionals of Scots clubs who had started their connection with the game in boyhood as caddies and had learned to swing a club while waiting for their patrons. They went on to become greenkeepers on the courses, made and sold equipment and coached amateur players; many of them were fine characters, winning respect and admiration from all who knew them. Not until 1890 was any amateur able to match their skill and win the Open.

The spread of the game naturally caused problems of organization and of government in the control of the rules. (To the outsider, golf appears to be a singularly uncomplicated game. It is a surprising fact that in a recently published volume containing the laws of all important games, the rules of golf fill many more pages than those of any other sport.) For a long time players were content to accept the authority of St Andrew's, though the Royal and Ancient Club, like the MCC in cricket, was very reluctant to assume any responsibility. But a change was to come. In the last years of the nineteenth century, the United States took up golf with an enthusiasm far surpassing anything known in Britain, resulting in some regrettable modifications in the nature of the game. The Americans take their sport very seriously, and they found some aspects of British golf not much to their liking. In this country most golfers have an affection for the friendliness of match play and foursomes, where each hole is a separate contest between opponents, and the match is decided by the number of holes won in the round. But a player may win his holes by narrow margins and lose others by wide ones, and then the match will go to the inferior player. This is anathema to the logical Americans, and they much prefer medal play, where the total for the round is the deciding factor. Moreover, British golf used to admit the stymie. The Americans considered that this was permitting an unnecessary intrusion of luck; so it had to go, and with it the last trace of humour vanished from the game.

The huge numbers of players in America opened up a profitable market for the manufacturers of equipment, and to advertise their products they poured large sums of money into the game to supply prizes for tournaments. This has resulted in the appearance of a new type of professional very different from the tough old greenkeepers of last century and sometimes less admirable characters than they were. These young men form a closed circuit, going round the world picking up the valuable prizes now available. They would despise the humble duties of the old professional, even the coaching; they can accumulate more than enough by winning tournaments and selling their names to advertisers. This has been accompanied by another surprising development in golf, its emergence as a great spectator sport; surprising, because while no one would deny the fascination of playing the game – it has the same attraction as the exercise of any other form of skill – to watch a man knocking a ball into a hole would seem to many to be a very moderate amusement. Television reveals the secret. The commentator is able to announce, 'Fifty thousand dollars depend on this putt.' The situation is the same as in those radio quizzes where similar amounts depend on a competitor's knowing the name of Henry VIII's third wife, or possessing some other equally useless piece of information. The viewer is able to enjoy the thrills of vicarious gambling with no feelings of guilt.

More than any other sport, golf has produced social problems. In Scotland the game in its early days was genuinely democratic, and to some extent it still is. Elsewhere the cost of modern equipment and especially the expense of laying out courses on valuable land near cities caused it to be restricted to the middle classes. The provision of municipal courses and of Artisan Golf Clubs, although they made the game accessible to the less well off, did nothing to solve the social problem, because there is little or no mingling of these players with the members of the private clubs. Moreover, the need to prevent overcrowding of courses caused the private clubs to limit the number of members; the easiest way of doing this was to raise subscriptions, and this tended further to restrict their membership to the wealthy. The extra revenue thus accruing is spent on constantly more lavish club-houses and attendant facilities, and membership becomes a status symbol and a business necessity in this country and even more in America. In many clubs today, the course is considerably less used than some of the other amenities, coming well after the bar and dining room, and sometimes after the card room as well. None of the proposals offered by the Sports Council for the provision of additional courses touches this problem, and in the jargon of the politicians, golf risks becoming socially divisive, a sad fate for any sport. (In a short story, 'Join the Club', in his book, *The Thing He Loves*, (1973), Brian Glanville has brought out into the open a long-held suspicion that anti-Jewish prejudice is strong in our suburban golf clubs, as it undoubtedly is in the USA. The subject calls for further investigation, since it is obviously relevant to any consideration of the place of sport in our society.)

Doctors sometimes prescribe golf to their elderly patients as a means of taking gentle exercise. In America this is becoming obsolete, because on many of their courses electric buggies now provide mechanical transport between tee and green, and the ageing citizens are deprived of their walk; this idea has not yet made much impact on British golf. The game is still prescribed as occupational therapy to those threatened with mental or psychic disorders. Perhaps it is in this light that golf should be regarded, rather than as a sport.

Croquet

This game has obvious affinities with golf; in one the ball is directed with a club at pegs and hoops, in the other at a hole in the ground. It is a better game than golf, in that there is genuine contention between opponents, who can interfere with one another's play. Both attack and defence are possible, and that is an essential element in sport.

Like most British games, croquet has its roots in the past. In the Middle Ages there was a game called closh, of which little is known except that it involved hitting a ball through a hoop. The same action was fundamental to the game of *pêle mêle*, borrowed from France at the time of the Restoration. On 2 April 1661 Pepys reports:

> To St James's Park, where I saw the Duke of York playing at Pele-mele, the first time that ever I saw the sport.

At a later point in the Diary he reveals some interesting details about the court on which it was played:

> [15 May 1663] I walked in the Park, discoursing with the keeper of the Pell Mell, who was sweeping of it; who told me of what the earth is mixed that do floor the Mall, and that over all there is cockle-shells powdered, and spread to keep it fast; which, however, in dry weather, turns to dust and deads the ball.

The use of powdered shell as a precursor of marl for binding the playing surface is noteworthy. Another entry throws light on the social niceties in the sporting world of the time:

> [5 January 1664] Afterwards to St James's Park, seeing people play at Pell Mell; where it pleased me mightily to hear a gallant, lately come from France, swear at one of his companions for suffering his man, a spruce blade, to be so saucy as to strike a ball while his master was playing on the Mall.

The date of this incident suggests that the game was energetic enough to keep the players warm; but on 3 May 1669 the Duke of York, who was engaged in a game which lasted an hour, called Pepys over for a discussion; this shows that, as in modern croquet, there were times when a player had moments to spare while his opponent was in play.

The word 'croquet' is first recorded by the *Oxford Dictionary* in 1858, in a quotation which shows that the game was well established by that time. In 1868 the All-England Croquet Club was founded and chose Wimbledon for its headquarters. Seven years later, as we have seen, it acted as foster-mother to the new game of Lawn Tennis. The cuckoo in the nest grew so strong that in the 1880s the Club dropped Croquet from its title, but when tennis suffered a temporary decline a few years later, croquet was restored to second place and the club became the Lawn Tennis and Croquet Club. However, control of the game passed to the Croquet Association, founded in 1896. The game has since had a small but enthusiastic following, and in recent years there have been signs that some members of the younger generation, dissatisfied with many modern developments in tennis, are turning to croquet instead.

Lacrosse

Lacrosse came to Britain from Canada, where the white settlers took it from the North American Indians. The Lacrosse Association of Canada was founded in 1867, and in that same year a team of Indians visited England to demonstrate the game and prompted the formation of the English Lacrosse Union in the next year. In this country the game is played mainly in London and Lancashire. At its best it is a graceful game, and it has been adopted by many girls' schools as an alternative to hockey as a winter pursuit.

Basketball, Netball and Volleyball

All these games have been imported into Britain and are invented rather than traditional. All can be played indoors as well as in the open air, and so are useful additions to the sports repertory. Basketball and netball are based on the same principle as football and hockey, of aiming a ball at a goal. The basic principle of volleyball is that of tennis, badminton and fives, preventing a ball from touching the ground within a given area; it is played with a larger ball and without rackets.

Credit for the invention of basketball, the most important of the three, is shared by Canada and the USA. James Naismith, its inventor, was a Canadian by birth but was working in the States when he devised the game. In these days when basketball, like so many other sports, has been exploited out of recognition by commercial interests, it is worth remembering that Naismith was a man of strong religious convictions, and that his motive in framing his game was, as one of his biographers put it, 'to assist youth to discover moral as well as physical strength through education'. A revealing anecdote relates that in 1907 a friend told him that he had just been appointed basketball coach to an American university: 'He fixed me with those blue-gray eyes and stated, "You don't coach basketball, you just play it."' Naismith lived until 1939, but such sentiments seem aeons away from us now.

Polo

This too is an imported game, of great antiquity. It was certainly played by Byzantine Emperors in the twelfth century; they probably derived it from the Persians, who were playing it in the sixth century A.D. There is evidence for its having been played in Rome in the fourth century A.D., and Romans may have taken it from the eastern parts of their Empire. Officers of the British Army in the days of the Indian Empire found it being played in princely circles in the sub-continent, took it up enthusiastically and brought it home with them.

The first match in England was played in 1870 on Hounslow Heath, with eight players on each side, and resulted in a victory for the Tenth Hussars over the Ninth Lancers by three goals to two. A contemporary wrote of the match, 'It was admitted by all who were looking on that the game was more remarkable for the strength of the language used by the players than for anything else.' Sir Winston Churchill was a keen player in his young days, and on the polo field developed many of those qualities which were to serve him well in later life.

Polo is played in the United States and in the Argentine, but for obvious reasons of the expense involved it has remained a game for the rich. However, with the spread of wealth in Britain and the great growth of interest in horsemanship among all classes, polo will probably gain in popularity too. It is strange that television has not yet exploited its possibilities as a spectator sport.

Baseball

Every American is convinced that his great national game is an American invention and he is driven to fury when an Englishman says, 'Baseball? Oh yes, our children play it; they call it rounders.' The statement is none the less exasperating for being true. The *Oxford Dictionary* defines baseball as 'The national field game of the United States; a more elaborate form of the English "rounders" '. The insult becomes even more deadly when, under 'rounders' the *Dictionary* gives as its first quotation, 'Rounders, besides an ordinary field, requires only a ball and a stick resembling a common rolling-pin'; in the folk-lore of English comedy, the rolling-pin is the traditional weapon which the masterful wife uses on her henpecked husband.

In fact the earliest recorded use of the term 'baseball' is in Jane Austen's *Northanger Abbey*, published in 1818 but written before 1800: 'It was not very wonderful that Catherine . . . should prefer cricket, base-ball, riding on horseback, and running about the country . . . to books.' It was many years later that the first American code of rules for the game was produced by the Knickerbocker Club of New York in 1845.

In the few places in Britain where baseball is played seriously, it is probably a legacy from the American forces stationed in those areas during the two great wars of this century.

10
Combat Sports

Wrestling

Boxing and wrestling no doubt originated as part of training for war, but by Homer's time they had already been sublimated into sports. A thousand years before Homer, a remarkable series of paintings in tombs at Beni Hasan in Egypt depicts wrestling obviously as a sport. For the Greeks wrestling was the most widely practised of their three combat events, being less painful than boxing or the *pankration* and giving every opportunity for the development of skill. The *palaestra* or wrestling school was the club-room of every Greek boy or man, where he would engage his friends in informal contests, just as today he would play a game of golf or squash. Plato gives us a charming picture of Socrates taking on his young friend Alcibiades in such a bout, and Plato himself was a wrestler only just below Olympic class.

The Greeks were fortunate in having a set of wrestling rules observed all over the Greek world – those of their Olympic Games. In Britain the sport has been prevented from attaining the position it deserves because our wrestlers have had an undue loyalty to their local rules, Cornwall and Devon, Cotswold, or Cumberland and Westmorland, and no national code has ever been agreed upon. The sport is of great antiquity in Britain. Well before the Norman Conquest, St Cuthbert was a wrestler; Chaucer has several references to the sport and reveals the traditional prize for it in his day, a ram. Of one of his Canterbury Pilgrims he writes:

> The Millere was a stout carl for the nones,
> Ful byg he was of brawn and eek of bones;
> That proved wel, for over-al, ther he cam
> At wrastlynge he wolde have awey the ram.

In his 'Tale of Sir Thopas', that delightful parody of a medieval romance, the poet describes his hero thus:

> Ther-to he was a good archeer;
> Of wrastlyng was ther noon his peer,
> Ther any ram shal stonde.

Chaucer knew too the pleasure that a match could give to a spectator, no wrestler himself, who liked to form his own opinion about which of two opponents was the better:

> For many a man that may not stonde a pulle,
> It liketh him at wrastlyng for to be,
> And demen yit wher he do bet or he.

Wrestling was clearly appreciated in Shakespeare's time, for in *As You Like It* he introduces the bout between Orlando and Charles obviously as much for the delectation of the audience as to further the plot of the play. This scene reveals that wrestling was then a dangerous sport. We are told that three of Charles' defeated opponents are left with little hope of surviving, and in the match with Orlando, Charles is carried off insensible after a single throw. We might regard this as merely a dramatist's exaggeration, but in 1556 Camden records, 'John Norweld, slayne at Blackhethe at a wrestlynge'.

Some encouragement was given to wrestling in the middle of the nineteenth century by the introduction of classes by weight, thus opening it to others besides heavyweights. In view of the honourable place of the sport in the ancient Games, wrestling was naturally included in the modern Olympics from the beginning, but this did little to promote it in Britain. The Olympic programme recognizes two codes, one of them the absurd Graeco-Roman style, which has nothing whatever to do with either Greece or Rome. Nor is the buffoonery of the phoney all-in wrestling, beloved of television viewers, likely to do anything for wrestling among serious lovers of sport.

The failure of wrestling to develop in Britain along with other sports at the end of the nineteenth century encouraged the importation from Japan of judo, which used to be called jiu-jitsu; this is growing steadily in importance and appeal. More recently karate and Kung Fu have been brought in from the Far East. Their attraction is perhaps not primarily sporting. In an age of increasing violence, these skills have the recommendation that they offer a means of defence against attackers of superior physical strength who are ignorant of the techniques of judo and karate.

Boxing

It is not easy to trace the early history of boxing in Britain, because of the difficulty of distinguishing boxing as a sport from fist fights used to settle a serious quarrel, but it would appear that boxing in any sense in which we understand it does not go back further than the beginning of the eighteenth century. About 1720 James Figg opened a gymnasium in Marylebone and included boxing among the exercises and diversions which he offered to his patrons. At the same time, prize fights were inaugurated, and for some years the dominating figure in these was Jack Broughton, who is said to have introduced boxing gloves about 1745. These were used only for practice, and for more than a century after their invention all prize fights were with bare fists. (It is interesting to note that Britain was not the innovator in this matter. In 1726 the Empress Catherine I of Russia issued a special decree regulating boxing contests. One of the duties of local authorities in the sport was to ensure that no hard objects were hidden in the boxing gloves.)

Broughton appears to have been a true sportsman, for he earned the nickname of 'Gentleman Jack'; the same title was later bestowed on an even more famous character, John Jackson, who had the distinction of teaching Lord Byron to box and of winning a mention in the poet's *Hints from Horace*:

> Men unpractised in exchanging knocks
> Must go to Jackson ere they dare to box.
> Whate'er the weapon, cudgel, fist, or foil,
> None reach expertness without years of toil.

Even more striking is the tribute which Byron pays him in a note to *Don Juan*: 'My old friend and corporeal pastor and master, John Jackson, Esq., Professor of Pugilism; who, I trust, still retains the strength and symmetry of his model of a form, together with his good-humour and athletic as well as mental accomplishments.'

Another poet, Tom Moore, records that Jackson 'made more than £1000 a year by teaching sparring'; £1000 was a very large sum in those days. Moore's use of the word 'sparring' is significant. Some years earlier, Dr Johnson in his *Dictionary* (1755) had given a characteristic definition of 'to spar' – 'To fight with prelusive strokes'. The object of the sport was to acquire skill in landing and parrying blows, and the relative importance attached to these, at least in early days, is indicated by the phrase 'the noble art of self-defence'. (The inventor of this expression is unknown. It is first found in a speech of Cobden, published in 1849, but he uses it ironically, and by putting it in inverted commas shows that he is quoting.) The violence of the blow delivered was of secondary importance. Even in prize fights a boxer's aim was to wear his opponent down until he withdrew from the contest – 'threw in the towel' or 'failed to come up to scratch'. Knock-outs were rare until the latter half of the nineteenth century. No doubt John Broughton's intention when he introduced his gloves was to save the features of his elegant young patrons from disfigurement, but boxing gloves have another function. Like the leather thongs wrapped round their hands by Greek boxers and the bandages worn under their gloves by the moderns, they protect the hands of the striker no less than the person of the struck. The bones of the hand are in general more fragile than those of the skull, and this no doubt contributed to the greater number of knock-outs in glove fights compared with those in bare-fisted bouts.

It has been suggested that the vogue for boxing among the young bucks of Byron's day hastened the decline of duelling in aristocratic circles, which occurred much earlier in Britain than in most European countries. Young men could settle their differences honourably in the boxing ring, without having recourse to deadly weapons. Such a notion cannot of course be proved; it is equally impossible to disprove.

Prize fighting, corrupt and rigged as it often was, had fallen into disrepute by the middle of the nineteenth century, but experienced a revival in the middle 1860s, largely through the patronage of the Marquess of Queensberry, who was responsible for a code of rules which regulated boxing for many years. At this time, gloves came into use for all matches, and classes by weight were introduced. Amateur boxing had been kept alive in the schools. Here again we are indebted for our knowledge to *Tom Brown's Schooldays*, in which it is recorded that at Rugby, 'Two or three nights in every week the gloves were brought out, either in the hall or fifth-form room'. The first match between Oxford and Cambridge took place in 1897.

But in recent years boxing, apart from prize fighting, has fallen under a cloud. The medical profession is convinced that even with large and well-padded gloves there is risk of damage to the brain, and many schools have abandoned it. If there is to be a revival, there will have to be a return to the sparring of the eighteenth century, with as much care taken to protect boxers from injury as is taken with fencers. As an amateur sport, boxing is now little more than a training ground for the professional ring, which still flourishes, much encouraged by television. But any viewer who watches on the screen one of the fights for the world heavyweight championship, must often as he listens to the animal screams of the spectators be reminded of Byron's words, 'The inhuman shout which hailed the wretch who won', and be amazed at the effrontery of our generation which dares to condemn the Roman enthusiasm for gladiators.

Fencing

From time immemorial the sword has been one of the chief weapons of war. For many centuries the infantryman with his sword and shield was the backbone of every army, until in the fourth century A.D. heavy cavalry, armed with sabre and lance, began to dominate the battlefield. As long as cavalry survived – until within living memory – the sabre was one of their principal weapons. Thus training with the sword has always been essential, and has prompted the development of swordsmanship as a sport. Contests with singlestick, backsword and quarterstaff, based on training for war, were part of the entertainment of the masses, now obsolete while the finer arts of sword-play were exploited in the sport which we call fencing.

It was not only in battle that skill with the sword was needed. Every traveller in the Middle Ages was exposed to attack by robbers and highwaymen. To carry a shield on a journey was burdensome, and early in the reign of Elizabeth, according to Stow, it was replaced by a dagger in the left hand which was primarily a defensive weapon to parry an enemy's sword but could also be used in counter-attack. Practice for fighting in this technique gave rise to the style of fencing seen in the match between Hamlet and Laertes. In more peaceful times the poniard was abandoned and the sword reduced in size to the rapier or smallsword which could be worn with less inconvenience. This was much used in the eighteenth century for duelling, so skill with it remained important. At the same time, fencing as a sport was greatly encouraged by the invention of the mask. Previously the weapons used in practice had been buttoned or 'bated', as we learn from *Hamlet*, but this did not prevent serious risk to the eyes; with the mask, fencers could enjoy much more freedom in play.

The three divisions of the modern sport of fencing embody the history of swordsmanship. The sabre is the counterpart of the cavalry weapon, the épée adheres most closely to the use of the sword in infantry fighting and duelling, while the foil is a stylized version of the smallsword for sporting purposes. In recent years the development of electrically linked equipment has made the task of the judges much easier. Britain has never led the world in this event, as the vocabulary of the sport makes clear, derived as it is mostly from Italy, Spain and France. But fencing commands a considerable and increasing following in this country.

Archery

The inclusion of archery in a chapter on combat sports may perhaps be justified by the long history of the bow as a weapon of war. As a sport, archery has had a curious record. In Homer, it is one of the events of the Funeral Games for Patroclus, but in later Greek history, though contests in archery are sometimes mentioned, it played no part in the regular athletic programme and was not included in the Olympic Games and other great festivals. No doubt this is partly accounted for by the fact that in Greek warfare as in Roman, archers were of only minor significance. In the Middle Ages in Britain, where the long bow was a prime weapon, archery was of great importance, and to encourage practice with it, attempts were often made to suppress other pastimes in its favour. When the bow gave way to firearms in war, archery lingered on as a sport. It was kept alive in England by the Royal Toxophilite Society, founded in 1781, and in Scotland by the Royal Company of Archers, which dates from 1676; the membership of these was largely aristocratic. In the middle of the nineteenth century, in common with all other sports, archery was organized and championships instituted both for men and women. Today it is an expanding sport and it has attained Olympic status.

The growth of keenness of competition has led to the development of bows which would hardly be recognized by the archers of Crécy as the tools of their craft. These elaborate and costly instruments put archery beyond the purse of many potential enthusiasts. Whenever the skill of the manufacturers of equipment in any activity begins to rival the skill of the user, the claim of the activity to be a true sport is open to question. For this reason it is legitimate to exclude from any book on sport those pursuits connected with the internal combustion engine, car and motor-cycle racing, power-boat racing, water skiing and aeroplane races. No one would deny the skill of those who use the equipment, but they are too much at the mercy of the manufacturers. In sport, it is the performer alone who matters.

(Above) Tennis. A men's doubles final in progress in No. 1 court before a capacity crowd at Wimbledon, still regarded as the most important tournament of all. *(Colorsport)*
John Conteh, at the Empire Pool Stadium, Wembley, where he won the World Light-Heavyweight title in 1974 after beating the Argentinian, Jorge Ahumada. *(Press Association)*

(Opposite) Sport and sponsorship. The Royal Navy found a novel form of advertising during the caber event at a Highland Games. *(Special Publicity Projects)*

(below) The Women's AAA Championships at Crystal Palace, 1974. Birds Eye sponsor the meeting and Cantabrian provide the hurdles. *(Press Association)*

11
Winter Sports

Strangely, in view of its climate, Britain played a considerable part in the development of modern winter sports. Skating on bone blades was practised in Norway and Holland over a thousand years ago, and Fitzstephen, in his account of twelfth-century London, writes of young men sliding on the ice of Moorfields with bones tied to their feet. The oldest organization for the sport in the world is the Edinburgh Skating Club, founded in 1642. Skating in England was encouraged at the Restoration by friends of Charles II who had acquired the art during their exile in Holland, where by this time it constituted the chief winter amusement. Pepys saw it for the first time in his life on 1 December 1662, and thought it 'a very pretty art'.

The first development of skating as a sport was in racing, which was certainly commonplace in Holland in the seventeenth century. The first recorded race in Britain was held in the Fens in 1814, and races are still held there whenever conditions allow. Figure skating appears to have been the chief British contribution. This was developed by well-to-do Britons who in Victorian days used to take winter holidays in Switzerland. Characteristically they made a team game of it. An orange from the picnic basket was placed on the ice as a centre, and round it two, four or even eight skaters performed the figures called by the captain, after the manner of square dancing. The style would seem strange nowadays; dignity was maintained at all costs. The employed leg was unbent, the unemployed leg carried close to it, the arms were folded across the chest or the hands clasped behind the back. Under these conditions a deep edge was impossible and the figures necessarily large. When indoor rinks became the chief centres of skating, the British technique had to be abandoned in favour of the free and passionate International style which now dominates our rinks. Ice hockey was taken through its experimental stages by the British in the same period, but it owes its modern development to Canada and the United States.

The growth in the number of indoor rinks, which reached its peak in the inter-war period of this century, had a curious result in practically killing skating as a popular amusement. Sixty years ago, whenever there was a hard frost, every sizable stretch of ice in the country became the centre of a scene recalling the great Dutch painters or Christmas at Dingley Dell in *Pickwick*. Even the poorest home seemed to be able to produce at least one pair of ancient skates; or there were always several enterprising men at the edge of the ice anxious to hire out skates and the use of a chair for putting them on. The few who did not wish to learn to skate went sliding, like Mr Pickwick and the unathletic Dr Johnson, who in his first term at Oxford went sliding on the ice in Christ Church Meadow when he ought to have been attending a tutorial. The hilarity of the proceedings was one of the few compensations for the discomforts of a cold spell. It is true that the skates were often anything but first-class. In 1806, J. Beresford in his *Miseries of Human Life* included 'Learning to cut the outside edge on skaits that have no edge to cut with'; many elderly men today, remembering their boyhood, will agree with him. But ordinary people in those days did not expect life to be perfect. However, as the cinema and television made the man in the street familiar with the art and skill of the greatest exponents, skating suffered the same fate as tennis, for the same reasons. Beginners at these sports expected to be able to achieve this skill immediately, and when they found they could not, they gave up the sport for something easier. Today a skater who knows a suitable place away from large cities often finds that he has a perfect stretch of ice to himself.

By far the most popular of winter sports nowadays is skiing; here too Britain played a part in the early stages, for it is said to have been a Scot who first took a pair of skis from Norway to Switzerland in the nineteenth century. It is a pity that so much emphasis is now placed on the competitive aspects of skiing, for Britain can never hope to compete with countries more happily endowed by their climate for the sport. It is true that the Cairngorms are now being developed to rival Continental centres, but the area is so remote from the great centres of population that the enjoyment of its facilities is necessarily expensive. Unfortunately some newspapers encourage their readers to suppose that the prestige of Britain depends on the performances of a few individuals resident abroad with unlimited opportunities for skiing who happen to have a British qualification. It would be far better if people enjoyed their fun in the snow without any such international preoccupations.

The greatest British contribution to winter sports is curling. Here the Scots have adapted their national game of bowls to the ice, making it sufficiently energetic to keep the players warm. Everyone who has ever seen it must envy those who have the opportunity of playing it regularly.

12

The Olympic Games

The Olympic Games play a part in modern sport which is perhaps disproportionate to their true worth, and the disproportion is growing greater. They were the dream child of one of the most remarkable figures in the history of sport, the French Baron Pierre de Coubertin, born in 1863. Like many of his countrymen, he was dismayed in childhood by the defeat of France in the Franco-Prussian war, and as a young man he looked round for an explanation, which he found in the poor physical condition of most young Frenchmen. As he searched for a basis for reform, he conceived an enthusiastic admiration for what was happening in Britain at the time, and particularly for the lead which the schools and universities were giving by fostering sport as a path to physical fitness; it is significant that one of his favourite books in his young days was a French translation of *Tom Brown's Schooldays*. For some years he concentrated on encouraging sport of all kinds in France, emphasizing the importance not only of skill but also of a spirit of true sportsmanship such as he detected in the British. An incident at Henley Regatta in the early 1890s tells us much about his character and outlook. In the final of the Stewards' Cup a French four had every prospect of winning when they were obstructed by their British opponents, who had run off course; de Coubertin persuaded his countrymen not to appeal for a foul.

Although the Baron's first efforts had been on behalf of his own people, his outlook soon widened and he began to conceive a vision of what sport might do for the world by promoting friendship among nations. With our hindsight it is easy to be cynical about this dream, but in those days the aim seemed to be within the realm of possibility. At that time international sport had not extended much beyond a few contests among English-speaking peoples, and there had been few signs of the dangers that lay ahead.

The method he chose to promote his international aims was a revival of the ancient Greek Olympics, for which his admiration was as deep as for British sport, but much less well founded. On this subject he was badly served by his authorities. Krause had been objective enough in assembling the evidence for Greek athletics, but in the intervening years, Curtius and others, moved by that sentimentality which has always been a weakness in the German character, had cloaked the subject in a rosy haze of sickly romanticism, presenting the Games as contests of handsome young athletes of the highest amateur principles striving without any ulterior motive for a worthless crown of olive leaves. It is a view for which there is no evidence whatever at any period. Certainly well before 300 B.C. the Games had become the preserve of a close body of professional athletes, as mercenary in outlook as any golf, tennis or football professional today. Had de Coubertin been accurately informed on these points, he would perhaps not have pitched his hopes so high.

Having gained support for his project, he assembled a small committee chosen by himself to organize the first festival. This body formed itself into the International Olympic Committee (IOC), still nominally the governing authority of the Games. Like the MCC and the Henley Stewards, whom he probably had in mind when he framed it, the IOC is self-electing and self-perpetuating. De Coubertin knew that this invited criticism; in defence of it he wrote, 'The very fact that this Committee is self-recruiting makes it immune to all political interference, and it is not swayed by intense nationalism.' Clearly he was well aware of some of the dangers that lay in wait for his movement in the future.

The obvious country for the revival of the Olympic Festival was Greece. Olympia itself, sole home of the Olympic Games in antiquity, was out of the question; the site had been partly excavated by German archaeologists, but the stadium still lay buried under several feet of alluvial soil, and there was no town within many miles where even the modest number of competitors expected could possibly be accommodated. If

Greece was to be the scene of the revival, the only conceivable centre was Athens. Considerable remains still existed of the ancient stadium used for the Panathenaic Games, the next most important meeting in ancient Greece after the four great 'Crown' Games, and this stadium was refurbished by a wealthy expatriate Greek from Alexandria. Some remodelling was called for. In antiquity a running track was a narrow rectangle, and in any race longer than a single length of the stadium, the runners turned round a post at each end of the arena. This would clearly not do for modern athletes; some seating along each side had to be sacrificed to allow the construction of a track of modern pattern with an area of dead ground in the centre and curves at each end. This may have been adequate for the modest performances of those days – the winner of the 400 metres took 54 seconds for the trip – but the curves are far too tight by modern standards. The stadium with its splendid marble seating still stands, and every visitor to Athens sees it, but it is the whitest of white elephants and will never again be used for any important athletics meeting.

This first modern Olympiad attracted a fair number of competitors. Eight nations were represented among the medallists, and the meeting was a reasonable success. It added two events to the modern programme. One of these was the discus, taken from ancient athletics. But the Greeks were naturally anxious to link these Games not only with the sport of antiquity but also with the achievements of their great historic past. These included two memorable feats of running at the time of the battle of Marathon, which saved Athens from destruction by the Persians in 490 B.C. The better attested of these is that shortly before the battle the Athenians sent off Pheidippides to run to Sparta to summon help. The distance is over 160 miles, and Herodotus states that Pheidippides arrived in Sparta 'on the second day'. A more picturesque but later story concerns another Athenian, Eucles, who ran from Athens to Marathon on the morning of the encounter, fought in the battle and then ran back to the city and announced the victory, dying as he did so. Later still the two stories were confused, and Pheidippides was credited with both feats. In 1896 the Greeks recalled these events by including a race from Marathon over the mountains to Athens, a distance of 24 miles, 1500 yards; this was the ancestor of all Marathon races.

These first Games certainly caused no sudden revolution in the world of sport. The second Olympiad was held in Paris in 1900 as part of an Industrial Fair – the earliest instance of the exploitation of the Olympics in the interest of commerce. In 1904 the Games crossed the Atlantic for the first time to St Louis; here too they were an item in an Industrial Exhibition. Hardly any competitors from Europe took part, and the USA made almost a clean sweep of the medals. There was a minor scandal over the Marathon. The American runner who finished first was proved to have accepted a lift from a car and was disqualified. In Paris four years before it had been widely suspected that the French winner of the Marathon had made use of his extensive knowledge of the back streets, acquired in the course of his duties as a baker's roundsman, to take several short cuts towards the end of the race. Until recently it was always supposed that the Marathon in 1896 had been above reproach, but just before his death in 1966 Sir George Robertson, who had composed a Pindaric Ode in celebration of that first Olympiad and had competed in the weight and discus, though he had never before in his life thrown either object, related a curious story in a BBC interview. The transcript of the tape runs thus:

> It was a remarkable race – the Marathon was accompanied by a lot of Greek officers on horseback – and my friend Flack was accompanied also by the butler from the British Minister on a bicycle. See what a funny sort of race it was. When they were about three miles from Athens, the bicycle man, the butler, said, 'I think I'll go back and see where the others are.' And he went back about a mile and there wasn't a soul in sight, so he came back to Flack and said, 'You can win this thing on your head.' And soon after that happened, up turned Louis, full of running, and proceeded to win the Marathon. Where he came from, none of us had any idea.

The strangest feature of this story is that in fact Flack did not finish among the first six, of whom five were Greeks and the other a Hungarian, G. Kellner. So before we accept this as historical fact, and deprive Spiridion Louis of the glory of his Olympic medal, it is well to remember that Sir George was over ninety years of age at the time of the interview, and that every elderly *raconteur* tends unconsciously to embroider his best anecdotes. He may well have confused his memories of the first Marathon with the stories of the second and third.

Any misgivings which might have been aroused by these rather unsatisfactory birth-pangs of the modern Olympics were largely set at rest by the fourth Games, held in London at the White City in 1908. The British had a longer experience than any other nation of running athletics meetings, and while not everything in the organization was perfect, the festival proceeded more smoothly than any of its predecessors, and there was no major scandal. The ground thus gained was consolidated at Stockholm in 1912. Then came the First World War, and the vision of international concord based on sport was shattered. But when peace was restored, the hope was entertained that this had been the 'war to end war', and the Olympic ideal seemed to accord well with the dreams which produced the League of Nations. Nothing occurred at the Antwerp Olympiad of 1920 to disturb this notion, but in the 1924 Games in Paris the ugliest forms of national rivalry showed themselves. There were disgraceful scenes, particularly in the boxing and fencing, and under the headline 'Olympic Games Doomed. Failure of the Ideal', *The Times* wrote, 'No one, it is to be feared, will feel justified in again appealing to the British public to support the sending of a full team to another Olympiad'. Perhaps it would have been better if the warning had been heeded and the revived Games brought to an end there and then.

It was in 1924 too that the first Winter Olympics were held, and there must be few today who would not agree that this was a mistake. The basis of the Olympic ideal is equality of opportunity for all potential competitors; the world is divided into countries which have facilities for winter sports and those which have none. Baron de Coubertin very properly but unsuccessfully opposed the introduction of these Games, which have become little more than a showcase for manufacturers of equipment.

The Amsterdam Olympiad of 1928, in which women's events were included for the first time, proved happier than Paris had been. Four years later the festival crossed the Atlantic for the second time, to Los Angeles. Even as recently as this, the Olympics commanded so little general attention that no journalists or broadcasters were sent from this country to cover the Games, and English newspapers contained little beyond the bare results. Los Angeles established one precedent;

for the first time an Olympic village was built to accommodate the competitors.

The real dangers of the Olympics first became apparent in Berlin in 1936. The Nazis used the Games to advertise their régime, and chauvinism was rampant. Fortunately the results of the events by no means conformed with the hopes of the organizers; that superb athlete, Jesse Owens, made nonsense of all Hitler's theories of Nordic superiority. After such a blatant exploitation of the festival for propaganda, many lovers of sport all over the world wondered what future could possibly await the Games, but then came the Second World War, and for some years all such speculation was academic.

With the return of peace, the hopes of 1918 were revived. The League of Nations, which had so signally failed to prevent the war, was replaced by the United Nations Organization, and the Olympic Committee once again entertained the dream that the Games might contribute to international understanding; they did their best to further this aim by awarding the first post-war Olympics to Britain in recognition of the part this country had played in resisting Hitler. In 1948 London was only beginning to repair the ravages of war, and no one expected that the Games could be mounted otherwise than austerely. The result showed how little the festival needs an elaborate and grandiose setting; it was one of the happiest of all Olympiads. The cynic would probably point out that the number of nations participating was limited. Some of the potentially obstreperous among them were excluded, others had not yet come into existence.

The modern Olympics had overcome their teething troubles and had successfully survived two great wars and the disasters of Paris and Berlin. In 1952 seeds of decline appeared again. Helsinki had been chosen in 1936 as the site of the 1940 Olympiad, and much work had been done on a stadium in the pretentious fashion set in Berlin, when the outbreak of war compelled its abandonment. So when in 1952 an Olympiad was again offered to Finland, the Olympic buildings needed only completion. Since then every host nation has felt constrained to outdo its predecessors in the magnificence of the setting provided for the Games, and has committed itself to vast expenditure with this aim in view. Architects' visions about the uses to which these buildings could be put when the Games were over have seldom been fulfilled, and capital cities, after building themselves almost into bankruptcy to entertain the Games, have found themselves saddled with stadia far beyond the needs of their people, and ancillary buildings for which no useful purpose could be discovered.

But Melbourne in 1956 was to show a far darker side of the Olympics than any mere set of pretentious buildings. Just as the Games there were about to open, Russia invaded Hungary in the vilest act of barefaced aggression since Hitler. Some people thought at the time, and perhaps still think, that the Games should have been abandoned immediately. Others think that a better solution would have been to exclude Russia from the meeting there and then. Most people prefer not to think about it at all. Russia was powerful, Hungary was weak; the International Olympic Committee did nothing. The Russians were allowed to compete; the Hungarians, whose countrymen at home were being butchered by Russians, naturally withdrew. The IOC, like the Priest and the Levite, averted their eyes and passed by on the other side. In 1956 the so-called Olympic ideal ceased to stand for anything. That the IOC, after swallowing this Russian camel, chose in subsequent years to strain at the South African gnat merely makes their cowardice on the earlier occasion the more contemptible.

It must be admitted that authority in the Games was already passing from the IOC. Early in the history of the modern Olympics, as the numbers of would-be entrants grew, it had become necessary to limit the number of competitors allowed to each country in each event, and the duty of nominating them had to be delegated to Olympic Associations in every country. Politically-inspired groups of these associations began to exert more and more pressure on the IOC, and in effect the control of the games has passed to them, as the fiasco of Munich showed.

The next three Olympiads, at Rome, Tokyo and Mexico City at least escaped any major catastrophe. Even the folly of choosing Mexico City in 1968 escaped the worst results predicted by the doctors for its high altitude, though the rioting which immediately preceded the Games there called for all the greasy apologetics which any disgraceful event connected with the Olympics can always evoke from interested parties. Each celebration of the festival was more costly and ostentatious than the last, and the pretence that the Olympics fostered good feeling and sportsmanship grew more and more hollow, until we came to the disaster of Munich in 1972. Here it should be said at once that the tragic murder of several members of Israel's team during the Games was no reflection on the Olympic ideal or on sport, as the Israelis themselves were the first to recognize. The assassins simply took advantage of conditions in the Olympic village which made their crime easy. But when that has been granted, there remains one disturbing recollection which is relevant to sport, the callous indifference of the majority of the competitors to what had happened in their midst.

Even if the murder of the Israelis had never taken place, there would still have been plenty happening at Munich to give urgency to the question of the future of the Games. Before the meeting started, there had been in Britain several squalid disputes about the selection of the teams, in archery, judo, yachting, fencing, cycling and swimming, and in the last-named of these there was also a scandal over the taking of drugs by some of the chosen competitors. In the Games themselves there were disputes in cycling, the pole jump and the modern pentathlon, and unsavoury brawls in water polo, basketball and hockey. It is idle to pretend that a festival which produces such results is performing any service to sport, to international understanding, or to any other desirable end.

Many of the weaknesses of human society arise from mankind's reluctance to recognize when institutions, which were founded with admirable intentions and from the most idealistic motives and which did good service in their early days, have ceased to perform any useful function and indeed have become positively harmful. The United Nations Organization, trade unions and the Commonwealth are obvious examples of this, and it is becoming increasingly clear that the Olympic Games fall into the same category. The problem of the future of the Games may solve itself. Countries become less and less anxious to undertake the task of accommodating this inflated festival, and it may well be that in the not very distant future no host nation will be forthcoming; or increasing chauvinism and diminishing control may lead to such an outbreak of violence and rioting among competitors and spectators that continuance would be unthinkable. Before the Olympics perish in this way with either a whimper or a bang, it is worth inquiring whether a better solution is possible. Substantially there are only two alternatives. The IOC might recognize that the Olympic festival has become unnecessary in the modern world, and indeed a threat to all the sporting ideals for which it is suposed to stand, and might wind up their charge with a dignified final ceremony; or the Games might be subjected to drastic reform.

There is much to be said for the view that a four-yearly festival is based on a state of affairs now obsolete. In antiquity, when communications were slow and difficult, there was every argument in favour of such an interval between celebrations of an event which aimed at bringing Greek competitors together from regions as far apart as the South of France and the Crimea. Even fifty years ago, to send a team to another continent was an undertaking costly in time as well as money, and there was still justification for preserving the ancient four-year interval. Today, however, when with the development of air travel, teams are constantly whisked to the other side of the world to play ping pong, this argument is no longer applicable. Nowadays too every sport organizes its own world championships, often held annually.

There is a further argument against the long interval. With increasing specialization and the constant raising of standards, the duration of an athlete's peak grows shorter and shorter, and it may well not include an Olympic year. It is clearly undesirable that an outstanding performer should be deprived of the supreme prize in sport by the accident of his year of birth. Nor is there any validity in the belief that a sport needs Olympic status for its prestige. Golf and tennis flourish without it, and Olympic soccer is admittedly a farce and contributes nothing to the world-wide popularity of the game. Equally weak is the theory that the Games are justified because they bring together practitioners of many sports; in practice they do nothing of the kind. Winter sports are completely separate in time and space, and even in the Games proper, for obvious reasons yachting, rowing, canoeing and the equestrian events have to be held at some distance apart; nor indeed do the competitors show any great longing to mingle with those in other sports.

If in spite of these considerations we reject total abandonment, the question remains whether there is any possibility of saving the Games by sweeping reforms. In any such attempt the aims of the reformers would need to be clearly envisaged. The first is to reduce the festival to manageable proportions. Even more important is to get rid of the chauvinism; this can be done only be scaling down every aspect of the Games and putting them into proper perspective. As we have seen, there was very little in the ancient Olympics which was worth imitating, but one principle of the Greek Games should be restored. They consisted wholly of contests between individuals; to return to this should be our first step; all team games should be eliminated. The first gain from this would be to increase the value of victory. No one would be able to gain an Olympic medal, as he can now, through someone else's efforts. Moreover it would strike a severe blow at nationalist hysteria. A team must represent some country; an individual need not be regarded as doing so. This aim would be helped by abandoning the hoisting of flags and the playing of national anthems.

There would, of course, be losses. Athletics would lose its relay races. But the part they now play is quite illogical. There are only two in the Olympic programme, 4 × 100m (the dullest of all relays) and 4 × 400m; except that they would inflate an already over-long list, there is no reason on earth for excluding the 4 × 200m, 4 × 800m and 4 × 1500m, to say nothing of hurdles. If they were all excluded from the Olympics, a World Championship Relay Meeting with a comprehensive programme would provide a wonderful occasion.

A further desirable improvement would be the elimination of all those events in which victory depends on the aesthetic estimates of a panel of judges – figure skating, diving and gymnastics; this applies not only to the Olympic Games but to the whole world of sport. It is essential to a sporting contest that the winner should be unmistakable. He reaches the tape first, he throws a missile further than anyone else, or he clears a height at which all others fail; competitors and spectators alike know what is happening, and there is no disputing the result. Competition is the very essence of sport, but in the realm of aesthetics competition has no place whatever. There are no absolute standards, and excellence is a matter of individual opinion. In figure skating and gymnastics, for instance, what seems to one spectator to be the acme of elegance appears to another to be pretentious posturing. Moreover, in any sphere of aesthetics, competition inevitably leads to ossification. The competitor is compelled to do not what his artistic conscience suggests to him, but what he knows will please the judges. At best, development in the art is hindered, at worst the art is diverted down a blind alley. In sport the standard of judging, especially in figure skating, is often derisory, and the effects on these sports are as deplorable as are the effects on music, poetry and drama of competition in those arts.

Now that success in the Olympics is more and more often the preliminary to embarking on a professional career in sport, the risk of corruption grows. Recently *The Times* published a slashing and well-merited attack on the judging in the World Figure Skating Championships, in which the author disclosed a new technique of bribery in the world of sport: 'Jacqueline de Bief, a former French and world champion, has revealed that she was sometimes offered generous marks in exchange for an amorous adventure.' In its Victorian heyday the newspaper could hardly have used more tactful language.

The impossibility of securing competent and honest judging in international and Olympic sport is even more obvious in boxing and wrestling. Moreover, victory in these events in the Olympics is only too often merely the puff preliminary to a career in the professional ring. They have caused constant disputes and bickering in the Olympic Games, and in spite of the distinction they enjoy of having been part of the programme of the Games in antiquity, there is every reason for excluding them today. Equally the fact that equestrian events figured in the Olympic festivals of the ancient world does not justify their retention now. The skill of the rider is not the only requirement for achieving victory; too much depends on the quality of the horse. The same consideration excludes yachting; too much depends on the boatbuilder. It is time too to realize that cycling has lost touch with life and is obsolete; the cycle has been killed by the car, and there is no point in trying to keep the corpse alive under the guise of sport.

We should then be left with modern Olympic Games composed of athletics and swimming – both with reformed programmes – and a regatta for sculling and canoeing, with schedules diversified by races over different distances and for different weight classes. Victory in such a festival would set the supreme crown on individual performance, as it did 2500 years ago. But whether the festival would retain sufficient prestige to justify its continuation alongside world championship meetings in separate sports is doubtful. Perhaps a quiet death and seemly burial for an institution which has outlived its usefulness is the best and kindest solution.

13
Sport and Broadcasting

During the last century and a half, improvement in means of communication has brought many changes to the world of sport. Railway, car and aeroplane have carried players and spectators more quickly and easily to sports meetings. Telegraph and telephone facilitated the arrangement of fixtures with clubs at a distance, and made it easier for club secretaries to collect their teams. In this century, radio and television have had the opposite effect to improvements in transport; they have taken sport to spectators in their own homes. They are such recent developments that the whole story of their contribution to sport is within the experience of many who are not yet in their dotage.

Radio transmission to the home started after the First World War, and received great encouragement from the General Strike of 1926; the lack of newspapers caused a rush to buy sets in order to keep in touch with what was happening. Soon after this date, the broadcasting of sport assumed some significance. It is true that the first occurrence of a sports item in the general news was earlier than this; on 14 November 1922 the bulletin included the scores of a billiard match then in progress. But it was in January 1927 that the first eye-witness report came over the air. H. T. B. Wakelam gave an account of the rugby match between England and Wales at Twickenham; later in that season, the same commentator reported on the Arsenal v. Sheffield United game at Highbury. In that year, too, the BBC, no doubt stimulated by the challenge of the technical problems of the undertaking at that time, broadcast a running commentary from a launch on the University Boat Race, with Guy Nickalls and John Snagge providing the descriptions. This tradition was carried over into television and has continued ever since. Unfortunately the race is usually decided before

Hammersmith is reached, and the later stages set the commentators a great problem in maintaining any interest, but on the rare occasions when the contest is close, the race provides an outstanding broadcasting experience.

The year 1927 also saw the first eye-witness report on cricket, given by P. F. Warner on a match between Essex and the New Zealand touring team at Leyton. Three years later, John Snagge undertook the same task for a Test match, against South Africa at the Oval, and this game revealed for the first time the difficulty which cricket presents to those who arrange programmes. On the day chosen for the broadcast, play had been so much interrupted by rain that Snagge had much ado to fill in his time and had to include an interview with the Oval groundsman. This problem became even more acute when the eye-witness report was replaced by a running commentary on the game in progress; the first of these took place in 1936.

Television broadcasts of sport started with tennis from Wimbledon and rugby from Twickenham in 1937, and the Test match against Australia at Lord's in 1938. But there were so few receiving sets in those times and reception was in general so poor that television had no real impact on sport. After the war the situation changed; better reception consequent upon technical advances made in war-time induced many more people to acquire sets, and television received the same stimulus from the Coronation in 1953 that radio had enjoyed from the General Strike. Then came colour and the fine screen, and the remarkable improvement in skill of the camera crews, which is often beyond praise.

On the broadest front, there is cause for disquiet about the position of television in the social scene. The danger is that it concentrates far too much power in far too few hands. This is most marked in the political sphere. In other respects, few of us have the same confidence in the BBC as we had in the days of Sir John Reith. But in the realm of sport, the advantages which television brings far outweigh anything that can be said against it. Games on television bring endless pleasure to the bedridden, the handicapped and the aged; for those who live in remote parts, the screen is the only way of keeping in touch with sport at top level.

Nor must we forget the part which sound radio has played and still plays in the development of sports broadcasting. For the blind it is irreplaceable, and in these days of transistors many others can enjoy a radio commentary on a match at a time when they are separated from their television sets. Not surprisingly, sport was slow to make its way on sound radio in the early days, for there is no human activity more purely visual. The radio commentator has to paint the whole picture, and try to conjure up the scene before his eyes in the imagination of his listeners. To help him with football matches in pre-war days, a plan or photograph of the field used to be published in the *Radio Times* with a grid of eight numbered squares superimposed on it, and an assistant was allotted to him to make this useful to listeners. Many will remember how, beneath the excited tones of the senior commentator describing the course of play, there could be heard a sepulchral voice like the ghost of Hamlet's father in the cellarage, 'Square Three'. Perhaps because the challenge presented by the difficulties is so great, the standard of radio commenting is high – often well above its television opposite. There must be many viewers, especially of rugby matches, who turn off the sound of their sets and listen to the radio commentary as they watch their screens.

The commentator we should all choose is one resembling the friend we like to have sitting next to us as we watch a match on the ground, but as no two people would agree on the qualities that friend should have, there will never be agreement about the ideal commentator. Most viewers would accept that some factual information is valuable, such as the name of a player who performs a notable feat; it is useful too, when a close-up of a scrum or line-out is shown, to be told whether a line visible on the screen is the half-way or the twenty-five. But there can be few who, at a most exciting moment of a match, want to be informed of a player's height, weight and age, and how many points he scored for his club last November; and still fewer who welcome the superfluous comment on the obvious, 'You do not need me to tell you that he will be disappointed at that', when a player has muffed a kick in front of the posts. We certainly do not want a soulless automaton for the commentary; excitement and enthusiasm at appropriate moments are very desirable. Yet on the whole the best advice to a television commentator is, 'If in doubt, say nowt.' It is better too if commentators can avoid adverse criticism of referees' and umpires' decisions, strong though the temptation may be at times to indulge in it. And it would be well if the play-back in slow motion of the incidents on which such decisions depend were abandoned. The task of these officials is hard enough at the best of times; if they are to be subjected to this form of trial by the mob, it will soon be impossible to persuade men of the right calibre to undertake the job.

Of all sports, athletics comes over best on television. The events tell their own story, and the commentator has an easy task. All he needs to do is to name the competitors, to avoid becoming obsessed with records and statistics, to eschew over-dramatization, and to beware of encouraging the 'cult of personality'. This last is also a danger for camera crews; the whole point of a race is the relative positions of the runners, and long-continued close-ups which show nothing but the leader miss this altogether. It is particularly exasperating when after the finish of a race the camera concentrates on the winner lying on the grass, while an excited commentator is describing a close fight for second place, a scene of which the viewers are being deprived. To be just to British cameramen, this is a fault more commonly seen when a broadcast is coming from abroad. In general, camera work is now so good that there is no longer any excuse for authorities failing to take strong action against runners guilty of deliberate fouls.

Cross-country running might well receive more attention. On the few occasions when it has been attempted, the effect has been spoiled by presenting innumerable shots of the leaders and completely neglecting the fact that it is a team sport. Even if only a short time is allotted to a race, the viewer should be given the chance to see most of the field.

Tennis is excellent television material, and the standard of commenting on it is high, if only because the commentators mostly know when to keep quiet and let the play speak for itself. Hockey might well be exploited further. The annual broadcast of a women's international match with its masses of schoolgirl spectators is a hilarious occasion, but the men are neglected. So too are rowing and canoeing, while swimming is given more than its due share. Most popular of all are the broadcasts of football of all three codes. These have the advantage that a match of eighty or ninety minutes can be presented in a truncated form which still gives a fair impression of the game as a whole. The skill with which the appropriate sections are selected and the joins concealed is admirable.

Of all these sports it can be said with certainty that broadcasting does the game itself no harm; indeed it may in time do positive good, if the dirtier players come to realize that their misdemeanours may be seen in close-up by a million eyes. The same unfortunately cannot be said of cricket; some of its saddest modern developments are accentuated and encouraged by broadcasting. Unlike football, cricket does not lend itself readily to presentation in abbreviated form. The 'highlights' of a Test match which are sometimes given in the middle of an ordinary news bulletin suggest that the proceedings are a swift succession of fours and sixes, of brilliant catches and the crash of falling wickets; this produces a totally misleading impression of what has really happened. The public now demand ball-by-ball commentary and complete television coverage of Test matches and contests in the new one-day competitions. This imposes an impossible task on commentators. No man unaided could maintain a monologue during the long hours of play, so the practice is to send in relays of commentators in pairs. In the expanses of dull play they pad the commentary with reminiscences and anecdotes, with statistics, jokes and observations on sparrows and spectators, like a couple of not very good cross-talk comedians from the music halls. They are doing their best and can easily be forgiven. When the score at the end of the first eight overs of a match is two leg-byes, Pindar himself could hardly produce a panegyric on the batsmen. The commentators are driven to endless discussions on the state of the wicket, how it is behaving now, how it will behave this evening and tomorrow and the day after that and the day after that. In extenuation of the paralytic inactivity of the batsmen they detect deadly subtleties in the bowling; the unfortunate incoming batsmen listen to this in their dressing room, and any courage they may have had evaporates. This was all very well ten years ago, when the flight of the ball could rarely be followed on the coarse screens then available, but with the finer reception today the viewer can see for himself that most of these viperish qualities of the bowling exist only in the imagination of the commentators and the batsmen, and his suspicions are often confirmed later when two tail-enders with no pretentions to batsmanship bang the stuff all over the field. Nine tenths of batting skill subsists in the mind and spirit of the batsman, as W. G. Grace's dictum reminds us: 'You've got to get at the bowler before the bowler gets at you.' Rarely nowadays do we see a cricketer attempt to follow this advice, and broadcasting must take a large share of the blame for this.

The task of abbreviating the video-tape of a football match for later presentation presents the editor with a difficult ethical problem. What is he to do about the more disgraceful fouls and scenes of violence which appear in the full version? If he excises all of them, he is not giving a true picture of the game, and viewers who read in the paper next day that the match was a particularly dirty one are bewildered, and mistakenly think that the journalist was prejudiced. On the other hand, the editor may rightly feel that the fouls in this match were probably no worse than many others perpetrated on the same afternoon in matches not being televised, and that it is unfair for one guilty player to be exposed and pilloried on the screen while the others escape. Most of us will be deeply thankful that we do not have to resolve this dilemma.

The complaint is sometimes made against broadcasting authorities that sport is allowed to occupy too much time on screen and radio. The charge deserves examination. There is nothing morally wrong in not being a lover of sport, even if some of us think that such people are missing a valuable element in the full life. The heartiest enthusiast for games would probably admit that there is something in the accusation, especially at times marked by such events as Test matches, the Olympic Games or the World Cup Soccer contest.

The BBC might well ask themselves whether they could meet this reasonable complaint, not by reducing the broadcasting of the events themselves, but by cutting out their dreadful previews and post-mortems, on which so much time is now wasted. Particularly should they eliminate those embarrassing interviews with winners and losers, many of whom have a vocabulary hardly extending beyond 'you know', 'sort of' and 'I mean to say'. Admittedly most of the fault lies with the interviewers. The fatuity of some of their questions passes belief. The greatest literary figure in the land might well boggle at being asked to compose an eloquent reply to the question, 'How glad did you feel when you realized you had won?' Small wonder that the ordinary games player can do little but stutter and yammer.

(To be fair to sports interviewers, the standard of their questions is no lower than that of BBC interviewers in other areas.) A further objection to these interviews is that they reveal that some of the leading figures in the world of sport are most unpleasant creatures. A moral purist might say that this is a good thing, because we must always have the truth at all costs; some of us would prefer to keep a few of our illusions.

14
Sport and Literature

The literature of sport is as old as literature itself. The earliest written works we possess, the poems of Homer, contain descriptions of sporting events, and there is a succession of such writing until our own day, when the output of printed matter on sport is enormous. Fortunately for the historian of the subject, most of it belongs to the category of what Charles Lamb called 'Biblia abiblia, books that are no books'. Such are the books of rules and statistics of games, magazines of chit-chat about the evanescent sporting scene, and all too many of the histories of sport. To this class too belong those rather pathetic little autobiographies which almost every professional in sport nowadays thinks it his duty to give to the world, generally aided by a 'ghost', to help his benefit fund. They contain a brief biography, a handful of anecdotes, a few platitudinous reflections about the present state of the game, and a long appendix of the statistics of a career. Provided that the authors steer clear of the petty squabbles of the dressing room, they are harmless enough; very occasionally, as with A. A. Mailey's *10 for 66 and All That*, a picture of a real character emerges. As a rough and ready test for our purposes we can ask the question, 'Will anyone who has read the book, apart from the author, ever wish to look into it again, except in search of information which he knows to be contained in it?' If not, then we can disregard it.

This process of elimination still leaves a very respectable body of books, of which a great majority are about cricket. The reason for this lies not in any lack of enthusiasm for other games in literary circles, but in the nature of sport itself. In most games, action is far swifter than any description can possibly match. The pace of cricket, on the other hand, even in its most agonizing moments, is leisurely. To read the famous account by Steel and Lyttelton of the hat trick by which F. C. Cobden won the University Match in 1870 takes about the same time as the over must have taken to bowl. Moreover, the greatest interest in sporting literature is not in action and incident. Every Saturday afternoon events occur on every football ground which are far more exciting than anything in cold print can possibly be.

Literature alone, however, can show us how the infinite varieties of human character reveal themselves in sport. In this lies the attraction of Homer's description of his Funeral Games, though the events of his athletic programme do not lend themselves particularly well to this purpose. Here cricket enjoys supreme advantages. As the game quietly proceeds, every player's characteristics gradually appear. The leisurely tempo allows a player's career to extend over a far longer period than is possible in most games; impetuous youth and mature experience combine in many teams, and leading players have many years during which to impress their idiosyncrasies on their fellows and on spectators. Compared with this, the active life of a footballer, athlete or rowing man is short, and every decade it becomes shorter as the demands of proficiency become more stringent. Character 'sketches' of contemporary footballers appear in shoals every week in magazines and newspapers, but, the laws of libel being what they are, these bear little resemblance to the originals, and by the time it is safe to paint the complete portrait, warts and all, the player has long been forgotten. The technique of the approach to the history of sport through thumbnail sketches of players was established by John Nyren in *The Cricketers of my Time* (1833), with his delight in depicting the richly varied qualities of the members of the Hambledon team. The method has been carried to a triumphant peak in our day by Sir Neville Cardus in his *Days in the Sun*, *The Summer Game*, and other works.

The history of sport has produced a vast volume of writing, but few books which come near deserving the title of 'classic'. J. Strutt set a worthy example in his *Sports and Pastimes of the People of England* (1801), with its careful citation of his sources. Strangely enough, one of the least satisfactory parts of the book is that dealing with cricket, but that deficiency has been more than adequately filled since his day. After Nyren came Pycroft's *The Cricket Field* (1851) and R. Daft's *Kings of Cricket* (1893), and on the statistical side, Lillywhite's *Scores and Biographies* and the successive volumes of *Wisden.* From our own day we have *The History of Cricket* by H. S. Altham and E. W. Swanton; this can be supplemented by Rowland Bowen's *Cricket,* which contains much curious information, but, unusually for a book on cricket, it is without charm.

The high standard set by Strutt for writing the early history of sport was well maintained by J. Marshall in his *Annals of Tennis.* This started as a series of articles in *The Field,* collected into a book in 1878. The game concerned was of course Royal Tennis; Lawn Tennis had only recently been invented at that date. (For the later game, Lord Aberdare's *The Story of Tennis* is a readable guide.) Rather strangely, although the sources are more readily available, modern games in general have fared less well. For football, G. Green's *Soccer: the World Game* (1953), M. Marples' *A History of Football* (1954) and T. Pawson's *One Hundred Years of the FA Cup* (1970) can be read with enjoyment as well as for information. Rugby has not been so well treated by historians, surprisingly in view of its close connection with the universities, nor have most other games. But the nineteenth century volumes of the Badminton Library on almost every sport still make very lively reading.

Much of the most competent writing about sport comes in the descriptions of games in our daily newspapers. This necessarily tends to be ephemeral, but accounts of matches of outstanding interest and importance are sometimes included in the anthologies of sports writing which are appearing in increasing numbers. A desire to emulate the excellence of this factual writing has tempted some authors of fiction to venture into the field, often, it must be admitted, without much success. Here too, cricket has supplied more material than other games. The extent of the fashion is revealed in G. Brodribb's chapter, *Cricket in Fiction,* in his *All Round the Wicket* (1951; a revised version can be found in A. Ross' *The Cricketer's Companion,* 1960). Few would disagree with his verdict that the outstanding novel about cricket is H. de Selincourt's *The Cricket Match,* which does for village cricket what Sir Neville Cardus has done with a different technique for the first-class game. Compared with this book, most other full-length cricket novels are very small beer indeed.

Generally, the most effective treatment of sport in fiction comes in episodes designed by an author to throw light on some aspect of his characters, in books in which sport plays only a small part – as it does in life. The best example of this is *Tom Brown's Schooldays*, the first school story in our literary history; in the opinion of many, none of its innumerable progeny has equalled it. Games occupy an important place in any schoolboy's life, and so they naturally figure in Tom's, but it is interesting to observe how the book differs from most of its successors. Games in school stories are usually won through the exploits of the hero, but not Tom's. In the football match on his first day at Rugby he is knocked out while failing to achieve a touch-down. He goes on a hare-and-hounds run, gets hopelessly lost and shamefacedly arrives back at school after dark. Even the cricket match against the MCC on Tom's last day at school, when he is captain of the XI, is recounted as the background to a conversation which the author clearly regards as more important. Of Tom's own achievements in the game we are told only that he 'made thirty or forty runs', and that he 'stumped the next man off a leg-shooter, and bowled small cobs to old Mr Aislabie'. (We should dearly like to know exactly what these 'small cobs' were; the word has escaped the net of the *Oxford Dictionary*, even of its latest supplement.) The School lose the match, but no one regards this as a tragedy. It has been said that every man has one good book in him, if only he will make it sufficiently autobiographical, and *Tom Brown's Schooldays* goes far to prove the truth of the dictum. Its sequel, *Tom Brown at Oxford*, is equally valuable to the historian of sport, but it is not a success; Hughes was no novelist, and when he comes to the love affairs of Tom and his friends, autobiography fails him. (The standard of the BBC's dramatizations of nineteenth-century novels is usually so high that it is necessary to warn those who have not read *Tom Brown's Schooldays* against the version of it presented on television, which bore little resemblance to the plot of the book and none at all to its spirit. It was a deplorable exhibition of blatant vulgarity.)

Another author who wrote of sport knowledgeably and put it into proper perspective was Ian Hay. Himself a public school master, he gives in his books a well-informed picture, perhaps somewhat idealized, of life at schools and universities at the beginning of this century. One of his last novels, *The First Hundred Thousand*, tells of Kitchener's Army and its fate on the Somme in 1916. Though he may not have realized it, he was describing the end of his era. There is an account of a rugby match in the book, and cricket and rugby, sympathetically depicted, play a part in several of his novels, but his outstanding achievement in this sphere is in the opening chapters of *A Man's Man*, where he describes a race in the Cambridge Mays from the point of view of a man rowing in them; true to the literary tradition of the time, the hero strokes his college eight to the headship of the river. Hay's description of the race deserves to stand alongside the picture of Dr Davie on the towpath.

Authors who include a cricket match as an episode in a novel are too often contented with a plot which is no more than a series of clichés, with the squire and the vicar playing their stereotyped parts and a local umpire with no pretence to impartiality. L. P. Hartley and Rex Warner follow this pattern, and even Siegfried Sassoon cannot avoid the conventional umpire. Miss Dorothy Sayers, in the match which marks the climax of *Murder Must Advertise*, is a welcome exception.

At the beginning of *Castle Gay*, John Buchan uses a rugby match to introduce – or reintroduce – a character from an earlier novel, Jaikie Galt, the former Gorbals Diehard but now a Cambridge Blue playing for Scotland against the Kangaroos, a touring side from the Dominions. The game follows the traditional pattern, with Jaikie snatching victory from defeat by scoring a try in the last minute. J. B. Priestley uses the same technique but a very different scene in the opening chapters of his *The Good Companions* (1930). One of the motives which send his hero, Jess Oakroyd, out on his travels is his disgust at the performance of the soccer team he favours, Bruddersford United, in a match against Bolton Wanderers. Priestley takes the opportunity to present a moving picture of the part which league football played in the life of working men in the industrial towns of the North during the years of the depression. Later in the book Jess meets a veteran player, Jock Campbell, formerly of the United, and in a few lines Priestley gives us a sketch of this man worthy to stand beside Cardus' vignettes of great cricket professionals. 'Such idealism as Mr Campbell had,' writes Priestley, 'centred about public houses; his one ambition now was to do what so many of his successful fellow gladiators had done, to find a nice little public house, not too far from a football ground, and turn himself into the landlord of it.' In the last act of his play, *Johnson Over Jordan*, Priestley gives us an equally telling portrait of an old cricket pro who has achieved Jock's ambition and is behind the bar of his public house.

For obvious reasons, the theatre has not been kind to sport, which has a drama all its own and demands its own stage. R. C. Sherriff made the plot of his play, *Badger's Green*, turn on a cricket match, but without great success. (His masterpiece, *Journey's End*, has at least a tenuous link with sport; it was written in the first place, not for the professional stage, but for performance by the members of Kingston Rowing Club; hence the all-male cast.) Ballet tried some forty years ago to make rugby football a theme for choreography, but the attempt was foiled because the dancers, whatever their kinetic accomplishments, could not be relied upon to give or take a pass. At about the same period, Marcel Marceau was far more successful with a wonderful mime of a soccer goalkeeper. But the finest presentation of sport on the stage was in *A Bit of a Test*, by Ben Travers. This was one of the famous series of farces at the Aldwych Theatre in the inter-war period, and by no means the best of them. The plot was not memorable, but no cricketer who saw it will ever forget the opening scene, laid in the dressing room of the pavilion at the Melbourne Cricket Ground at the end of the first day's play in the Test match, with Ralph Lynn as England's leading amateur batsman and Robertson Hare as England's captain, spin bowler and night watchman.

Sport played a considerable part in the genesis of one of the most famous books of the nineteenth century. At the time when Dickens was beginning to make a name for himself as a result of *Sketches by Boz*, there was a vogue for humorous sporting prints, and Dickens was invited by a publisher to supply the accompanying letterpress for a series of these, which were to be executed by an artist of established reputation, Robert Seymour; the incidents depicted were to be associated with the members of a group to be called the Nimrod Club. The idea had some attraction for Dickens, but he protested that 'although born and partly bred in the country, I was no great sportsman' – the plates were to depict mainly field sports – and even before the artist's tragic death he succeeded in having the plan changed so that the plates would arise out of the text and not the other way round, and that he should be allowed to describe 'a freer range of English scenes and people'. The result was *The*

Pickwick Papers. During the short time when negotiations were in progress, Seymour's plan obviously started Dicken's imagination working on ideas for it, and some of these appear in *Pickwick*, generally with Mr Winkle as the anti-hero. It is possible that the cricket match between All Muggleton and Dingley Dell owes something to the same source. The description of the game has been much overrated. Dickens clearly knew little about cricket, was not interested in it and quickly tired of the incident. It is true that the law permitting an innings to be declared closed did not yet exist, but an account of a match in which only one side bats and the other 'gives in' can hardly be considered the pinnacle of sporting literature, no matter who wrote it.

This episode illustrates a curious point about the literature of the subject. Sport has a rich treasure of wit and humour, but all of it depends on the games themselves being taken seriously. Attempts to make the games funny almost invariably result in a dreary waggishness. A. G. Macdonell's description of a cricket match in *England, Their England* has been similarly over-praised; much of it has the heavy facetiousness of a fourth-form schoolboy. (Macdonell's really important contribution to the literature of cricket came in his *How Like An Angel*, a withering satire on the Australian attitude at the time of the so-called 'bodyline' Test matches; it is required reading for all concerned with cricket, whether in Australia or elsewhere.) P. G. Wodehouse, probably the greatest master of the technique of comic writing who has ever lived, wrote about cricket and golf in his early books; he never committed the error of making the games themselves farcical, whatever may have gone on around them. R. C. Robertson-Glasgow, most charming of all writers who have devoted themselves to the lighter side of cricket, was equally guiltless in this respect.

The place of sport in social life is best revealed almost by accident in the biographies and autobiographies of men and women who have achieved eminence in the wide world and in whose lives sport has played some part. A bibliography of such books would be immense; a good example of them is *Cambridge Doctor*, by R. Salisbury Woods (1962). The author was a Cambridge Athletics Blue before the First World War and represented Britain as a weight-putter in the Olympics of 1928. He had a distinguished career as a doctor on active service in both wars, and otherwise mostly in general practice in Cambridge. Not surprisingly, he was the father figure of the Cambridge University Athletic Club in the inter-war period and for some years after the Second World War. His reminiscences show the contribution which sport at top level could make to a well-rounded life, and also throw much light on the changing rôle of sport in the life of the country as a whole during the last half-century. For those who prefer to have their opinions on such subjects formed for them, there is a great and growing body of writing on the sociology, psychology and philosophy of sport. The major prophet of the subject is a Dutchman, J. Huizinga, whose work, *Homo Ludens* (1938), was translated into English in 1949. It has produced a vast offspring of books and doctoral theses, especially across the Atlantic; here are 'biblia abiblia' a-plenty. The ordinary reader will probably find all he wants to know on these topics lucidly set out in *Sport in Society*, by P. C. McIntosh.

Since the Second World War a great change has come over the literature of sport, as over literature generally. From the beginning of Western civilization, the arts have usually been based on the tacit assumption that life is fundamentally worth living and can indeed be splendid, and that it is the function of art, even when its subject is tragic, to convince mankind of this truth. There have always been individuals who could not share this confidence, and from time to time society has fallen into the same despair and concluded with the Greek epigrammatist:

> What then remains, but that we still should cry
> Not to be born, or, being born, to die?

We are living now in such a trough. In literary circles, hope is looked on as almost indecent, and the sole aim of most of our novelists, dramatists and versifiers is to explore the squalid aspects of life in the interests of some fancied revelation of truth. From their point of view this has one advantage. Most of their unsavoury explorations are thinly veiled pornography, and there is always a ready market for dirt.

The literature of sport has kept in step with this movement, and is faithfully exploring the meaner aspects of the sporting scene. David Storey in *This Sporting Life* and in the play *The Changing Room* paints a grim picture of Rugby League football. Hugh Atkinson does the same for the Olympics. His book,

The Games (1967), is a *roman à clef*, a mixture of fact and fiction for which the author uses the term 'faction'. In it Avery Brundage, Keino, Elliott, Cerutti and Bikila Abebe are easily recognizable under their pseudonyms, while the principal character, Henry Hayes, is invented. The plot is loaded with political corruption, hypnotism by coaches, sex tests and drugs; the book is over-written throughout. At the climax, Hayes runs off course in the final stages of the marathon race within sight of the stadium. Not much more agreeable in its picture of modern athletics, though rather better written, is *The Olympian*, by Brian Glanville.

The title of a short story by Alan Sillitoe, *The Loneliness of the Long Distance Runner*, seems to promise an interesting study of the thoughts and emotions of a typical athlete. In fact it is about a borstal boy who loses a race intentionally in order to spite the Governor; it has nothing to tell us about sport. Faced with such books, one can only fall back on the old critic's cliché, 'Those who like this kind of thing will find this just the kind of thing they like.' Defenders of this latest phase in fiction constantly make the accusation that the older writers shut their eyes to the darker aspects of sport. This is simply untrue. In the earliest account of a game in our literature, Tom Brown's match at Rugby, Hughes tells us that at half-time, 'Some of the leaders visit their coats, and apply innocent-looking ginger-beer bottles to their mouths. It is no ginger-beer though, I fear, and will do you no good. One short mad rush, and then a stitch in the side, and no more honest play; that's what comes of those bottles.' 'No more honest play' is surely significant enough.

And we must not forget the 'Dark Chapter' in the Reverend James Pycroft's *The Cricket Field* (1851), which reveals a degree of corruption unknown as yet in our day. The older authors were not blind to this side of the sports scene, but they kept it in due proportion to the pleasanter aspects, and so gave a balanced picture of the world of sport. One thing is certain. The older literature of sport attracted the right sort of youngsters to an enthusiasm for games; they are repelled by its modern counterpart, which makes sport attractive only to those who want to make as much money as possible from it and have no scruples about the methods they use in doing so.

Literary critics have often pointed out that the Christian religion, though it appeals to man's deepest feelings and has produced some of the noblest prose ever written, has inspired singularly little poetry which is unquestionably of the highest rank. The same is true of sport. Plenty of verse has been written about it, but very little of it can be called poetry. The greatest lover of Homer will not often find himself turning to the Funeral Games, unless he is an historian of sport, and there are even fewer signs of the poetic afflatus in the games described by Homer's Greek and Roman imitators. In our own country, in verse as in prose, cricket has claimed the greatest share of attention, and sufficient has been written in this field to fill five hundred pages of L. Frewin's anthology, *The Poetry of Cricket*. Some of it is not much more than doggerel, most if it makes very pleasant reading, but rarely indeed does it touch the heights. Much of the best of cricket's humour is found in its verse. On the serious side, the poetry – and indeed the prose – of cricket bears out the judgement that the fundamental subject of all great art is the triumph of time. The slight melancholy of the golden glow of a summer's evening and the closing overs of a match suffuses much of it, and the recurrent theme is:

O my Hornby and my Barlow long ago!

The old cricketer, sometimes in a contented old age enriched by his memories, sometimes a pathetic figure, reduced by drink and poverty to a state in sad contrast to his former glories, appears time and time again; or it may be a cricketer of high promise dying young, as in Edmund Blunden's 'Pride of the Village'.

There are no descriptions of cricket matches in verse today; the long narrative poem is out of fashion. James Love's account of the game between Kent and All England in 1744 is a charming period piece, but nothing of the kind would be possible nowadays, and it must be admitted that Love's work, technically considered, exhibits few of the merits and most of the defects of the couplet verse of his time. The only successful piece of sporting narrative in verse from our own day is John Masefield's 'Right Royal', a romantic description of a steeplechase, in which the anapaestic rhythm vividly suggests the galloping horses, and their names give the same splendour to the poem as Milton's use of very different names produces in some parts of *Paradise Lost*. It is difficult to imagine the same treatment being used for a poem about a race with human runners, and our popular ball games appear to this generation to be equally unsuitable material for narrative verse.

Compared with cricket, these games have inspired little verse of any other kind. John Betjeman has a pleasant trifle, 'Seaside Golf', but most of his interest in sport emerges in his admiration of athletic young women. There is Clemency, the General's daughter, sailing her dinghy on Beaulieu River, and Miss Joan Hunter Dunn, heroine of 'A Subaltern's Love-song'. There is 'The Olympic Girl':

> The sort of girl I like to see
> Smiles down from her great height at me.
> She stands in strong, athletic pose
> And wrinkles her *retroussé* nose.

and Pam in 'Pot Pourri from a Surrey Garden', with her arm, 'as firm and hairy as Hendren's':

> Pam, I adore you, Pam, you great big mountainous sports girl,
> Whizzing them over the net, full of the strength of five.

The Poet Laureate brings to his sporting poems a touch of intellectual detachment which is not common in this field, where much of the work tends to be extrovert and often rather naïve, as is appropriate. Sport is children's play carried forward into adult life, and too much celebration is unwelcome; whether in action or in literature, it should always preserve something of its origin in the innocence of childhood. There is a short stanza, once the battle-horse of many a speaker at a school prize-giving:

> For when the One Great Scorer comes
> To write against your name,
> He marks – not that you won or lost –
> But how you played the game.

The high moral tone of this passage and the use of the word 'Scorer' probably cause most people to think that the metaphor is from cricket. It fact, the stanza is from 'Alumnus Football' by an American, Grant Rice. We may smile at its ingenuousness; we might perhaps also remember that it may be true. The present generation does not take kindly to moral instruction. Edmund Blunden, wishing to make the same point for young cricketers about the importance of playing the game, did not dare to use the modern idiom, but felt constrained to put his excellent advice into the form of a pastiche, 'Couplets for Learners as they might have been written in 1753':

> . . . Be this your Counsel then: Succeed with Grace
> And should you fail, fail with a gen'rous Face . . .
>
> Deny no Praise even if 'tis at your Cost,
> A Match that makes for Friendship is well lost . . .

The volume of verse about football is small, but it includes one short masterpiece. Gordon Jeffery in his 'Men on the Terraces' has done for league football what Priestley did for it in prose forty years earlier. It is perhaps significant of the state of football in our time that Jeffery falls into the mood of nostalgia which we encounter so often in the literature of cricket:

> Rain fell sadly throughout the match;
> Two goals were shared, but nobody cared,
> Or seemed to care, about the match.
> Why did we stay on the terraces,
> Watching a game not worth the name?
>
> Surely there are better places?
> More admirable ways of using
> Saturday afternoon, than choosing
> To watch men playing a game they're paid for?
> Is that what Englishmen were made for?
>
> But sometimes during the dullest play
> Something comes back from an earlier day.
> A fleeting moment, a hint of grace
> Brings back a feeling, a time, a place . . .
>
> We are more than what we seem,
> Men on the terraces, soaking wet.
> We have glimpsed part of our golden dream,
> Our April glory. Together, yet
> Private, as the thoughts recall
> The hopes and dreams of what we were
> Or wanted to be, in the far-off days.
>
> A forward slips on the rain-soaked ground,
> The goalkeeper safely gathers the ball . . .
> Slowly the thoughts of yesteryear
> Flicker and fade in the smoke and the haze
> Lowering over the football ground.

15
The Future

Of all the paradoxes in the world of sport, one of the most remarkable is that while every game we play has its traditional roots far back in the past, the great nexus of organized sport which is so important in the social scene in every country of the world today is of very recent growth. It is also a matter of legitimate pride to us that the origin of this movement of organization lay in Britain.

In 1860 there were only two sports sufficiently well ordered to have a code of rules accepted all over the country – cricket and rowing. By 1885, athletics, soccer and rugby, Lawn Tennis, golf, cycling and swimming all had associations whose authority to make rules and arrange competitions was recognized throughout Britain. In modern jargon, this quarter of a century in Britain witnessed a sports explosion. Even those who take a jaundiced view of all games have to admit the contribution which sport has made to the social life of the whole world in the last hundred years, a contribution for which our great-grandfathers were responsible. Belittling the Victorians and their achievement is an infallible sign of a fifth-rate mind.

It was no accident, of course, that this enthusiasm for games started in the public schools and universities and in the social class from which these institutions drew their members. They were the only people who had the leisure and the money to allow them to develop their interest in sport at all fully. But it was an accident – and a lucky one – that the outburst came at a time when the religious movements of the first half of the nineteenth century had had a profound effect on undergraduate life.

As a result, the games then developing were deeply infused

with those qualities which we sum up in the term 'sportsmanship' – willingness to keep the rules, magnanimity in victory, cheerfulness in defeat and so on. These undergraduates knew that in a few years' time they would have entered on careers which would put into their hands the government and running of a great country and a great empire. They would be Members of Parliament or top civil servants, magistrates or judges or officers in the armed services of the Crown, or they would be administering or defending huge overseas domains; others would be serving the community less spectacularly as doctors, parsons or schoolmasters. During their last fling of freedom, the realization of the responsibilities awaiting them gave them every inducement to put their sport into proper perspective. We have no reason to believe that they were less keen or less anxious to win any game they happened to be playing than are their successors today. But when a man knew that in a couple of years he might be administering a large district in India, he was not likely to attribute undue importance to winning or losing a football match.

This was the healthy and balanced attitude towards sport which these young men brought to the clubs which they founded in their efforts to extend their enjoyment of games to those less privileged than themselves. The boys and young men who played for these clubs naturally caught the sporting spirit from them – the young are very imitative – and to this day a respect for fair play is deeply engrained in the British character, except where it has yielded to exaggerated partisanship and a desire to see the home team win at all costs.

Towards the end of the nineteenth century, organized sport was taken up by many European countries and by North America, and in the first quarter of this century it spread over most of the world. Fortunately this happened at a time when the tradition of sportsmanship was still strong in Britain. Because this was a conception new to several countries, they had no word for it in their language and so borrowed the term with the idea. To this day, *Le fairplay* is international linguistic currency, another fact of which we in this country may be modestly proud.

The origin of our games in Victorian England has had other results which can still be observed; some of them are valuable. The Victorians laid great stress on conventions, among them those of dress, and they carried these on to the sports field. Oxford University Rugby Football Club has always played in dark blue jerseys with white collars; in the 1880s the team used to take the field with these collars starched, though the effect must have vanished in the first few minutes of the game. (My authority for this is my father, who for fifty years seldom missed an OURFC home match.) This appears mildly comic to us now, but there can be few cricketers who are not glad that their game still preserves its traditional uniform of 'whites'. The world of sport is full of wit and humour, yet a certain degree of formality and dignity is a very desirable element in it. All-in wrestling and the Harlem Globetrotters show us what happens when this element is lost, and professional tennis in America is already following the same course.

Today it is unfashionable to say so, but it nevertheless remains true, that the greatest gift of these Victorian pioneers to sport was their insistence on the importance of being a good loser. In any game in which there is a winner there must be at least one loser; without losers, sport would be impossible. As a player approaches maturity in his thought and feeling about sport, he acknowledges more and more that he owes a debt to the games from which he has derived so much enjoyment, and one of the ways in which he pays this debt is by frequently accepting the rôle of loser. He realizes that here is another of sport's paradoxes. He may perhaps have gone through a season as a member of a side with an unbeaten record, but he will not necessarily remember that season with most pleasure. In every game he has played, his supreme desire has been to win, yet in retrospect, in many of the games which he recalls with greatest satisfaction he was on the losing side.

Nowadays any leading sportsman or woman who is being interviewed on television feels it obligatory to declare, 'I am a bad loser', and this is always received with sycophantic admiration by the interviewer. In a few cases the statement has the sole merit of being true. Much more often it is made because fashion dictates it. One young girl athlete proclaimed proudly to the world that she hated all her opponents. It might occur to these poor victims of platitude and cliché that if they so much dislike losing, there are two remedies open to them. They can eschew competitive sport entirely, or they can confine their efforts to those levels where they know that they will meet no one but their inferiors in skill. We have all met some who take the latter course; they are not very admirable creatures. Most players are only too eager to match themselves against those whom they know to be their superiors; it gives them the chance of admiring their opponent's skill at close quarters. On rare occasions it may happen that they manage to defeat a better man or a better team, and such a victory has a sweetness all its own. The price to be paid for it is an occasional defeat at the hands of the less skilled. That is one of the reasons why such a defeat should be accepted with a good grace.

Such were the ideals of conduct which sportsmen of the twentieth century inherited from their Victorian predecessors, and this was the accepted code for professionals and amateurs alike at least until the Second World War, even if here and there standards were already weakening. Naturally not every player always lived up to these ideals. There were black sheep, amateur no less than professional, but they were known and not much liked by their fellows, while spectators showed an uncanny ability to detect them, and the favourites of the crowds were always players whose sportsmanship was as marked as their skill. Yet, as we can see now, in sport and elsewhere the nation was living on its moral capital. Moreover, emphasis was moving from the conception of sport as enjoyment for the players to sport for the entertainment of spectators. This movement was accelerated in the years immediately after 1946, when crowds at all sporting fixtures grew enormously in numbers. This in turn brought large amounts of money into sport, and among other unfortunate consequences changed the character of the professional. It is fair to say that before 1939 most professionals accepted that status because the only way in which they could play the games they loved at top level was by doing so. No one except boxers and jockeys made more out of sport than a decent living. Now, however, sport began to promise wealth, and inevitably attracted many who were richly endowed with skills for games but had no real interest in sport and certainly no love of it; they have brought to sport the trade union outlook, maximum wages for minimum hours of play.

It should be said at once that there is nothing improper in playing games for pay to entertain spectators; the professional who does this is on the same footing as the actor, singer, ballet dancer, juggler, conjuror or orchestral player. To play cricket to entertain spectators is as legitimate as to play the violin to entertain an audience. But there is an important difference. To accept money for playing the violin has no effect whatever on music; to accept money for playing cricket changes the whole character of cricket from a game played for the enjoyment of the players to entertainment laid on for spectators.

One of the difficulties of discussing sport is the ambiguity of the term itself, rivalling that of the word 'love'. The relevant section of the *Oxford Dictionary*, published in 1914, distinguished twenty-four meanings of 'sport', the 1933 supplement added another, and no doubt the next supplement will discover still more. We have no concise way of differentiating games played for the enjoyment of the players from games designed to earn money for the players by attracting spectators. Discussion would be easier if we invented a term 'spenter' for the latter, reserving for 'sport' its basic significance, 'that which a man does to disport or amuse himself'. In logical terms, the entertainment of spectators is the essence of 'spenter'; if the players enjoy it, that is an accident. The essence of sport is the enjoyment of the players; if spectators also enjoy it, that is accidental.

The post-war boom in spectator games began to diminish in the middle 1950s, and the decline has continued steadily. The managements of 'spenter' clubs found themselves with failing resources to meet the heavy commitments they had undertaken. Faced with this crisis, they looked round desperately for a solution, and found it by selling the 'spenter' industry body and soul to advertisers, concealing what they were doing – even from themselves, one suspects – by disguising it under the term 'sponsorship'.

Because an advertising campaign usually results in a temporary increase in the profits of an individual company, a generation which believes profits to be the supreme achievement of the human race regards all advertising as unquestionably a Good Thing. In fact the advertising industry of today operates a gigantic confidence trick played on society. An insane fiscal policy which prevents companies from increasing dividends leaves large sums in the hands of directors, and one way of disposing of these is to use them in large-scale advertising which will build up goodwill in preparation for a happier future. The least laborious way of conducting this advertising is to hand out largesse to the governing bodies of 'spenter' to enable them to run competitions bearing the name of the advertiser.

As a natural result of this policy there has been a wild rush by everyone connected with sport to get a hand in the kitty. A second effect has been to attract a number of undesirable characters into the world of 'spenter', and their evil communications are speedily corrupting the good manners of those already in it. The glint of gold has blinded the eyes of even such bodies as the MCC to the dangers of accepting these treacherous gifts. It cannot be said too often that the man who pays the piper calls the tune, and the control of sport will soon be wholly in the hands of men whose interest in it does not extend beyond the consideration of how it can be exploited to increase profits. Already first-class cricket is in chaos, and is becoming an affair of one-day matches promoted by rival advertisers because they attract the crowds. The County Championship, the proud pinnacle of the game for a century, has ceased to be attractive to spectators, and soon it will have to go; no one will subsidize it. Moreover, there may at any time be a great financial slump, or an enlightened Chancellor of the Exchequer may decide that taxation of commercial advertising would not only produce considerable revenue but would also confer a great benefit on society, a thing which taxation does all too rarely. In either case the subsidies to 'spenter' from commerce will cease abruptly, and the shoddy edifice which is being built on these unsubstantial foundations will immediately crash.

The injection of all this money has caused the winning of games to be financially important; in these circumstances, the good loser naturally disappears. Tactics become fouler and fouler. Today, in the language of radio commentators or sports journalists, the adjective 'professional', when it does not mean 'dull', means 'dirty'. Foul play on the field is accompanied by ever-increasing hooliganism on the terraces. Decent spectators stay away, and crowd numbers fall further. Worse still, youngsters of generous instincts, the very best material for the future of sport, are more and more turning away from the commercialized squalor of the traditional team games of cricket and football, and are devoting themselves to such pursuits as mountaineering, orienteering and non-competitive sailing and canoeing. All these are admirable activities, but in a society where so much depends on combined effort, there is a great deal to be said for team games and the attitude of mind which they unconsciously engender. Even if we disregard such sociological and psychological considerations, anyone who played these games fifty years ago will want the coming generation to enjoy them too, and will feel that if the young abandon the traditional games, they will be missing something good.

If any improvement is to come, the first necessity is to grasp how bad is the present state of affairs, to reject the bland platitudes and complacent predictions of those who have a vested interest in its continuance, and to face the fact that if reform does not come quickly, it will soon be too late. The second step is to realize how very small is the number of players in the world of 'spenter' compared with the total of those who play the games; yet control of the games is wholly in the hands of the 'spenter' minority. Fifty years ago, everyone who played a game aspired to do so at the highest level. Today that is no longer true. No doubt the majority of players who are not in the small circle of 'spenter' are outside it because they lack the skill necessary to gain entry. But nowadays there are many players of potentially sufficient skill who simply do not want to have any truck with that squalid world. These are the key figures in the situation.

Any scheme of reform must start with acceptance of the fundamental difference between sport and 'spenter'. It will not set its aims impossibly high and endeavour to reform the latter; 'spenter' must be left to look after itself, and sport must make a clean break from it. Players and clubs will have to decide which of the two worlds they belong to. A man who wants to play games simply to enjoy himself will join a sports club. Clubs and players who hope to make money out of games will continue to exist as hangers-on of the 'spenter' world.

We already have plenty of examples of how not to tackle the problem. The FA took the lead in the surrender to 'spenter' when early in this century they abandoned any qualification by birth or residence for football clubs. The MCC held out against this until recently, and then they plunged county cricket into the same anarchy by their farcical 'special registration'. They then assumed the lead in the surrender when in 1962 they took the supremely silly step, presumably in pursuit of some supposed principle of egalitarianism, of abolishing the distinction between amateur and professional. Nothing whatever has been gained by this action, and much has been lost. It is almost incredible that the FA, after ten years of the cricket experience had shown its utter failure, should have taken the same step and abolished the status of amateur. It is already clear that this will achieve nothing except the elimination of the Amateur Cup and all amateur leagues.

These melancholy mistakes help us to see the lines which any improvement in the world of sport must follow. Those who have no desire ever to participate in 'spenter' must cut adrift and organize their games to please themselves. In soccer the AFA already exists as a focal point for the movement in that game. In cricket, the MCC, which should have been the leader in preserving the best traditions, has sold itself entirely to 'spenter', and a new controlling organization will have to be brought into being. Fortunately there are plenty of clubs such as the Free Foresters and I Zingari whose members still play the game for pure enjoyment; they could provide the executive for the new association which is required. A leading aim of these new organizations should be a drastic reduction in the number of league and cup competitions, if not their complete abandonment. All the most enjoyable cricket is already played without any such stimulus. Rugby football is at this moment showing how much a game suffers by their introduction.

In any such scheme of reform we should naturally remember what happened a century ago, and look to the schools and universities for leadership and support. Today 'schools' does not mean only public schools, nor are universities limited to Oxford and Cambridge; grammar and comprehensive schools and modern universities are already making a great contribution to sport, and a still more important part awaits them. Although there are a handful of graduates playing in 'spenter', it can be assumed that the vast majority of undergraduates still envisage careers for themselves in which sport will play its proper rôle of spare-time recreation enjoyed for its own sake and nothing more. So too in schools, the upper forms have a high proportion of pupils who aim at similar careers, whether through a university or not. The higher forms provide the school first teams, and these set the tone for the attitude to sport throughout the school. It is the nature of the young to be idealistic, and today, we are told, their idealism is turning them more and more against the totally commercial orientation of life which they see around them. Sport is essentially the preserve of the young; they should take courage, and insist that their idealism and their revolt against commercialism find expression first of all in this sphere.

As we have seen, the movement in schools and universities which a hundred years ago brought into being the modern world of sport was accompanied by – if indeed it was not the result of – a deepening of social, moral and religious awareness in the young of those days. At the moment, those who base their opinions on television and the sensational press take a gloomy view of the young, and see few signs of any such movement today. Even if their pessimism were justified, it is well to remember that fashions of all kinds among the young change very quickly. What happened in the nineteenth century may happen again in the twentieth.

Any mention of sport in schools at once evokes the question of the relation between games and physical education. No book is more widely studied in academic circles today than Plato's *Republic*, and every reader is well aware that in the curriculum of a Greek school in the fifth century B.C., physical training ('gymnastic') was on the same level of importance as instruction in literacy ('grammar') and in arts and sciences ('music'), and that on this curriculum Plato based the education of his philosopher kings. The important position of 'gymnastic' in Greek and Roman education was helped by the circumstance that for many centuries a citizen might find himself fighting for his city or country, and his survival then depended on his physical fitness. When the Roman Empire collapsed, education passed wholly into the hands of the Church, and with the official attitude heavily in favour of the mortification of the flesh, physical education was rigorously excluded from the curriculum.

With the Renaissance, humanist reformers were loud in their praise of Plato's ideals and the Greek three-fold curriculum, but such was the force of conservatism in educational circles that nothing was done. The headmaster Mulcaster might recommend football, John Milton in his *Tractate of Education* might advocate fencing, wrestling, horsemanship and military drill in schools, but physical training gained no entry into our educational establishments. At the universities, football and other games were still prohibited throughout the eighteenth century. In the schools, games were at best tolerated, at worst banned – football was not permitted at Shrewsbury until 1836. Then in the middle of the nineteenth century, educational authorities in Britain realized that there was much to be said for the ideas of Plato and the Greeks about physical excellence as an aim in training the young. Perhaps unfortunately, this movement coincided with the outburst of enthusiasm for games which was to have such important results for the whole world. The public schools discovered that games were good and contributed to the health of their pupils. *Mens sana in corpore sano* was quoted at every speech day. Headmasters followed a logical line of reasoning; if games were good, then all boys should be made to play games. This notion had another attraction. Authorities at boarding schools are convinced, probably rightly, that boys who have nothing specific to do at any time will be up to no good; games gave them something to do.

Compulsory games at school may be difficult to justify theoretically, but any harm they may have done has been grossly exaggerated. The idea that those who were compelled to play games at school never played after they had left is completely untrue. It has no more basis than would a suggestion that anyone compelled to learn to read at school never reads anything when school days are behind him. The worst effect of the practice of using compulsory games as the physical element in a complete education was that it fostered the fallacy that games are the best or at least an adequate form of physical training, which they are not. Towards the end of the nineteenth century, far better methods and systems of achieving physical fitness were worked out in countries where games were less highly regarded than in Britain. They were slow to be adopted here, and Britain still lags far behind most civilized countries in her standards of physical training. Today teachers of the subject in our schools regard it as their first duty, often as their only duty, to coach the school's teams, and the pupils of no great ability at games are sadly neglected, though they are the unfortunates who need help most. The sooner the conceptions of sport and of physical education are separated, the better for both. There is every justification for making physical training compulsory and important; if that is done, games will look after themselves.

About the future of international sport it is not easy to be confident. Contests in which teams represent their countries will continue to belong to the realm of 'spenter'; they may well come to an end in the next few years, as the rioting and hooliganism which seem to be their inescapable accompaniment outgrow the ability of the police to deal with them. It is much to be hoped, however, that meetings between schools, universities and clubs of different nations will survive and extend – contests on the lines of those which Oxford and Cambridge have enjoyed for many years against their opposite numbers in USA. These will be in the domain of sport, not 'spenter'; if Britain gives a clear lead, the necessity for the distinction will in all probability be felt in other countries. Already much hard thinking on the subject is being done across the Atlantic, both in Canada and USA. In the States, for example, the position of sport in the universities is under close examination, and the institution of 'sports scholarships' is coming in for much criticism from thoughtful academics.

Herein lies the promise for the future. The world of sport needs far fewer maudlin speeches at club dinners, far fewer syrupy platitudes from journalists, and far more clear thinking. But clear thinking is an arduous task which all of us willingly dodge.

Index

Compiled by Adam Elgar

advertising, *see* sponsorship
Alexander the Great, 15–17, 30
amateurism, 44, 52–3, 67–8, 80, 85–7, 112–15, 116, 129, 140, 217
Amateur Rowing Association, *see* rowing
Amateur Swimming Association, 100
America's Cup, 98
Apollinaris, Sidonius, Bishop of Clermont, 22
archery, 102, 135, 175–6
Armstrong W. W., 60–1, 63
Ashes, the, *see* cricket
Association Football (soccer): AFA, 115; Amateur Cup, 113; bladders, early use of, 102; Cambridge Rules, 107–8; clubs, 107–8; Corinthian FC, 113–15; FA Cup, 11, 108; FA formed, 108; FIFA, 116; Football League, 114; hurling, 104–5; Italian, 103–4; laws, 109–10, 117–18; literature of, 200; Medieval, 103; money and, 119–21; Olympics, 116; Romans and, 19; 'soccer', derivation of term, 109; tactics, 110–11; television and, 194–5; Universities and, 105–6; World Cup, 12, 114, 116
athletics: AAA, 140–1; AAC, 140; Achilles Club, 142–3; amateurism, 140–1; cross-country running, 150–2, 194; cycling, 152–3; discus throwing, 145–7; Exeter College sports, 137–8; goal running, 143; hammer throwing, 145; handicapping, 141; high jumping, 141, 148; javelin throwing, 147–8; Marathon, 182–3; pole vaulting, 148–9; putting (the 'stone', the shot), 144–5; relay races, 189; running footmen, 136; stakes in, 136–7, 140; television and, 194
walking, 149–50
Austen, Jane, 169

Baddeley, V. C. Clinton, 95, 202
badminton, 158
Badminton Library, 134, 137, 200
Balfour, Rt. Hon. A. J., 154
ball games: in ancient Britain, 19; in Greece and Rome, 17; *see also* separate sports
Bannister, Dr Roger, 139
Bardi, Giovanni de', 103–4
baseball, 168–9
basketball, 167–8
Beauclerk, Rev. Lord Frederick, 46–7
Betjeman, Sir John, 208
betting, *see* corrupt practices
Bligh, Hon. Ivo, 58
Bloxham, M. H., 122
Blunden, Edmund, 207–9
Boat Race, University, 33, 49, 81–4, 191–2

Bosanquet, B. J., 59, 62
Bourne, Dr G. C., 90–1
Bouverie, E. O. P. (*Encyclopaedia of Sport*), 31–2
bowls, 159–60, 179
boxing, 172–4
Bradman, Sir Donald, 62–3, 73
Buller, Sydney, 72–3
Byron, Lord, 172–4

Campbell, F. W., 108–9
canoeing, 96–7
Cardus, Sir Neville, 13, 40, 53, 78, 199–200
Carew (*Survey of Cornwall*), 104–5
chariot racing, 17–19, 22, 151
Charles I, King, 28
Charles II, King, 29–30, 177
Chaucer, Geoffrey, 24–5, 170–1
Chesterton, G. K., 9
Church, the Christian, 16, 20; athletics and, 122, 135; cricket and, 48–50, 75–7; football and, 111; Non-conformism, 48–9; puritanism, 21–2, 24, 35–7; Royal Tennis and, 23–34; rugby and, 133
Cinnamus (Byzantine historian), 27
clubs, 12, 33, 51–2; *see also* separate sports
Cole, W. S., 82
corrupt practices: betting, 9, 41, 42–3, 46–9, 77, 80, 85, 120, 136–7; bribery, 120–1, 190; unfair tactics, 63–6, 72–3, 117–18, 215; *see also* sponsorship
Coubertin, Baron Pierre de, 142, 180–1, 184
Cowes, 97–8
cricket: All England team, 42; Antioch, first recorded game at, 37; Ashes, the, 58; betting, 42–3; 'bodyline', 63–6; bowling, development of, 73–4; 'British Champion', 41–2, 44; broadcasting and, 192, 195–6; the Church and 48–50, 75–7; county clubs, 51–2, 54–7, 71–2; County Cricket Council, 55; county rivalry, 42; earliest appearance of, 36–7; international matches, the first, 57–9; laws of, 38–41, 43; literature of, 198 ff.; Lord's cricket ground, 43, 46–7, 49, 55, 58, 74, 192; MCC, 43, 54–5, 64–5, 68, 71, 181, 215–17; Oxford and Cambridge and, 48–50; puritanism and, 37; social background of, 41–9; stakes in, 37; Test matches, 59 ff., 69; throwing, 72–3; umpires, 39–41, 43, 72–3; Wales and, 57; women's, 74–5
croquet, 165–7
curling, 179
Cuthbert, St, 170

Daft, Richard (*Kings of Cricket*), 75, 199
Dickens, Charles: (*The Pickwick Papers*), 31, 33, 130, 178, 203–4; (*David Copperfield*), 150
Dublin, Trinity College, 106

Ellis, W. W., *see* Rugby Football
Erasmus, 27
Eton College, 24, 30, 81, 88–9, 91, 94, 107, 111
Eton Fives, *see* Fives
Exeter Cathedral, petition of, 24

Fairbairn, Steve, 89–90
fencing, 174–5
Field Tennis, 34
Fives, 24, 30
football, *see* Association Football, Rugby Football

Galen, 102
gambling, *see* corrupt practices
Gibb, James, 158
Goldwin (*In Certamen Pilae*), 37–9
golf, 162–5
Gower, John, 25
Grace, Dr W. G., 71, 78, 196

Graveney, T. A., 68
Greek athletics, 16–18, 21–2, 135, 138, 144, 146; swimming, 99; wrestling, 170
gymnastics, 189

Hammond, W. R., 53
Harris, David, 73–4
Hart-Dyke, Sir William, 31–2
Herod I, King of Judaea, 70
Hobbs, Sir Jack, 6, 53
hockey, 160–1
Homer, 17, 135, 146, 170, 175
Hughes, Thomas, 122–3; *see also* *Tom Brown at Oxford*, etc.

international sport, *see* sport, international

Jackson, A. N. S., 6
Jackson, John, 172
Jackson, N. L., 113–14
James I, King, 36, 136, 162
Jardine, Douglas, 63–6
Jockey Club, 43
Johnson, Dr Samuel, 44, 79–80, 138, 149, 172, 178
journalism, 13–14, 53, 61, 68, 77, 151–2
judo, 174
Jupp, V. W. C., 52

karate, 174
Krause, J. H. (*Die Gymnastik der Hellenen*), 138
Kung Fu, 174

lacrosse, 167
Lampeter, St David's College, 132–3
lawn tennis, 28, 154–8, 166–7
Longhurst, Henry, 13
Lord, Thomas, 43
Lord's cricket ground, *see* cricket
Love, James, 42, 45, 207

McNeill, R. J. (*Encyclopaedia Britannica*), 31–2
Mailey, A. A., 198

money in sport, *see* corrupt practices, *also* sponsorship
Mulcaster, Richard (*Positions*), 104–5, 218–19

Naismith, James, 167–8
Napier, Rev. J. R., 76
netball, 167
Nyren, John (*Cricketers of My Time*), 41, 45–6, 73–4, 199
Nyren, Richard, 45–6

Olympic Games:
aims of, 180–1, 184–5; ancient, 64, 70, 135, 139, 170, 181, 190; modern, 12; Berlin, *1936*, 185; canoeing, 97; football, 116; founding of, 142, 180–2; Greece, *1896*, 181–3; gymnastics, 189–90; IOC, 181, 186; literature of, 205–6; London, *1908*, 184; *1948*, 105; Munich, *1972*, 187; Paris, *1900*, 183; *1924*, 184; reforms of, 188–9; rowing, 85, 91, 93; seventeenth century, 136; skating (figure), 189–90; swimming, 100; Winter Olympics, 184, 188; wrestling, 171
Oxford and Cambridge, contests between:
athletics, 138–40; boxing, 173; Cricket Match, 33, 49, 56, 67, 107, 124; lawn tennis, 155; rackets, 35; Rugby, 122, 125, 129, 134; *see also* Boat Race
Oxford Movement, 49

Paul, St, 21
Pepys, Samuel, 29–30, 136, 160, 163, 166, 177
Plato, 170, 218
Pliny the Younger, 17, 80–1
polo, 27, 161, 168
professionalism, 25, 44, 46–8, 51–3, 67–8, 85–7, 111–15, 127–8, 136, 140, 213–15
punting, 95–6
Pycroft, Rev. James, 46–7, 199, 206

Queensberry, Marquess of, 173
Quiller-Couch, Sir Arthur, 87–8

rackets, *see* Royal Tennis
radio broadcasting, 191–3, 196
Ranjitsinjhi, K. S., 62, 72–3
Richmond, 2nd Duke of, 38–9
Richmond, 4th Duke of, 43–4
Robertson, Sir George, 183
Roman Empire, 15–19, 22, 69–70, 99
rounders, 168–9
rowing:
Amateur Rowing Association, 85–7; bumping races, 82–3, 94–5; first competitions, 79; Henley, 80, 83–5, 91–4, 180–1; Holme Pierrepont, 94; innovations, 87–91; National ARA, 86–7; Olympics, 85, 91, 93; professionalism, 85–7; regattas, 79–80; schools and, 81, 84; stakes in, 80, 85; University Boat Race, *see* Boat Race
Royal Tennis:
competitions in, 33; decline in seventeenth century, 35; manner of play, 23; origins, 23–4, 26; popularity, growth of, 24–6; professionalism, 25; racket, development of, 26–7; rackets, the game of, 30–4; royal patronage, 29–30; sales of equipment, 25–6; scoring, 28–9
Rugby Football:
competitions, 134; Ellis, W. W., 122–4; literature of, 200 ff.; Magdalen College School, 126; professionalism, 127–8; Rugby League, 128, 131, 134; Rugby Union, 108, 121, 127–8; scoring, 124–5, 129; soccer and, 131–2; tactics, development of, 125–7; Wales and, 125, 132–4
rules, 12–13, 33; *see also* separate sports, formation of

sailing, 97–9
Sayers, Dorothy L.:
(*Gaudy Night*), 96; (*Murder Must Advertise*), 202
Scaino (*Trattato della Palla*), 28–9, 32, 103–4
Shakespeare, William, 26, 35, 44, 99, 102, 143, 159–60, 171, 174–5
Shearman, Montague, 134, 137, 140
Sheppard, Rt Rev. David, 75–7
skating, 177–8, 189–90
skiing, 178–9
Southey, Robert, 97
spectators, 9, 52, 54, 67–9, 77, 164, 213–15
'spenter', 214–17, 220
sponsorship, 69–71, 119, 214–15
sport and society, 41–9, 53–5, 101, 111–12, 127–8, 131–2, 140, 164–5, 215 ff
sport, international, 9–10, 12, 56 ff, 91–3, 116–19; *see also* Olympic Games
squash, 34
Strutt, J., 106, 162–3, 199
Swanton E. W., 13, 200
swimming, 99–101

table tennis, 158–9
television, 174, 192–7, 212
tennis, *see* Field Tennis, lawn tennis, Royal Tennis, table tennis
Tom Brown at Oxford, 83, 86, 201
Tom Brown's Schooldays, 48, 83, 103–5, 122–4, 130, 136, 150, 173, 180, 201, 206

umpires (cricket), *see* cricket

volleyball, 167

Wakefield, Lord, 109, 130
Warre, Dr, 88–9
water polo, 100
Wesley, John, 48–50
Wingfield, Major, 154
Wisden, 199
Woolley, Frank, 53, 71
Wordsworth, Charles, 49–50
wrestling, 170–2